The Phonology of English as an International Language:
New Models, New Norms, New Goals

Jennifer Jenkins

OXFORD
UNIVERSITY PRESS

OXFORD

UNIVERSITY PRESS

Great Clarendon Street, Oxford OX2 6DP

Oxford University Press is a department of the University of Oxford.
It furthers the University's objective of excellence in research, scholarship,
and education by publishing worldwide in

Oxford New York

Auckland Cape Town Dar es Salaam Hong Kong Karachi
Kuala Lumpur Madrid Melbourne Mexico City Nairobi
New Delhi Shanghai Taipei Toronto

With offices in

Argentina Austria Brazil Chile Czech Republic France Greece
Guatemala Hungary Italy Japan Poland Portugal Singapore
South Korea Switzerland Thailand Turkey Ukraine Vietnam

OXFORD and OXFORD ENGLISH are registered trade marks of
Oxford University Press in the UK and in certain other countries

© Oxford University Press 2000

The moral rights of the author have been asserted

Database right Oxford University Press (maker)

First published 2000
2009
10 9 8 7 6 5

No unauthorized photocopying

Any websites referred to in this publication are in the public domain and
their addresses are provided by Oxford University Press for information only.
Oxford University Press disclaims any responsibility for the content

ISBN-13: 978 0 19 442164 5

Printed in China

Contents

Acknowledgements

Many people have contributed in their different ways to this book. First, I would like to acknowledge my debt to all the learners of English who provided the data, especially learners at Angloschool, Birkbeck College, Imperial College, and King's College London. Without them, the book could not have been written. In addition, the students on my master's and undergraduate courses at King's College London over recent years have shown a lively interest in the project, asking probing questions and making perceptive comments which enabled me to refine my core proposals.

I would also like to thank my colleagues at King's, especially Sara Garcia-Peralta, John Field, and Neil Murray, for their generous encouragement. Many colleagues working in the field of phonology and phonetics around the world have been helpful and supportive. Special thanks are due to Judy Gilbert, Bryan Jenner, John Levis, Maya Leon Meis, Jonathan Marks, Larry Morgan, Paul Tench, Michael Vaughan-Rees, and Robin Walker. Barbara Seidlhofer has been a source of inspiration and a mine of information, and also provided invaluable comments on a substantial chunk of the final draft.

Much of the research on which the book is based was carried out during my doctoral studies at the Institute of Education, University of London. My gratitude goes to John Norrish for his guidance and generous support at that time, and to fellow students Koo Yew Lie and Arifa Rahman for the insights they gave me during our numerous discussions.

I would like to express my sincere thanks to those at OUP who have been involved in the book, and especially to Cristina Whitecross for her constant encouragement, to Julia Sallabank for her patience, energy, and dedication during the preparation of the manuscript, and to Anne Conybeare for all her help in the earlier stages. Above all, I owe an immense debt to Henry Widdowson. His commitment from the start and his generosity in the sharing of his wisdom and time have had a profound influence on the development of my ideas.

The author and publisher are grateful to the following copyright holders who have given permission to reproduce extracts and adaptations of copyright material:

Blackwell Publishers for an extract from 'Double Standards: teacher education in the Expanding Circle' by B. Seidlhofer from *World Englishes* 18/2: 238 (Blackwell Publishers).

Oxford University Press for extracts from 'Sociolinguistics and Second Language Learning' by Lesley Milroy from *Language and Understanding* © G. Brown, K. Malmkjaer, A. Pollitt, and J. Williams 1994; Language Teaching: A Scheme for Teacher Education: *Pronunciation* by Christiane Dalton and Barbara Seidlhofer © Oxford University Press 1994; and *Communication in the Language Classroom* by Tony Lynch © Tony Lynch 1996.

The Society of Authors as the literary representative of the estate of L. P. Hartley for an extract from *The Go-Between*.

The Times Higher Education Supplement for an extract from 'English is as English does', a review of A. Pennycook: *The Cultural Politics of English as an International Language* (Longman, 1994), published in the *THES* Book Review Section 7 July 1999.

Although every effort has been made to trace and contact copyright holders before publication, this has not been possible in some cases. We apologize for any apparent infringement of copyright and if notified, the publisher will be pleased to rectify any errors or omissions at the earliest opportunity.

To John, Nick, and Harriet

Introduction

For the first time in the history of the English language, second language speakers outnumber those for whom it is the mother tongue, and interaction in English increasingly involves no first language speakers whatsoever. The expansion of the use of English in this direction has been documented and discussed by applied linguists throughout the past decade (see, for example, Crystal 1988; Rampton 1990; Phillipson 1992; Widdowson 1994a; Brumfit 1995; Sridhar 1996; Crystal 1997). Precise figures vary, according to which authority one consults, how the different second language users of English are categorized, and in particular, at what level of proficiency these users are considered to be speakers of English at all. Nevertheless, the trend remains clear. Indeed, Crystal suggests that if one accepts a criterion of 'reasonable competence', there may be as many as 1,350 million second language speakers compared to around 337 million first language speakers. Even the most conservative estimate based on 'native-like fluency' would still place second language speakers at around 335 million (1997: 60–1). Either way, this trend is likely to continue apace in the 21st Century.

The only really surprising element, then, is the relative failure of English Language Teaching (ELT) pedagogy—with the exception of the teaching of Business English (see Alexander 1996)[1]—to adjust its methodologies in line with this changing pattern, in which the goal of learning is more often to be able to use English as a lingua franca in communication with other 'non-native speakers', i.e. as an international language, than as a foreign language in communication with its 'native speakers'. Since it is in their pronunciation that the existing and emerging second language (L2) varieties diverge most from each other linguistically, it is arguably this linguistic area that most threatens intelligibility. This is the area, therefore, that most demands attention if international communication is to be successfully promoted through the English language as the trend continues into the new century. Meanwhile, the majority of EFL teacher training and education courses, both preservice and inservice, persist with phonology syllabuses that assume a 'native-speaker' interlocutor. They therefore involve elements that are unnecessary, unrealistic, and, at worst, harmful for preparing teachers to equip their learners with pronunciation skills appropriate to an international use of English.

The purpose of this book is to explore the phonology of English from an international perspective. This is done in two stages. The first, which involves description and analysis, is essentially an examination of how speakers of English as an International Language (EIL) behave phonologically, by means of data drawn from lingua franca contexts. The second stage moves on to a reconsideration of the problems of mutual phonological intelligibility and acceptability, with the aim of facilitating the use of EIL. This involves recommendation and, to an extent, prescription in the discussion of specific new goals for pronunciation teaching.

It will quickly become evident that the concept of mutual intelligibility for EIL is itself problematic for two main reasons. First, it poses a major pedagogic dilemma. Attempts to work towards the promotion and preservation of mutual international intelligibility will inevitably conflict with the growing intellectual and socio-psychological needs to accord the burgeoning L2[2] varieties of English parity with first language (L1) varieties as acceptable norms. The solution proposed here is the establishing of a set of 'nuclear norms' for all L2 speakers of English (and receptively for L1 speakers also), thus in many ways the phonological counterpart of Quirk's (1982) proposals for grammar. Outside this nuclear core, speakers would then be unconstrained in their use of L1 features of pronunciation, in other words, of local phonological norms. However, the second problem is that phonological intelligibility is itself extremely difficult to isolate and pin down. This, in turn, means that the identification of a set of nuclear norms to guarantee mutual phonological intelligibility in international contexts is likely to be a complex process.

Nevertheless, once we have identified such a phonological core, we will be able to advocate and implement a far more realistic approach to phonology within ELT pedagogy. It will be possible to establish a clearer distinction between learners' productive and receptive phonology, with pronunciation syllabuses no longer being required to embrace large numbers of fine details in an attempt to guide learners to approximate the speech of 'native speakers'.

In addition, it will become easier to incorporate notions of 'teachability' and 'learnability' into pronunciation teaching. Some phonological features, like nuclear stress, will be categorized as 'teachable' because of the clear-cut, generative nature of their rules, and others, like pitch movement, as 'learnable' (acquirable) outside the classroom—though only after a good deal of exposure to the language—because of the complexities involved. This, in turn, will enable pronunciation teaching and materials to shift the focus from 'what is convenient for teachers to teach' to 'what is effective for learners to learn' (Seidlhofer and Dalton 1995: 145). We will see also that it is possible for ELT pedagogy to exploit accommodation, itself an area much overlooked and under-researched in relation to second language pronunciation teaching, not only for its mediating role in EIL intelligibility, but also for its as yet unrecognized contribution to L2 phonological acquisition.

The book begins by discussing the issue of the changed ownership of English and the implications of the growth of EIL as they relate specifically to phonological intelligibility. In the second chapter, we briefly consider the problem of negative attitudes towards language variation in general. The second chapter goes on to study in greater detail the effects of phonological variation, here between speakers of different L1s (inter-speaker variation) and, in Chapter 3, within individual speakers according to sociolinguistic context and socio-psychological need (intra-speaker variation).

Having examined what L2 speakers actually do, we move on in Chapter 4 to a discussion of intelligibility as the basis for establishing which core features of pronunciation are likely to promote successful communication in EIL. Then, in Chapter 5, we consider the complexity and extent of pronunciation transfer and its implications for the feasibility of teaching the core. In Chapter 6, bearing in mind the discussions of the two previous chapters, we settle down to the business of identifying the phonological core in detail. In Chapter 7, we turn to the problem of devising procedures for the ELT classroom which will encourage the negotiation of intelligibility and, thus, the use of the core in both the production and reception of speech. We conclude, in Chapter 8, with a discussion of the urgent need for theorists and practitioners alike to take EIL phonology seriously and to translate its implications into radical proposals for pedagogy, instead of continuing to promote ways of describing and teaching pronunciation which have become irrelevant to the changed role of English in the multilingual world.

It should now be apparent that the issue of phonology for international English is one which has significance for the whole future of the English language on a worldwide scale. Nevertheless, not only has it been largely ignored pedagogically, but it has only rarely filtered through into ELT theoretical literature. This is, no doubt, partly the result of the fact that pronunciation has itself been marginalized during recent years as a result of difficulties in aligning it with and incorporating it into communicative approaches to language teaching.

Undoubtedly, some important discussion has taken place since the late 1970s among a small circle of writers, including Brumfit (1982, 1995); Kachru (1985, 1992); Quirk (1985); Smith (1983, 1992); Strevens (1980); and Widdowson (1982, 1984, 1994a), *à propos* the ownership of English and problems of mutual intelligibility, particularly as they relate to ESL contexts. However, even in the works of these authors, the crucial phonological issue tends to be relegated to a brief footnote or paragraph. It has thus been left largely to be played out in society newsletters, such as that of the International Association of Teachers of English as a Foreign Language (IATEFL) and its Pronunciation Special Interest Group's publication *Speak Out*, which by their very nature reach a relatively small readership. A further purpose of this book is therefore to rekindle a wider theoretical interest in phonology and thereby stimulate theoretical discussion of phonology for EIL.

One final introductory point: the title of this book is an intended echo of Pennycook's *The Cultural Politics of English as an International Language* (1994). His book has been profoundly influential on the development of my own thoughts. However, while I share many of his views, I come to some different conclusions: English *is* the international language at present, so rather than argue in terms of the past why this should not be, I prefer to look ahead to ways in which we can make the language more cross-culturally democratic, under the 'ownership' (in Widdowsonian terms) of all who use it for communication, regardless of who or where they are. This firmly places me, pedagogically speaking, in the opposite camp to that of 'real English' which, I believe, has at present the effect of deflecting attention away from the nature of EIL.

In attempting to 'democratize' the English language, I identify pronunciation as the area of greatest prejudice and preconception, and the one most resistant to change on all sides. So, although many of the issues at stake are at heart cultural and political, they are embedded in and symbolized externally by phonology and phonological attitudes. It is, therefore, to changes in these that we must look if English is to achieve true integrity as an international language, and thus we have another major motivation for giving EIL phonology a high profile.

Notes

1 In this respect note Widdowson's argument that 'English as an international language is English for specific purposes' (1997: 144).

2 The term 'L2' is used throughout to contrast with 'L1', i.e. to indicate English that has not been learnt as a first language or 'mother tongue'. It does not distinguish between the ESL (English as a Second Language) and EFL (English as a Foreign Language) varieties of English.

1 The background: Changing patterns in the use of English

English is England's language but the world's treasure.

Liu Dailin, Deputy Dean of the Foreign Language Department
at the China Central Radio and TV University, quoted in the
EL Gazette, September 1996

The historical shift

The teaching of English to speakers of other languages has a history
stretching back to the late 15th Century. From that time onwards, English
has been taught, albeit intermittently, to people for whom it was not their
mother tongue, whether to further trading and commercial interests,
promote empire, facilitate the everyday survival of refugees and other
migrants, or for a combination of these causes.

Until fairly recently, the goal of such teaching was straightforward:
learners wished primarily to be able to communicate effectively with native
speakers of English, who were considered by all to be the owners of the
language, guardians of its standards, and arbiters of acceptable pedagogic
norms. This was the situation regardless of the status of English as a
'foreign' or 'second' language, respectively EFL (taught to those for whom
English had no internal function in their L1 country) and ESL (taught either
to those for whom English had an internal function in their L1 country or
to those who had emigrated to English L1 countries). In order to achieve
their goal, it was considered essential for these 'non-native speakers' to
approximate as closely as possible to the native standard, particularly with
regard to pronunciation and, in the 20th Century, very often with respect
to a single prestige accent, Received Pronunciation (RP).

However, in recent years, worldwide political and commercial
developments, in particular the massive increase in American economic
domination, have begun to present a serious challenge to the traditional
roles of English and consequently to the goals of its pedagogy. This is not
the place for a detailed account of events and, for such, the reader is

referred to the works of Phillipson (1992), Pennycook (1994), and Crystal (1997). For our present purposes, it will suffice to outline two main phases of change.

First, the dismantling of the British empire in ESL countries, particularly in the Indian subcontinent, was accompanied not by the abandoning of the English language in favour of the L1 (or L1s), but by the more active promotion of local, and thus L1-influenced, varieties of English. Inevitably, tensions have arisen within such countries between the desire, on the one hand, to accept a range of local English accents from speakers of different L1s such as Punjabi and Bengali, and, on the other, to retain intelligibility among them. Talking specifically about the problem in India, Bansal comments that while 'the view that the only suitable model is British RP is not shared by all educated people in the country ... it is felt that some reasonable standard should be insisted upon to ensure effective communication'. Likewise, on an international scale he considers that 'it is desirable to establish certain minimum standards of mutual intelligibility among the various dialects of English spoken in the world' (1990: 229–30).

Second, and still more recently, these same tensions have begun to emerge in the context of EFL. Here, English has rapidly metamorphosed in the past half century from a foreign language into an international one. Its most frequent use outside the L1 countries (the 'English as a Native Language', or ENL, countries, like the UK, the USA, Canada, and Australasia) and the ESL countries is between speakers *neither* of whom learnt it as an L1. Thus, it differs crucially from other foreign languages such as Spanish, Russian, Japanese, and so on, which continue to be learnt predominantly for communication with their L1 speakers, usually in the L1 country.

To complicate matters even further, this situation is also becoming more common among speakers of ESL, several of whose countries (for example, Malaysia, the Philippines, India, Pakistan) are in the process of switching from a purely *intra*-national use of English to an *inter*-national one, essentially to facilitate trade with countries where English is not spoken as an L1. Pakistan, for instance, now trades extensively with a number of countries in the Far East, especially Japan, using English as a lingua franca. Thus, although the ESL countries are not the central concern of this book, they play an important part in the development of EIL in terms of both their own internationalization and their early role in the bid for the recognition of L2 varieties of English.

Changing ownership; changing terminology

In recognition of the changes outlined above, a number of more forward-thinking and less parochial applied linguists have begun to call into question the whole issue of who owns the English language and, consequently, who is entitled to prescribe the standards against which use is to be measured. No one denies the 'rights' of so-called 'native speakers' to establish their own standards for use in interaction with other 'native speakers' (ENL), and even with 'non-native speakers' (EFL). However, the important question is: who should make such decisions for communication wholly between 'non-native speakers', i.e. for English as an International Language?

The view that 'native speakers' do not own EIL has been held for a number of years. Smith, for example, asserted as long ago as 1976, in relation to ESL, that 'English belongs to the world … . It is yours (no matter who you are) as much as it is mine (no matter who I am)' (1983: 2). Brumfit more recently argues that:

> Not only has 'English' become international in the last half century, but scholarship about English has also become international: the ownership of an interest in English has become international. We are no longer a language community which is associated with a national community or even with a family of nations such as the Commonwealth aspired to be. We are an international community …
> (1995: 16)

This position is expressed most emphatically by Widdowson who, having explained precisely why English is now an international language ('it serves a whole range of different communities and their institutional purposes, and these transcend traditional communal and cultural boundaries'), continues by arguing forcefully against native speaker control:

> How English develops in the world is no business whatever of native speakers in England, the United States, or anywhere else. They have no say in the matter, no right to intervene or pass judgement. They are irrelevant. The very fact that English is an international language means that no nation can have custody over it. To grant such custody of the language is necessarily to arrest its development and so undermine its international status. It is a matter of considerable pride and satisfaction for native speakers of English that their language is an international means of communication. But the point is that it is only international to the extent that it is not their language. It is not a possession which they lease out to others, while still retaining the freehold. Other people actually own it.
> (1994a: 385)

Views of this sort are slowly gaining support among scholars. Within the EFL community, it is largely 'native-speaker' linguists themselves who have begun to 'examine critically the construct of the native speaker' and to question the latter's identity, authority, and the appropriacy of its norms (Kramsch 1998: 19). 'Non-native speakers' appear, on the other hand, to be rather more reticent. (It is noticeable, though, that the same is not true of the ESL countries, which have a much longer history of English use coupled with linguistic imperialism, and whose members speak out more vociferously against control by the L1 'centre'). Many 'non-native speakers', particularly among the teaching fraternity, hold the view that desirable English is indeed that variety spoken by its natives. This seems to relate to a lack of confidence for, according to Kramsch, 'non-native teachers and students alike are intimidated by the native-speaker norm and understandably try to approximate this norm during the course of their work together' (1993: 9). We even find expression of the opinion that it is patronizing to suggest they should do otherwise and aim to acquire anything short of 'native-like' proficiency:

> In the Expanding Circle[1] ... the ideal goal is to imitate the native speaker of the standard language as closely as possible. Speaking English is simply not related to cultural identity. It is rather an exponent of one's academic and language-learning abilities. It would, therefore, be far from a compliment to tell a Spanish person that his or her variety is Spanish English. It would imply that his or her acquisition of the language left something to be desired.
> (Andreasson 1994: 402)

While this view is not by any means universal (see the social-psychological discussion in the next section), it is one sometimes held by teachers and prospective teachers. The situation is complex and sensitive, and L1 speakers of English would do well to guard against unwittingly appearing to patronize L2 speakers. In this context, Bisong's (1995) reaction to Phillipson's (1992) claims of British linguistic imperialism in Nigeria is a case in point. Bisong finds the latter both patronizing and misguided, and argues that English is simply one of a number of languages available to Nigerians, a part of their 'rich linguistic repertoire'. They learn it 'for pragmatic reasons to do with maximizing their chances of success in a multilingual and multicultural society', a type of society whose complex nature is not easily comprehended by the monolingual mind.

One of the principal areas on which the ownership debate has recently focused is the anachronistic terminology in use to describe the users and uses of English. I speak here particularly of the terms 'native speaker', 'non-native speaker', and 'English as a Foreign Language'. Taking each in turn, I will outline the objections that have been made and suggest more realistic alternatives.

First, 'native speaker'. Kramsch argues that 'The notion of a generic native speaker has become so diversified that it has lost its meaning' (1993: 49). While this may not necessarily represent the situation for all languages, it clearly holds good for English. The term, for example, fails to recognize that many varieties of English in outer circle countries, such as Singapore, are spoken not only as official languages but also in the home (see Brown 1991). Again, it ignores the fact that English is often one of several languages available in the repertoires of the multilingual populations of, for example, India and African countries (see the discussion of Bisong 1995 above). In such contexts, it is often difficult to ascertain which language is a person's L1 and which their L2. The term perpetuates the idea that monolingualism is the norm when, in fact, precisely the opposite is true for the world at large. And, as Rampton (1990) points out, it implies the ethnic Anglo speaker as a reference point against which all other Englishes should be measured, which cannot be acceptable or appropriate for a language that has passed into world ownership.

Similarly, it is entirely inappropriate, indeed offensive, to label as 'non-native speakers' those who have learnt English as a second or foreign language and achieved bilingual status as fluent, proficient users. The perpetuation of the native/non-native dichotomy causes negative perceptions and self-perceptions of 'non-native' teachers and a lack of confidence in and of 'non-native' theory builders. It leads to 'non-natives' being refused places on EFL teacher training courses,[2] limited publication of their articles in prestigious international journals (cf. Block 1996), a simplistic view of what constitutes an error, and deficiencies in English language testing programmes, because speakers are being measured against an unrealistic and irrelevant standard.

Rampton (1990) discusses a number of possible alternatives. However, a problem with these suggestions arises with the negative connotations of their opposites. For example, his 'expert speaker' for a fluent speaker implies the use of 'non-expert speaker' for a less fluent one, thus imposing just as much of a value judgement as does 'non-native speaker'. My own suggestion is to reconceptualize the issue, turn the traditional terminology on its head, and replace the two terms as follows.

For those L1 speakers of English who speak no other language fluently, I suggest substituting the term 'native speaker' with 'monolingual English speaker' (MES). L1 standards would remain operable here but not be used to measure L2 varieties of English. This would mean, to take a controversial example, that just because MESs generally use weak forms (thus pronouncing the vowel sound in words like *to*, *from*, and *of* as schwa /ə/), an L2 speaker would not automatically be expected to do so. Since these pronunciation features do not appear to contribute to international intelligibility (see Chapter 6), the speaker would not be criticized or penalized for *not* doing so.

On the other hand, for both those 'native speakers' who speak another language fluently and for 'non-native speakers' who speak English fluently, I suggest 'bilingual English speaker' (BES). While these are likely to be shortened to MS and BS, the intermediate 'E', strictly speaking, is necessary. This is because it distinguishes English from other modern languages, which are genuinely foreign in that they are learnt and used predominantly for communication with their L1 speakers, and which, therefore, do indeed have non-native speakers. Further, it is crucial for the third term, 'non-bilingual English speaker' (NBES), to allow for the fact that a speaker may be bilingual, but not in English. This term bears none of the negative implications of 'non-native' but instead provides a neutral, factual description. It tacitly acknowledges that many L2 speakers of English may have no desire to speak it fluently, let alone like a 'native', and that their English may have progressed to the level at which it serves their particular international communicative purpose.

This categorization is not without its problems. In particular, where should the line be drawn between BES and NBES and, more importantly, who should draw it? However, it has two great advantages. Firstly, the term MES is less favourable than BES, reflecting the fact that monolingualism is not the world norm nor the preferable condition. Secondly, BES removes the artificial distinction (in an international context) between speakers of L1 varieties of English and proficient speakers of L2 varieties. In this connection, there is an urgent need to redefine the term 'bilingual' for English, such that it no longer implies 'equally competent in two languages', an interpretation which itself leads to diffidence on the part of proficient BESs to describe themselves as bilingual. Rather, the term should mean that the speaker has attained a specified degree of proficiency in both languages, although in practice probably going well beyond this level in one of them. Such a removal of the native/non-native distinction is likely to have a positive influence on teaching, teacher education, and theory building.

Throughout this book, I will continue to use the terms 'native speaker' (or 'NS') and 'non-native speaker' (or 'NNS') (enclosed by inverted commas) when discussing my sources. But in an endeavour to practise what I preach, otherwise, wherever feasible—and bearing in mind that they present new concepts for the reader—I will use the more appropriate terms 'BES/MES' and 'NBES' when discussing my own work. On those occasions where it is necessary to distinguish between those bilinguals for whom English is an L1 and those for whom it is an L2, I will use the (I hope) more neutral terms 'L1 speaker' and 'L2 speaker'.

Moving now to 'EFL', the term does not express the principal purpose of learning English today, and unless it is genuinely used to describe native/non-native interaction as the pedagogical aim, the word 'foreign' has a number of negative implications. According to Gika, 'we teach this language to help people communicate easily, talk to each other without linguistic and even cultural barriers, understand each other better ... to bring people closer', and the term 'foreign' is unhelpful in this context. She asks, 'how foreign can it be internationally, since people all over the world communicate in English?' (1996: 15).

One possible alternative to EFL simply involves reversing the second and third letters to arrive at ELF, or 'English as a Lingua Franca'. This term would have a number of immediate advantages: ELF emphasizes the role of English in communication between speakers from different L1s, i.e. the primary reason for learning English today; it suggests the idea of community as opposed to alienness; it emphasizes that people have something in common rather than their differences; it implies that 'mixing' languages is acceptable (which was, in fact, what the original *lingua francas* did) and thus that there is nothing inherently wrong in retaining certain characteristics of the L1, such as accent; finally, the Latin name symbolically removes the ownership of English from the Anglos both to no one and, in effect, to everyone. These outcomes are all highly appropriate for a language that performs an international function. However, it remains to be seen whether ELF ultimately catches on. In the meantime, I will for present purposes restrict its use to describing the core of pronunciation features that I identify in Chapter 6 as a model for international English phonology—the 'Lingua Franca Core', and will continue to use the more widely-acknowledged EIL.

English, then, is an international language owned by all who use it and in this connection the terminology issue is one of great import. It is not possible to label someone as a 'foreigner' or a 'non-native' and believe that he or she has equal rights to the language. These words both reflect an underlying attitude and, in turn, feed into it and influence it still further. As Alexander argues, 'Such terms now simply block understanding rather than allowing English teachers wherever they may originate and wherever they may work to acknowledge that English as an International Language (EIL) is here to stay' (1996: 35).

Appropriate pedagogy for an international language

In view of these worldwide transitions in the function, contexts of use, and ownership of English, it was inevitable that people would ultimately begin to question traditional EFL pronunciation goals. The two main issues at stake were, and still are, first, the extent to which it is relevant to try to instil L1 pronunciation norms into learners who are rarely likely to communicate with an L1 (especially an RP) speaker of English; and second, how to promote international intelligibility in the face of the vast expansion in the numbers of EFL varieties and their speakers. In other words, how do we identify for pedagogy the 'minimum standards of mutual intelligibility', to which Bansal (1990) refers, without recourse to an L1 model?

It was, as described above, within the context of ESL that these issues were first raised, with writers such as Smith (for example, 1983) and Bansal (for example, 1990) speaking out against the insistence on the teaching of RP but remaining, at the same time, anxious about the diversification of English accents within the dialects of the ESL countries. While concerns for mutual intelligibility have not by any means dissipated, the battle has largely been won in the ELT literature in terms of the acceptance by the English L1 countries of the inappropriacy of UK, USA, and Antipodean pronunciation norms for the ESL countries. However, this acceptance derives in part from a failure to appreciate the international uses of English for many members of the latter countries: in other words, the myth persists that their English performs only country-internal functions and that there is still a distinct EFL–ESL divide. Moreover, it does not extend to an acceptance of such L2 pronunciation (or other linguistic) norms for those ESL speakers who have emigrated to the L1 countries.

Moving on to the EFL context, we find at present among the teaching profession little, if any, willingness to accept any aspect of L2 phonological variation as a desirable end-product of teaching. The most widely accepted view among teachers, if not necessarily of their learners or some applied linguists, is that of Quirk:

> ... while 'Japanese English', 'German English', 'Russian English' may be facts of performance linguistics, there is no reason for setting them up as facts of institutional linguistics or as models for the learners in the countries (1982: 27).

I shall discuss Quirk's view in relation to the ESL varieties in the following chapter.

In a much-cited paper, Kachru discusses the sociolinguistic spread of the world's users of English in terms of three concentric circles (see also Phillipson's (1992) division into the 'core' and 'periphery'). Kachru's 'inner circle' is made up of the ENL countries (see above) and is 'norm-providing'; his 'outer circle' consists of the ESL countries and is 'norm-developing'; and his 'expanding circle' comprises the EFL countries and is 'norm-dependent' in the sense that the criteria by which usage is judged are imported from the ENL countries, primarily the UK and USA. This latter circle is 'currently expanding rapidly and has resulted in numerous performance (or EFL) varieties of English' (1985: 16–17). Their speakers are thus the producers of Quirk's 'performance linguistics' (see the previous paragraph).

In describing Kachru's model, Crystal argues that 'the question of whether autonomous norms can develop in a foreign language situation (such as Japan) remains unresolved' (1995: 364). This represents a significant, if not overly dramatic, theoretical shift from Quirk's and Kachru's positions, which seem to discount any suggestion of making L2 varieties the goal of teaching in the expanding (as opposed to the inner) circle, to one which tentatively acknowledges the possibility. Indeed, in the field of cultural studies this sort of theoretical shift in attitude towards foreign language norms is well advanced, and is even beginning to filter through to the EFL classroom. The writings of Byram (for example, 1989); Prodromou (1988); and Kramsch (for example, 1993, 1998), among others, are influencing a change in pedagogical attitudes, such that learners are no longer automatically expected to acquire the English L2 cultural baggage along with linguistic and communicative competence, but are often 'permitted' to apply the language to their own cultural norms. And in the most forward-thinking classrooms learners are being encouraged to develop what Kramsch describes as 'intercultural competence'. This is achieved, for example, through contrastive work, exposure to a range of cultures, and the use of literature and drama. Such learners develop a receptive awareness of the fact of difference in cultural norms across L1/cultural groupings, while at the same time gaining insight into the nature of the norms of their own L1/culture. While there is no suggestion that learners should normally apply the cultural baggage of other groups to their own English production, this awareness should not only increase their tolerance of difference but should also enable them to accommodate mutually, in small but significant ways, towards members of other groups, as they engage in EIL interaction.

Against all this, the focus on what the 'natives' do, which is so predominant a feature of EFL pronunciation teaching,[3] appears backward-looking and inappropriate for an international language, not least because research in social psychology has demonstrated clearly the links between accent and personal and group identity (for example, Edwards 1982, and see below). However, popular attitudes to accent are, as the social-psychological literature tells us, firmly entrenched and very slow to alter. In terms of the English language, this phenomenon has in the past been most evident in the split between attitudes towards RP and GA and those towards other accents, whether L1 regional or L2 foreign accents. As regards British L1 accents, a recent survey by the Institute of Personnel and Development reveals that job recruiters still discriminate against people with 'strong regional accents—especially those from Liverpool, Glasgow, or Birmingham' or with strong 'working class accents', and a recruitment consultant advises such people to 'upgrade' (*The Guardian*, 2 January 1997).[4] Such accent-based discrimination occurs in other ENL (English as a Native Language) countries, most notably the USA, where speakers of Black English varieties are particularly negatively perceived as compared with speakers of standard English or 'white' varieties, such as New Yorkese (see, for example, Eisenstein and Verdi 1983; Lippi-Green 1997).

The British situation has undoubtedly improved regarding much L1 regional variation. As a leader in *The Guardian* pointed out the day after reporting the above survey, 'Fifty years ago the employment as a BBC news reader of a man with a Yorkshire accent roused middle England to fury. Today Yorkshire, unlike Scouse or Brummie, is rarely a problem'. Although intelligibility is often cited as the reason for negative attitudes towards certain accents today, such as Liverpool, Birmingham, and Glasgow, it is not always clear which is the chicken and which the egg. Admittedly, some L1 accents are more difficult to understand relative to others, partly from lack of exposure, and partly from the extent of their own deviations from the shared common core of L1 phonological features crucial to intelligibility (see Chapter 4)—note the need for the regional Scottish dialogue in the film *Trainspotting* to be subtitled for an American audience in 1996. However, as Wolff (1959) demonstrated long ago, intelligibility is not necessarily reciprocal and may be the result rather than the cause of negative social-psychological attitudes which have, themselves, reduced the receiver's motivation to make an effort to understand.

If popular attitudes towards L1 accents of English have been so slow to change, it is not surprising, then, that L2 accents are still regarded negatively even by the majority of EFL teachers (though British teachers no longer support *en masse* the exclusive use of RP in the classroom). They are seen as unfortunate facts of deviant L2 performance rather than as acceptable examples of L2 'regional' variation with the potential to serve—at least in some of their features—as teaching models (see Brown 1991: 56). Meanwhile, those who write pronunciation materials for the EFL market have a vested interest in preserving the phonological status quo, with its emphasis on the need for learners to acquire all the features of 'native speaker' (RP or General American) pronunciation, including connected speech, rhythm, and intonation patterns, regardless of their (ir)relevance to EIL intelligibility (see Chapter 4 for a discussion of this resistance to change and of the need to restore the balance between segmental and suprasegmental phonology for EIL).

However, in recent years, one of the potentially most significant and interesting phonological developments has been the increasing antipathy of a small but growing number of British phonologists, sociolinguists, and EFL teachers towards the perpetuation of RP as the teaching model for L2 learners of English and the point of reference against which their pronunciation should be judged. RP, the minority prestige accent (or, more accurately, group of accents) with its origins in the public school system and a social élite from London and the Home Counties (though nowadays not regional in use), has provoked criticism for a number of reasons quite apart from the irrelevance and, for some, the embarrassment of its social origins or its stigma in certain intranational contexts. For example, Macaulay (1988: 115) points out that RP is spoken by only a tiny minority of English users and argues that it would be better if present-day linguists and phoneticians 'overcame their fascination with the accent of an elite minority and concerned themselves more with the speech of the majority of the population'. According to Crystal (1995), less than three per cent of the British population speak RP in its pure form, with many educated people having developed an accent known as 'modified RP'—a combination of RP and regional features. Indeed, Daniels (1995) refers to RP speakers as the 'phantom speakers of English' because of the unlikelihood of a learner's coming into contact with one of them. If regional accents have now become the L1 rule and RP the exception, there seems to be little reason to base the teaching of L2 English on an RP model, other than the fact that 'even in the inner circle only a specific elite group is considered as "norm makers", or as models for emulation' (Kachru 1985: 17).

A second argument against the use of RP in teaching is that it is by no means the easiest accent for an L2 learner to acquire, either productively or receptively, as compared with certain regional accents, such as Scottish English (see page 17). It lacks any close relationship with English orthography, contains a relatively large number of diphthongs, and elides the /r/ sound after vowels. Weak forms, a feature of both RP and General American (GA) but (contrary to popular opinion) not common to all native varieties of English, present both productive and receptive problems for learners, as we will see in Chapter 6.

A third argument concerns the fact that RP has altered over time. With clear distinctions between the speech of older and younger speakers of RP there is a risk of equipping learners with old-fashioned pronunciation. A further problem relating to this last point is that the most recent changes to RP are not being incorporated into teaching materials. Examples include: the loss of the diphthong /ʊə/ as in the word 'poor', which is now more likely to share the vowel sound /ɔː/ of the word 'core'; the lengthening of the previously clipped final vowel sound /ɪ/ in words ending in 'y', such as 'happy', 'very'; the phonetic (but again not phonemic) change to the diphthong /əʊ/ when followed by /l/ in words like 'cold' and 'goal' such that the sound becomes [ɔʊ].[5] And this is apart from the more extreme changes in the direction of 'Estuary English' such as /l/ vocalization, where the /l/ following a vowel in words like 'beautiful' and 'milk' is pronounced /ʊ/ (see Brown 1991: 93–5). Interestingly, Crystal (1996) considers that, regardless of the wishes of the standard-setting élite, it is possible that the English language, even ENL, is beginning to be influenced by international pronunciations. Should this be so and should the process continue, the implications for the whole English pronunciation system are immense.

Returning to the field of social psychology mentioned above, we find the attitudes of some teachers and their students unfavourable to the use of RP. A growing number of 'native' EFL teachers who speak other varieties of English are no longer prepared to accept that they should either 'upgrade' to an RP accent for teaching purposes or use their own regional accent, but explain to their students how items should be pronounced 'properly', thus implying that their own speech is in some way inferior. The situation in this respect as regards 'non-native' teachers is rather more complex and, because it links up with so many other issues that I will be considering later in the book, I will not discuss it further here except to make two points. Firstly, these teachers know from the personal experience of learning English as an L2 how important a role pronunciation plays in both productive and receptive intelligibility, and therefore tend to focus on it far more in the classroom than do 'native' teachers. Secondly, they tend, for various reasons again relating to personal experience, to insist on a rather higher degree of 'correctness' than do 'native' teachers. Both these points will be taken up again later.

Moving on to the learners themselves, we cannot escape the close links between language and identity. According to Widdowson, the reason why any attempt to reduce English to 'an entirely neutral medium for the conveyance of information' is doomed to failure is precisely because 'as soon as the human factor intrudes, the language grows, changes, varies, becomes subject to the identifying need of speakers to express their own identity' (1982: 11–12). Accent is particularly closely bound up with both personal and group identity, the group in this case being those sharing the learner's mother tongue. A survey by Porter and Garvin (1989) reveals that while some L2 speakers genuinely do desire to acquire an RP accent, many more, when asked, admit to preferring to retain something of their L1 accent. For the Japanese tertiary level learners of English in Benson's (1991) study, English with a Japanese accent is the second most preferred goal, and in both Benson's study and that of Starks and Paltridge (1994), an American English accent is preferred as a learning goal rather than a British (i.e. RP) one.

Learners who in all other respects achieve a very high degree of proficiency in English frequently retain a number of L1 phonological features. Although motor control is likely to be an element in this process (see Chapter 2), identity is probably the more salient issue. As Dalton and Seidlhofer argue, 'Pronunciation is so much a matter of self-image that students may prefer to keep their accent deliberately, in order to retain their self-respect or to gain the approval of their peers'. Therefore, insisting on learners conforming to target-language pronunciation norms and renouncing those of their mother tongue 'may even be seen as forcing them to reject their own identity' (1994a: 7). Daniels (1995) poetically suggests that in retaining 'the sounds, the rhythms and the intonation of our mother tongue', we avoid cutting 'the umbilical cord which ties us to our mother'. It should be added at this point that the context of learning, in terms of whether the learner is in a monolingual classroom (usually in their own L1 country) or in a multilingual classroom (more often in an L1 English country), also plays a part here. This issue will be explored more fully in later chapters.

The EIL phonological problem: where do we go next?

Thus far, we have established a number of things. English is now learnt and spoken most frequently to serve international functions among L2 speakers in international contexts. Its L1 speakers have therefore forfeited the right to dictate standards of pronunciation for L2 use. Moreover, the main L1 accent on which EFL (as opposed to ESL) pedagogy has hitherto been centred, i.e. RP, is not even widely used among L1 speakers and is therefore unlikely to be appropriate as the basis for L2 pedagogy. And there are, in any case, sound social-psychological reasons for not pushing learners of English to attempt to approximate an L1 accent too closely, but any alternative must, above all, be capable of promoting mutual intelligibility. Clearly, then, the optimum situation will be one in which EIL can both express the identities of its (L2) speakers and be a successful means for communication, much as any language reconciles, for the greater part among its L1 speakers, the opposing forces of the desire to establish 'wider networks of communication' and to preserve the speaker's 'particular identity' (Widdowson 1982: 9).[6]

Given that RP appears not to satisfy the various criteria that would render it an appropriate pedagogic model for EIL, we need to consider the alternatives. One option is the use of a Scottish or GA model since, with fewer diphthongs and closer orthographic links, these are probably easier for L2 learners to acquire and understand. They also lack the negative connotations of RP (Brown 1991). For these two reasons, Abercrombie proposed Scottish English as an EFL teaching model as long ago as 1956. Modiano has more recently advocated replacing British English with Mid-Atlantic English as the pedagogic standard for Europe, since this is 'a form of the language in which decidedly British pronunciations have been neutralized' (1996: 207). Another option is for learners to focus on any L1 regional variety that appeals to them (Daniels 1995), perhaps including that of one of their teachers. A third option is that of 'cloning', whereby learners model their pronunciation on that of someone they admire, not necessarily a 'native' speaker, but someone whose accent is easily intelligible. This could include speakers heard only on recorded teaching materials, such as the journalist Kate Adie, who features in the *Headway* series (see Jenkins and Kenworthy 1998).

An interesting approach to the problem from an ESL rather than EFL perspective, and referring to the language in general rather than pronunciation alone, is that of Bhatia, who argues:

> In the emerging language learning and teaching contexts of variation in the use of English across the international boundaries, it is necessary to recognize nativized norms for intranational functions within specific speech communities, and then to build a norm for international use on such models, rather than enforcing or creating a different norm in addition to that.
> (1997: 318)

Bhatia's proposal is taken up again in Chapter 6 below, where the Lingua Franca Core is discussed.

A further possibility involves distinguishing between a 'model' and a 'norm'. According to Dalton and Seidlhofer:

> If we treat RP and/or General American as a norm, we connect them strongly with ideas of correctness. The norm is invariable and has to be imitated independently of any considerations of language use. The aim, however unrealistic, is 100 percent attainment of the norm, which is regarded as an end in itself.

On the other hand:

> If we treat RP and/or General American as a model, we use them as points of reference and models for guidance. We decide to approximate to them more or less according to the demands of a specific situation or a specific purpose. In other words, a model is always connected to language in use and is therefore variable. Pronunciation models are pedagogic means to achieve the end of effective communication for specific learners. Ideas of correctness do not really apply—a pronunciation is simply more or less appropriate to a specific use of language.
> (1994b: 2.6–2.7)

In this sense, RP (or, indeed, GA) would serve in the classroom as the teaching model, providing points of reference to prevent learners from diverging too far away from each other and thus from a common pronunciation core safeguarding intelligibility. Learners would in turn be expected to adjust their accents further towards either the L1 or the L2 according to the context of interaction. This is an interesting possibility and ties in closely with the direction I will be proposing, particularly in its associations with accommodation theory. However, the fact remains that despite being the most frequently and fully described accent of British English, RP is now considered by a large majority to be obsolete and, even if it were not, we are soon likely to reach a situation where there are very few teachers able to provide a first-hand demonstration. Meanwhile, it is unlikely in the foreseeable future that the British would condone a move towards an American, or even a Scottish, accent for the world's largest group of English speakers, the NBESs. On the other hand, if we opt for one of the multi-model approaches, the safeguarding of mutual intelligibility becomes still more problematic.

The conundrum, then, remains and becomes ever more urgent as the number of new varieties of EIL continues to grow rapidly, thus increasing the amount of interaction taking place worldwide among NBESs—so that they are now the world's major group of English speakers. Any solution, however, must consider carefully the particular nature of the interactions of this group, and base its proposals on an examination of what its speakers actually do, rather than on what people think they do.

Interaction between NBESs has a number of characteristics that distinguish it from interaction involving BESs (of either 'native speaker' or 'non-native speaker' origin). For this reason, I prefer to make a distinction between interaction among NBESs and 'EIL' (which describes purpose rather than result) and to describe such interaction as 'Interlanguage Talk' (ILT). The term was first used by Krashen (1981, 1982), and subsequently by Long and Porter (1985) and Ellis (1994), to describe the simplified linguistic code in which acquirers of second languages speak to one another. My own use of the term refers specifically to the speech of NBESs from different L1s as they engage in interaction. These are members of the 'expanding circle' whose English has either fossilized at some point along the interlanguage continuum before achieving bilingual status, or is still in the process of moving in the latter direction, probably by means of continued language instruction. The term is not intended to refer to the speech of members of the outer circle, i.e. of those groups who speak established 'ESL' varieties of English. Their language is no more fossilized than that, for example, of L1 speakers of English from Australia or Scotland (but see Chapter 2, pages 30–2, for Quirk's and Selinker's completely different approach to ESL variation).

ILT is seen as problematic because of the amount of miscommunication it generates. Schwartz, for example, argues that while breakdowns in communication are not uncommon between L1 speakers of English, 'second language learners are faced with an additional burden to interaction—the imperfect command of the language of communication'. As a result, their conversations are 'often characterized by errors and problems of understanding' (1980: 138–9). Likewise, Varonis and Gass point out that ILT differs from both 'native/native' and 'non-native/native' interaction not only in that ILT interlocutors 'spend more time negotiating than the other pairs', but also because 'their non-understandings involve more work in the resolution' (1985a: 83). Lynch (1996: Chapter 6) provides a couple of good examples of this sort of thing, both of which interestingly involve loss of intelligibility through pronunciation error.

Indeed, pronunciation appears to play a very major role in problematic ILT. This is not surprising when one considers that the different L2 varieties of English are characterized by the transfer of L1 pronunciation features, which can vary markedly from one variety to another. On the other hand, these different varieties have far more in common with one another in terms of grammar, the learning of which tends to follow common developmental routes to a far greater extent than does the learning of phonology (see Ioup 1984). In terms of production, then, ILT is likely to be characterized by a substantial amount of differential L1 phonological transfer, itself leading to mutual intelligibility problems. This is borne out by a study I carried out among a multilingual group of postgraduate students at London University some years ago (reported in Jenkins 1995). Pronunciation emerged as by far the greatest factor in unintelligibility, and the difficulty tended to increase with the gap between interlocutors' first languages.[7] This study was followed up with several further years of research into ILT, some of which is reported in the next chapter, which confirmed the original finding of pronunciation as a—probably *the*—critical factor in unintelligibility in ILT.

The ILT pronunciation problem is compounded on the reception side by the NBES's tendency to process information in a bottom-up rather than a top-down manner (see Chapter 4 for empirical evidence). While most people would nowadays support an interactive processing model rather than one which is purely top-down or bottom-up, it seems that NBESs do not follow the same pattern. Difficulties which they encounter with top-down skills, particularly in relation to making use of contextual cues, both linguistic and extra-linguistic, and linguistic redundancy, force them back to an over-reliance on bottom-up skills which, in turn, leads them to focus too firmly on the acoustic signal. As Brown argues:

> For complex social and psychological reasons, they are less sure that they have grasped the topic being spoken of, the opinion being expressed about it, and the reasons for the speaker wanting to talk about it. They are less sure of the relevance of their own past experience in helping them to arrive at an interpretation. On top of all that, they are less sure of the forms of the language ... For all these reasons foreign learners are less able to bring to bear 'top-down' processing in forming an interpretation and, hence, are more reliant on 'bottom-up' processing.
> (1990: 59–60)

This is perhaps something of an oversimplification in that NBESs at different stages are likely to apply the two types of processing in different combinations. Nevertheless, they do as a group appear to place an inordinate amount of attention on the incoming signal, such that when this signal is distorted by a non-shared pronunciation error, intelligibility problems are virtually inevitable. Moreover, this is not restricted to phonological error, since NBESs have a narrower band of allophonic tolerance than either MESs or BESs, so that phonetic errors may also be problematic. This is linked closely to the fact that the majority of NBESs have not been exposed to a range of other NBES accents and the types of phonological and phonetic transfer they contain. It is precisely this lack of exposure which causes them to focus on bottom-up information. For, as Lynch points out, 'in unusual situations, such as ... dealing with an unfamiliar accent ... we may be obliged to pay greater attention to bottom-up information' (1996: 22).

The ILT intelligibility problem thus involves both production and reception, and in replacing an L1 teaching model, we need to take both fully into account. If we can identify precisely which phonological and phonetic features affect intelligibility for ILT hearers (and these will not necessarily be the same as for L1 English speakers—only ILT data can provide this crucial information)—we can then devise pedagogic measures to facilitate the accurate production of these by ILT speakers.[8] In other words, we can establish some sort of pronunciation core of intelligibility such that exists among L1 varieties of English (see Chapter 6) and then set about finding ways to encourage speakers to adjust their speech in its direction 'as and when necessary; and here, accommodation processes also have an essential role.

Indeed, it may well be that Speech Accommodation Theory (SAT) potentially has the greatest contribution of all to make to ILT pronunciation and, thus, to EIL. According to this theory, which, in more recent years, has become more broadly based and known as Communication Accommodation Theory or CAT (see Giles and Coupland 1991), speakers may adjust their speech either in the direction of that of their interlocutors (convergence) or away from that of their interlocutors (divergence). The former process, that of convergence, is the one that is of particular interest to us in the context of EIL.

The original motivation found to account for convergence was the desire to be liked. This desire can operate both at an interpersonal level, i.e. the desire to be liked by one's interlocutor, and at group level, i.e. the desire for membership of the community represented by an interlocutor. In the accommodation literature, however, group identity is more commonly associated with the process of divergence: a speaker diverges from the speech of an interlocutor in order to distance himself from the latter and thus preserve his own sense of group identity. Subsequently, the wish to be understood has come to be considered an equally salient motivation for convergence as the desire to be liked. Both motivations are central to EIL. They are also mutually inseparable owing to the fact that, by definition, interlocutors are bidding for membership of an international community rather than of one or other's L1 community. Thus, the issue of group identity coincides with the desire for intelligibility in ILT and together they alter the accommodation conditions (see Chapter 7).

It seems likely that the whole future of the English language is to an extent bound up with the process of convergence. On the one hand, speakers need to be able to adapt and adjust their speech to make it more comprehensible—and, no doubt, acceptable—to particular interlocutors in particular settings. This includes the ability to adjust towards a more standard form of pronunciation and, indeed, it would patronize speakers with both L2 and ethnic minority accents such as Ebonics (see Todd 1997), to suggest otherwise. On the other hand, receivers, including teachers, need to develop a greater tolerance (in both senses) of difference, and the ability to adapt and adjust their expectations according to interlocutor and setting. Bhatia argues in his proposal that we consider international English 'a kind of superstructure rather than an entirely new concept' (see pages 17–18).

The best way to enable this 'superstructure' to be added is 'by making the learner aware of cross-cultural variations in the use of English and by maximizing his or her ability to negotiate, accommodate and accept plurality of norms' (1997: 318).

With the rapid increase in the number of different varieties of English in the world, each with its own accent, few people, if any, are guaranteed to be exposed pedagogically to every single accent that they are likely to encounter. Flexibility is therefore the key. In the rest of this book, I will explore not only the possibility of establishing a phonological core for EIL, but also how pedagogic procedures can help speakers of English to acquire such flexibility.

Notes

1 This term, taken from Kachru (1985), loosely refers to those countries whose people speak English as a Foreign Language rather than as an official and/or second language. See page 12 for full details of Kachru's representation of the sociolinguistic spread of the world's users of English as three concentric circles, the 'inner', 'outer' and 'expanding' circles.

2 The University of Cambridge Local Examinations Syndicate in 1996 combined their schemes for the training of 'native' and 'non-native' teachers. However, it remains to be seen how the directors of these training courses respond.

3 This has also become one of the main purposes of the growing number of corpora of English, such as the British National Corpus, COBUILD, and CANCODE. Their automatic application to the teaching of English, welcomed by 'inner circle' teachers (possibly because of the 'expert' status it bestows on them and the natural advantage it accords them over 'non-native' teachers) is a questionable step for EIL (cf. Widdowson 1991; Prodromou 1996 a, b).

4 It should be added that the reverse situation sometimes obtains: an RP accent can be a distinct disadvantage in fields such as popular music and certain branches of the media, and may provoke ridicule and hostility in Australia (cf. Brown 1991: 31).

5 Throughout the book, square brackets are used both for phonetic symbols and to denote actual speech realizations. Slanting brackets are used only for abstract phonemic distinctions.

6 Nevertheless, we must not exaggerate the success of L1 communication: as we saw in the previous section, the L1 varieties of English do not enjoy one hundred per cent mutual intelligibility, and more should not be demanded of L2 than of L1 speakers.

7 Germanic languages (for example, Dutch and Danish) and Romance languages (for example, Spanish and Italian) can be considered to have

smaller gaps within their groupings than the gaps, for example, between Dutch and Spanish, or Italian and Japanese.

8 This is not to suggest that the intelligibility problem will be identical for each hearer regardless of their L2. Clearly, this will depend not only on the NBES's stage of interlanguage development, but also on their L1. Nevertheless, it should be possible to isolate a minimum set of features whose correct production will guarantee phonological/phonetic intelligibility for all NBESs, regardless of their L1.

2 The variation problem 1: Inter-speaker variation

Variety's the very spice of life,
That gives it all its flavour.

Cowper, *The Task* Book II, 'The Time-piece', line 606 (1785)

Contrary to the view expressed by Cowper, the terms 'variability', 'variation', and even 'variety' have always held certain negative connotations. In many walks of life they are, or have been for periods of their history, associated with some degree of unreliability, lowering of standards, or falling wide of an accepted norm. Evidence of such is provided by a large number of dictionary definitions. *The Shorter Oxford English Dictionary* (Onions 1973), for example, cites an 1832 biological definition of 'variability' as: 'capability in plants or animals of variation or *deviation* from a type'. 'variable' is defined as: '*liable* or apt to vary or change; *susceptible* of variation; mutable, *changeable, fluctuating, uncertain*' and, relating to persons, as: 'Apt to change from one opinion or course of action to another; *inconstant, fickle, unreliable*' (late Middle English). Again, 'variation' is defined as: 'difference, *divergence*, or *discrepancy* between two or more things or persons' (1637), and in biology as: '*deviation* or *divergence* in the structure, character, or function of an organism from those typical of or usual in the species or group' (1859). Among the OED definitions of 'variety' is that of 1579: 'tendency to change; *fickleness*'. Definitions of the verb 'to vary' include the words '*diverge, divergence, disagree, dissent, inconsistent,* and *discrepancy*', while the late Middle English definition of this verb has a very familiar contemporary ring: 'to *differ, diverge,* or *depart,* in respect of practice or observance (from some standard)'. (Emphasis added to items bearing derogatory associations within definitions.)

Human nature, on this evidence at least, seems to have a strong tendency to favour conformity to standards, uniformity, and conservatism, and to disfavour non-conformity, diversity, and change. Because language is so closely bound up with human identity and attitudes, it is inevitable that we should commonly encounter among speakers of standard English(es) strongly held and deeply entrenched convictions as to the superiority of language which adheres to established linguistic norms and the inferiority of language which departs from them. When Jean Aitchison was so bold as to express, in her BBC Reith Lectures in 1996, the view now accepted by most linguists that language variation and change are natural processes rather than symptoms of degeneration and decay, she received many outraged responses from the general public. The following, quoted in an article by Aitchison herself in *The Times Higher Education Supplement*, is a typical example: 'Madam, how dare you distort, desecrate and defile the English language as you did in your recent Reith lecture' (15 March 1996: 19). The following year, John Honey maintained that 'standard English is not merely one variety among many, but instead derives its value from a set of qualities which are not shared by other, non-standard dialects' (1997: 5). He followed this up with an appearance on the BBC2 programme *Oldies* in December 1997, where he announced that 'we' now know for certain that some three or four dialects of English are intrinsically superior in quality to all the others. This sort of view is evident in the discrimination against speakers of English with certain regional accents that is still rife in the UK and USA in job interview situations (see pages 13–14). And L2 variation is the target of still stronger prejudice, even in the usually progressive *Guardian* newspaper. For example, in his review of the BBC2 programme *The Ballad of Yoko and John*, Adam Sweeting claims, with reference to the (admittedly Japanese-) English of Yoko Ono, that 'the significance of a rare interview with Yoko was dissipated by the difficulty of deciphering *her mauling of the English language*' (Supplement, 7 January 1998: 19; emphasis added).

The problem, though, is not simply that many speakers of standard English favour linguistic conservatism and uniformity. It is compounded by the fact that although they may experience variation as an *intra*-speaker phenomenon in their own L1 use, it is not something they consciously recognize, particularly in relation to pronunciation. Yet this variation in pronunciation, morphology, syntax, and lexis is apparently 'so acute that the same individual, playing various social roles, may frequently display forms of standard and non-standard Englishes in different contexts' (Brown *et al.* 1994: 154). Patterned variation is 'a ubiquitous characteristic of the contemporary language ... rather than merely a marginal phenomenon', 'language is inherently variable, and variant choices carry clear social meanings' (Milroy 1994: 167). This applies, as Milroy points out, especially to the speech channel and, more particularly, at the phonological level, where the standardization process is least successful. However, where pronunciation is concerned, many L1 language teachers regard with suspicion, and 'lay' speakers interpret as criticism, any suggestion that they employ such variation in their own speech.

On the other hand, while the majority of L1 English speakers are not sensitive to their own *intra*-speaker variations, they are quick to notice the *inter*-speaker variations of L2 speakers. These they interpret as monolithic deviations from the 'rightful' L1 standard, and do not appreciate the significance of the variability. Again, this is particularly true of pronunciation where it reflects the majority view of speakers of any L1 accent, not only of those who speak the standard prestige variety. In the field of second language acquisition, where authorities are well aware of the synchronic variation in L2 speech, similar attitudes surface to some extent in the use of terms like 'free variation' and 'systematic variation' (cf. Ellis 1994) to denote variation in grammatical *correctness* in the target language. Thus, grammatical variation in interlanguage (IL), both between L2 and L1 speakers (inter-speaker variation) and within the speech of an individual speaker (intra-speaker variation), is often viewed by the experts as something to be explained in order to reduce and, preferably, eradicate it.

However, two concepts hitherto unrecognized in EFL, but fundamental to international uses of English, will emerge from this and the following chapters. Firstly, that of *acceptable L2 inter-speaker variation*: while inter-speaker phonological variation can certainly impede communication in EIL, particularly in interlanguage talk (ILT), it is no longer appropriate to regard all such variation from the L1 as automatically deviant. Much of it comprises acceptable regional variation on a par with that which we find among L1 accents of English (where, incidentally, inter-speaker variation can also present an obstacle to intelligibility). It should go without saying that an L2 speaker of English who has attained BES status (and whose production cannot therefore be considered an IL) does not exhibit 'deviant' pronunciation, but rather L2 regional variation, along with some degree of variation in standardness of the type exhibited by L1 speakers. It is at the NBES level, where speakers still retain ILs, that the phonological and phonetic forms that occur can be judged for 'correctness'. And, from a study of the types of inter-speaker variation occurring in ILT and their effects on intelligibility, we will be able to establish later on (Chapter 6) which variants are acceptable as regional ones and which are not. Thence we will be able to redefine the concept of phonological acceptability for EIL and consider the implications for pedagogy and assessment.

The second, and possibly still more fundamental—and surprising— concept for EIL, is that of *beneficial intra-speaker variation*. By employing accommodative processes, speakers may vary their pronunciation in such a way that their phonological variation constitutes a solution rather than a problem, as we will see both here in relation to same-L1 and different-L1 interlocutors, and in the following chapter in relation to different task types. But before considering why and how this is so, we will need to look more closely at these two types of IL variation, inter-speaker (this chapter) and intra-speaker (Chapter 3), in order to examine the ways in which they operate and to assess their effects on intelligibility.

Inter-speaker variation

L2 inter-speaker variation is the type of variation with which most people are familiar. Essentially, it involves the transfer of features of the particular L1 onto the production (and, of course, reception) of the target language.[1] It is most noticeable phonologically, where the resulting IL accent tends to form a stereotype for the whole L2 group of speakers in the collective mind of the L1 community. Meanwhile, L2 speakers are also aware of their inter-speaker variation, both in their own pronunciation and—generally to a far greater extent—in that of speakers from L1s other than their own. This leads to frequent comments in multilingual settings about the mutual unintelligibility of other speakers' IL pronunciations, particularly when exposure to the ILs concerned has been limited and/or (for reasons which will later become clear) the interaction takes place in groups rather than dyads. Worryingly, if Trudgill's (1998) assessment of the developing situation is correct, while homogeneity is on the increase among World Englishes at the lexical and grammatical levels, the gap is widening at the phonological level.

Hitherto, L2 inter-speaker phonological variation, or phonological transfer, has been discussed in terms of variation from a standard native model, with such variation being considered lack of correctness. This contrasts largely with the situation relating to L1 variation, where regional pronunciation norms may, and often do, cause attitude judgements of inappropriacy, rather than grammatical judgements of incorrectness (though note, the same cannot be said of L1 regional morphology and syntax, where non-standardness is indeed regarded as inaccuracy).

As soon as we begin discussing the English language in an international context, however, it becomes crucial to redefine L2—and possibly also L1—phonological correctness. This means reconsidering the issue in relation to the wider context of international phonological norms, rather than continuing to focus narrowly, and often obsessively, on the norms of a minority of speakers, RP or GA, within a minority English-speaking community (Britain or the USA), although the USA represents a more substantial minority than does Britain. And in view of the close links between accent and personal and group identity that were discussed in the previous chapter, the need for such redefinition of phonological correctness could be said to amount to a moral obligation.

Medgyes argues that 'there are as many equal varieties of English as there are countries where English is spoken as a first or second language—and a lot more, if dialects and sociolects are also taken into account' (1992: 340). I doubt, though, that he intends us to infer from this that 'anything goes'. We are still faced with the task of distinguishing between an interlanguage, whose speaker remains at the level of an NBES (non-bilingual English speaker: see Chapter 1) and an EIL regional variety, whose speaker has progressed to BES (bilingual English speaker) status, while—in all likelihood—retaining numerous phonological and phonetic features of the L1, which will distinguish her speech from that of BESs from other L2 'equal varieties'. This is because, as is widely acknowledged, L2 varieties of English differ most noticeably in their pronunciation. The crucial challenge for EIL phonological research, then, is to identify those areas in which differences among the manifold international varieties of English (including L1 varieties) are benign and those in which they pose a potential threat to international intelligibility, particularly for those who remain NBESs, and whose interactions thus remain at the level of interlanguage talk. Having accomplished this, we will be in a far stronger position to make claims on behalf of L2 regional norms.

We may also be able to identify within the L2 varieties common phonological features necessary for adoption by L1 speakers of English when they themselves engage in international communication. It is conceivable that such features will ultimately become formalized within a new international variety, such as the 'World Standard Spoken English' (WSSE), predicted by Crystal (1997: 138), and/or lead to a redefinition of the concept of standard English, such that it is able to embrace 'divergent' L2 features. (See Ahulu 1997, who argues strongly and convincingly in favour of the latter move, though he is admittedly referring to grammar in general rather than phonology in particular). These developments are especially plausible where large numbers of L2 varieties share the same non-L1 phonological features, such as /θ/ and /ð/ substitutions or avoidance of weak forms. It is important, if English is to have an international future, that we find out what the L2 varieties have in common and then build on this information in pedagogy (for the expression of similar views, see Ufomata 1990; Sure 1992; Bhatia 1997).

In fact, it seems that the latter process has already begun. Local L2 English norms are emerging for the first time, or at least being offered professional support, in regions where the language has a strong international function as well as an intranational one, such as Kenya, Sierra Leone, South Africa, and, to some extent, Europe. Experts from these and other L2 English backgrounds have started putting forward strong arguments for the right of their local variety of English to be norm-setting rather than norm-dependent: see Sure (1992) for the claim that Kenyan English should be the standard against which Kenyan learners' English performance is measured; Berns (1995) on the nativizing process among European varieties of English and the possibility of a new institutionalized norm-setting variety, 'European English'; Conteh-Morgan (1997) on the nativization process of English in Sierra Leone; Hibbert and Makoni (1997) on arguments against standard English as the norm for South African Englishes. Perhaps situations such as the following, described by an Austrian teacher of English in Vienna, will be hard to find ten years or so from now:

I've been here at ... very very long and this has been a tradition that you're supposed to approximate the native speaker, and unless you approximate the native British speaker you are sort of regarded as inferior. And I think that's where attitudes need to change. I don't see why a good EFL teacher, Austrian English teacher, shouldn't have a trace of an accent of his local variety of English. We're talking about international English, we're talking about English as a global language, and we're still keeping to this idea that the Austrian teacher—I mean I was brought up in that tradition—*you must sound more British than the British.* (contributor to open discussion on English as an International Language, British Council/IATEFL *ELT Links* Symposium, Vienna, September 1996; emphasis added)

It can only be hoped that the change of attitude this speaker refers to will not be too long in coming, and that L2 teachers of English will no longer be regarded as 'inferior' because they retain something of their 'local variety of English'.

ESL varieties and the interlanguage controversy

At this point, we need to make an important distinction between foreign language (EFL) and second language (ESL) varieties of English. In Chapter 1, we considered Kachru's three-concentric circle model of English users. Kachru (1985, see page 12) distinguishes between English speakers in the outer circle, for whom English performs essential intranational functions, and those in the expanding circle, who learn the language for use predominantly outside their own country in communication with L1 speakers and (more often) L2 speakers from other language backgrounds.

It is undoubtedly true that in a number of ESL countries such as Bangladesh, there are many learners of English who have not yet reached their target production, and who thus still have interlanguages. However, we should be careful not to confuse the inaccuracies of their production with the more stable regional pronunciation varieties used by fluent speakers of non-British or American varieties of outer circle English. Unsurprisingly, more conventional authorities such as Quirk (for example, 1990) and Selinker (for example, 1972, 1992) consider varieties like Indian English to be fossilized versions of standard British or American English. For example, in an article which elicited outraged responses from writers in both outer and expanding circles, Quirk attacks what he calls 'liberation linguistics' (roughly, the acceptance of non-standard Englishes as legitimate varieties) and, according to Kachru (1991), implicitly invokes the concept of 'deficit linguistics' (roughly, the assumption that linguistic non-standardness equals incorrectness). Regardless of proficiency level, Quirk then bunches the ESL varieties together with EFL varieties, such as Russian English, French English, and Japanese English, labelling them all 'non-native varieties of English', claiming that these varieties 'are inherently unstable, ranged along a qualitative cline, with each speaker seeking to move to a point where the varietal characteristics reach vanishing point, and where thus, ironically, each variety is best manifest in those who by commonsense measures speak it worst' (1990: 5–6).

On the other hand, a number of less conservative language experts see the ESL varieties in a very different light. Riney, for example, quoting Selinker's (1972) definition, argues that the term 'interlanguage' should be reserved for 'developing systems of language learners "based on the observable output which results from a learner's attempted production of a TL [target language] norm"'. He himself advocates the introduction of 'the terms (*sic*) 'additional language' to refer to the more stabilized systems of competent speakers of second or additional languages' from countries, such as Singapore, India, or even Holland, 'whose target language norm is, as time goes on, less and less likely to be a native speaker one based in the UK or the USA' (1997: 238).

Nelson condemns Selinker's (1972) claim 'that interlanguage (IL) competence "in whole groups of individuals" may become fossilized, "resulting in the emergence of a new dialect ([as] Indian English), where fossilized IL competences [*sic*] may be the normal situation".' (1995: 273). Nelson rightly considers this to be 'a rather devalued use of the characterization "normal"' (ibid.) and goes on implicitly to support Y. Kachru's argument that:

> The question of why a stable system should be characterized as an IL is not answered. It is also not clear what the difference is between 'stable' and 'fossilized': that which is fossilized is surely unchanging and therefore stable! Additionally, if 'an entirely fossilized IL competence' refers to a community ... it is difficult to see why it is an IL and why it is 'fossilized'. Presumably American English developed as an IL among a large portion of the immigrant population from the non-English-speaking parts of Europe. Does that mean that American English represents an 'entirely fossilized IL'? (1993: 266)

This seems to be pure common sense, though two further points need to be made in connection with ESL and EIL. Firstly, fluent English speaker groups in the expanding circle (my BESs, or bilingual English speakers) deserve to be treated similarly to competent speaker groups in the outer circle. Their English is no less stable than that of the latter; nor does it exhibit, any more than they do, characteristics common to ILs, such as phonological blends not occurring in either the L1 or the L2, for example, the Korean English IL affricate /dð/ for the phoneme /ð/ (Ahn 1998: 302–3).

Secondly, while many would agree that the validity of the ESL varieties for intranational use is now established beyond doubt, it does not follow that these varieties are acceptable (or appropriate) in their unadulterated form for international use. As was discussed in the previous chapter, the gap is closing between ESL and EFL varieties (though not in the sense implied by Quirk above) as speakers from both types of community engage increasingly in international communication. Just as members of the inner circle will find it necessary to make phonological adjustments to render themselves intelligible on the international circuit, so will members from the outer circle be obliged to modify their speech in certain ways if they wish to be understood by speakers of varieties of English other than their own. To that extent, some of the suggestions made in this book will be relevant to their (international) language needs.

Phonological inter-speaker variation and its effects on interlanguage talk

The time has come for us to examine in greater detail the ways in which NBES inter-speaker pronunciation may vary from the L1, and the extent to which such variation can impede intelligibility when NBESs interact with one another. Looking first at segmental variation and then at suprasegmental, we will not distinguish at present between acceptable variation and unacceptable error; but to avoid excessive circumlocution and political correctness, all L2 phonological variation from L1 forms will be described indiscriminately as 'error', 'deviation', and 'variant'. However, the reader is advised to bear in mind that in Chapter 4, the status of these deviations will be reconsidered according to their effects (or lack of them) on intelligibility in ILT. Hence some are likely to be designated acceptable L2 regional variants rather than errors.

Inter-speaker segmental variation and its effects

It has been widely argued for some years now that segmental (i.e. phonemic and phonetic) variation has a rather less serious effect on the intelligibility of L2 English speech than suprasegmental (i.e. prosodic, including stress, rhythm, intonation, and features of connected speech).[2] This debate will be taken up in greater detail in later chapters. For the moment, I will simply point out that to date no serious comprehensive investigation of the relative contribution to intelligibility of these two areas has been conducted at all, let alone within the context of ILT.

Habit formation plays a major role in the production of L2 sounds with muscular habits that have always operated to produce the sounds of the L1 being automatically activated in L2 production. Although NBESs often cope well with the articulation of L2 sounds when they have sufficient planning time to focus cognitively on them and thus exert control over them, as soon as they release this control in order to focus their attention on the content of their message, the old habits tend automatically to return. This situation continues until and unless sufficient practice of L2 sounds leads to the formation of new habits which, for the majority of NBESs, will not occur throughout the entire L2 phonological system.

Sounds that are phonetically very different from those in the L1 are initially likely to prove most difficult to produce, since the articulators must be activated in new ways. On the other hand, where there is any degree of similarity between L1 and L2 sounds, there is a tendency to identify the two, and thence to categorize the new sounds in terms of the old. Selinker considers that the making of such 'interlingual identifications' is 'a basic, if not *the* basic, SLA learning strategy' (1992: 260; emphasis in original). While the process of interlingual identification makes for greater ease of articulation at first, ultimately it holds the threat of fossilization. This may manifest itself simply in a slight degree of foreign accent, but may have implications for intelligibility, especially in ILT. Examples where this has proved to be the case are the Japanese pronunciation of the voiceless glottal fricative /h/ as the voiceless bilabial fricative [ɸ] before /uː/ as in the word 'who'; and the Spanish pronunciation of bilabial plosive /b/ as the voiced bilabial fricative [β] as in 'table'.

In order to master an L2 sound, a learner has to acquire both physiological knowledge regarding its articulation and an understanding of its place in the phonological system to which it belongs. This involves not only the acquisition of sounds which do not exist in the L1, but also—more problematically—the recognition and ability to deal with the often complex overlap between the L1 and L2 systems. This complexity manifests itself in two major ways. Firstly, two distinct phonemes (i.e. sounds which distinguish meaning) in the learner's L1 may be reduced to allophonic status (i.e. different realizations of the same phoneme) in English. For example, clear [l] and dark [ɫ] are phonemes in Russian but allophones of the same /l/ phoneme in English as in, respectively, 'lip' and 'pill'. If these two such allophones are distributed wrongly in a syllable, the effect, if any, is generally one of oddness rather than unintelligibility. Secondly, two or more allophones in the learner's L1 may have full phonemic status in English, for example, [n], [m], and [ŋ] in Japanese, as in the English words 'sun', 'sum', and 'sung'. In this case, incorrect distribution of the sounds is very likely to result in unintelligibility. The latter situation is particularly troublesome, since learners may not be aware of any difference in the articulation of sounds which are purely allophonic in their L1—much as the average L1 speaker of English is not aware of articulating the phoneme /n/ in three different ways depending on its phonetic environment (i.e. as a dental, an alveolar, and a post-alveolar in the words 'tenth', 'find', and 'range' respectively). Learners therefore have great difficulty in distinguishing such sounds perceptively as phonemes of a second language.

In the previous hypothetical example, although production would also prove difficult prior to extensive instruction, it would almost certainly precede perception. We cannot assume that because NBESs are able to produce sound contrasts, they can necessarily discriminate aurally between them; indeed, the opposite is not infrequently true (for example, the often-cited Japanese-English discrimination problem with /l/ and /r/). Even for L1 learners of sound systems, there is evidence that the auditory level is not necessarily primary (see page 47), so that 'acoustic differences cannot be readily perceived until the corresponding articulatory gestures have been learnt' (Ladefoged 1967: 167). Further problems commonly arise for NBESs both where two distinct phonemes of English are articulated phonetically very close together, for example /p/ and /b/ in initial position (the main difference being that the former is aspirated before a vowel sound while the latter is not), and where two or more phonetic realizations of one phoneme are articulated in very different ways, for example clear [l] and dark [ɫ].

It may be argued that to perceive or produce these distinctions to any degree of precision is unnecessary, since the context will compensate for any deficiency in the form of the message itself. But a striking feature of the data which are produced below to support the categories of L2 phonological and phonetic deviation is the fact that in the majority of cases, a clear context—linguistic, extra-linguistic, or both—was available at the time the deviant form was produced. In spite of the presence of such a context, these forms regularly led to intelligibility problems for those receivers who did not share the speaker's L1. Those receivers who spoke the same L1 as the latter generally (but not always) found the deviation intelligible. The role of context in ILT will be discussed at much greater length in Chapter 4.

We can categorize segmental deviation types conveniently into three groupings:

1 sound *substitution* and *conflation*;
2 *consonant deletion* (or *elision*);
3 *addition*.

Deviations involving *substitution* (for example, Japanese /l/ for /r/ and vice versa) and *conflation* (for example, both /θ/ and /s/ being pronounced /s/) tend to be caused by the kinds of phonemic and articulatory difficulties described above. In the case of *consonant deletion* a sound may be omitted altogether, such as the omission of the /r/ in 'price', typically by a Taiwanese speaker of English. Alternatively, the elided sound may be replaced by a glottal stop /ʔ/ as in the Chinese-English pronunciation of 'duck' as /dʌʔ/. *Addition* can be of two types: *epenthesis* and *paragoge*. *Epenthesis* refers to the intrusive sound placed between two other sounds to facilitate a 'difficult' articulation. It passes unnoticed in L1 speech, for example, the epenthetic /t/ in the word 'mince' /mɪnts/ or the /p/ in 'comfy' /kʌmpfɪ/. In L2 speech it is most often a vowel that is inserted. For example, an Arab speaker of English may insert a vowel between the /p/ and /l/ in the word 'place', thus pronouncing it as /pɪleɪs/. *Paragoge* involves the addition of a sound to the end of a word. For example, a Korean speaker of English typically pronounces the word 'luggage' as [lʌgidʒi]. Deviations involving consonant deletion and epenthesis or paragoge are closely connected with differences in permitted syllable structure between the L1 and English, with an open CV (consonant-vowel) structure tending to be universally preferred (see below, pages 37 and 101).

An intelligibility problem may result from a unique deviation source, that is, a deviant sound substitution/conflation, or deletion, or addition within a single word. More commonly, though, unintelligibility is the result of multiple such segmental deviations, either within a single word or among consecutive words.

Sound substitution and conflation

Where deviations involve sound substitutions within single words, the outcome often depends on whether or not a substitution results in a non-word. For example, the day after his driving test, a Korean student came into class with a downcast expression and announced 'I pailed'. On a different occasion, the same student asked a Japanese student at the start of the mid-morning break, 'Do you want a copy?' In the former type of situation, where the error 'pailed' is a non-word (if we exclude the homophone 'paled', which these students were unlikely to know), a BES would immediately recognize that an error had occurred and would probably be able to make the necessary mental adjustment in order to interpret the word correctly. NBESs, on the other hand, may, and indeed did on this occasion, have more of a problem. While they were aware that they had not understood, they did not have sufficient L2 lexical knowledge to appreciate the non-word status of 'pailed', and therefore to search their mental lexicons for viable alternatives. In fact, one of the group followed up 'I pailed' with the question: 'Did you pass your driving test?'.

More problematic, though, is the second example, where both a BES and NBES receiver could (and did) simply misunderstand the intended message (in this case, a 'coffee' rather than a '(photo)copy' was being offered). Again, though, the BES (or MES) receiver has the advantage, since she is more likely to make use of contextual cues in arriving at an interpretation. In fact, even when the context is manifestly clear, NBESs still seem more likely to place their trust in an acoustic signal (in other words, the exact speech sounds which are transmitted, see Chapter 4).

Even where certain deviations occurring in isolation would not normally lead to non-understanding, when combined with others within the same word, the combination frequently causes too much distraction. For example, in isolation the substitution of /t/ for /θ/, or *schwa paragoge* (the addition of word-final /ə/), rarely seem to cause problems of understanding for the NBES recipient. However, during a discussion between a Korean and a Taiwanese student of English on the subject of crime, the Korean student referred to 'cartheft' as /kɑː 'tepətə/. His Taiwanese interlocutor was completely unable to grasp the meaning (which she admitted in a follow-up discussion) and simply twice repeated the speaker's word with the same erroneous pronunciation. (Note that word stress is also involved: see page 39).

Potentially still more problematic for intelligibility is a word group containing a range of substitutions and conflations, which, with each individual deviation further compounding the problem, may be rendered totally incomprehensible to both NBES and BES interlocutors. For example, a Japanese student ended a short presentation on the subject of the European Union with a humorous, unprepared one-liner that sounded very much like 'Don lies a fizz off score'. Despite many years of exposure to Japanese-English ILs, I did not understand the sentence until it had been repeated four times.[3] On the other hand, one Japanese student in the group understood immediately, while the others needed only a single repetition. However, the non-Japanese NBESs (European, Iranian, Korean, Taiwanese) were completely mystified until the sentence had been 'translated' for them into: 'Don't rise (i.e. raise) the fees of school (i.e. school fees)'.

This is, of course, an extreme example, with a pronunciation error (or errors) in every word along with lexical and grammatical oddity. These involve a combination of consonant substitution, reduction in vowel quantity, and phonetic approximation (i.e. allophonic rather than phonemic deviation): 'don't' was pronounced with a short nasalized [ɔ̃] and deletion of /nt/; the [ɹ] in 'rise' was substituted with [l]; 'fees' and 'school' lost their vowel length, while the vowel of 'school' was also opened to [ɔ] and the final [ɫ] was deleted; the vowel of 'of' was not weakened, nor was the consonant voiced; and because so much else was in doubt, the conflation of /ð/ with /z/ in 'the' also contributed to the general lack of intelligibility. Interestingly, though, the grammar errors caused no intelligibility problems for these NBESs: they understood the meaning of 'Don't rise the fees of school' instantly. Such lack of effect of grammar error on ILT intelligibility is a recurring feature throughout the ILT data that I have collected over the years. Possible reasons for this phenomenon will be explored in Chapter 4.

The previous example contains an instance of phonetic approximation which was difficult to interpret. In fact, the majority of phonetic approximations seem to lead to foreign accent alone rather than to unintelligibility, and can therefore be ignored unless a learner wishes to acquire 'native-like' pronunciation (perhaps because he—or more probably she—intends to teach English, or is an immigrant to an ENL country and wants to assimilate as fully as possible to the second language and culture). On the other hand, in a small number of cases, phonetic L1 transfer may cause unintelligibility, as happened in the previous example. Moreover, such phonetic deviations as do occur seem to cause more of a problem for NBESs than for BESs/MESs. This is because the latter have a wider band of phonetic tolerance and range of awareness of the available options than do the former, and are therefore better able to categorize different phonetic realizations as belonging to the same English phoneme. By contrast, NBESs tend to hear phonetic differences as categorical, i.e. phonemic. Although this phenomenon appears to be less of an issue than phonemic substitution in the ILT data, several comprehension difficulties were caused, for example, by approximations of word-final /n/ by Japanese speakers (as above), and by Spanish-English approximations of /b/ with [β], such that 'book' was pronounced [βʊk] and 'table', [teɪβɫ].

Syllable simplification: consonant deletion and sound addition

These two processes will be discussed together as they are the two methods used by NBESs to simplify English syllables. NBES simplification of English syllable structure is, in fact, potentially far more damaging to ILT interaction than substitution and conflation. As was pointed out above (page 35), the chief cause of such simplification is the structure of L1 syllables, with the universal preference for an open-syllable CV pattern. Speakers of CV languages tend to select one of two ways to simplify the syllables of a non-CV language: consonant deletion (with or without the insertion of a glottal stop to replace an elided consonant) or addition (by epenthesis—the addition of a sound word-initially or between sounds, and by paragoge—the addition of a vowel word-finally, with schwa paragoge being found only in ILs and not in first languages). Some NBESs employ a combination of these two strategies, possibly depending on their degree of proficiency in English (with deletion tending to be an earlier process and addition a later one) and the internal structure of the syllable in question. However, the majority opt for one or the other, depending on the structure of L1 syllables.

Fluent speakers of English (whether MES or BES) also simplify syllables by means of the process of elision. Although this process bears some similarity to that of NBES consonant deletion, the similarity is generally superficial: L1 English elision is a highly rule-governed process and while L2 English consonant deletion is also strictly constrained, it is governed by the rules of the speaker's L1 rather than those of English (cf. Brown 1990: 76). Epenthesis and paragoge tend to increase intelligibility by reducing ambiguity and aiding recoverability of the original form (for further discussion see below, pages 65–6 and 116–19). This is borne out by every occurrence of these strategies in the ILT field data, other than the example of 'cartheft' cited above (where epenthesis served to emphasize the deviant conflation of /f/ with /p/ and thus compounded the intelligibility problem).

On the other hand, even in the presence of strong contextual cues such as the availability of the problem words in written form and the framework of a clear, familiar topic, the majority of deletions in the data resulted in non-understanding for all different-L1 receivers, even those who employ the strategy of deletion in their own ILs (for example, Mandarin and Taiwanese speakers). Similar findings result from the study of Suenobo et al. (1992) of the relative effects of errors of consonant deletion, substitution, and epenthesis by Japanese speakers of English on 'native speaker' listeners. While consonant deletion was found to cause the highest rate of misperception, epenthesis led to the highest rate of perception and, in context, was actually found to increase intelligibility. Such findings lend support to Gimson's frequently cited claim (for example, 1978) that it is consonants rather than vowels which carry the message at segmental level.

Where deletion occurred in the ILT data in isolation and in word-final position, it seemed to have a slightly less serious effect, particularly if it was substituted by a glottal stop. This type of deviation occurred frequently with final /n/, /nd/, /nt/, and /m/ even before a following vowel sound. Taiwanese speakers, for example, produced the 'don't' in 'I don't agree' as [dɔʔ], 'kind of' as [kaɪʔɒv], and 'time' in 'long time ago' as [taɪʔ]. On the other hand, deletion in word-initial position was far more likely to cause a comprehension problem, even where it was the only error. This is partly because deletion is not permissible in this position in L1 English syllable structure, and partly because a glottal stop was rarely, if ever, used in this environment to signal the loss of a sound. When there was more than one such error within a word or word group, or when errors of deletion combined with other categories of error, there were always serious repercussions for the understanding of receivers from different L1 backgrounds.

For example, after being shown a film of the Peking Opera on video as part of a classroom presentation, a Japanese student asked the Taiwanese presenter whether the opera was based on a true story. The latter replied that it was just [fɪʔʃɔ], and although the Japanese student knew the word 'fiction', she was unable to interpret it when simplified by medial and final deletion, and merely echoed it as [fɪʃɔ]. Again, in a discussion of students' favourite television programmes, even though all the different categories of programmes were written on the whiteboard, the category 'children's programmes' was rendered completely unintelligible when pronounced (by another Taiwanese speaker) as [ʃʊɹeʔ pɒgwæʔ]. As in many of the previous examples, I (the teacher) was able to interpret the deviant/erroneous pronunciation well ahead of those students who did not share the speaker's L1. This was no doubt partly because I was better able to make use of the contextual cues, and partly because I had had more extensive prior exposure to the ILs of the speakers concerned; it can also be attributed to the fact that, unlike the situation for NBESs, my process of interpretation was not complicated by the presence of a second IL, i.e. the receiver's as well as the speaker's, falling wide of the target in a different direction.

The view that 'Most segmental errors, though noticeable, do not interfere with communication' (Daniels 1995: 8), is thus something of an overstatement. As Rost points out, even among fluent speakers (he is, in fact, discussing L1 speakers), 'most mishearings can be identified as occurring at a segmental level', even though higher level phenomena, such as schematic effects, may also be involved (1990: 52). And as has been demonstrated above (and see Chapter 4), segmental transfer errors can prove highly detrimental to successful communication in English, particularly in ILT. However, some suprasegmental errors hold a similar potential, and it is to the latter category that we now turn.

Inter-speaker suprasegmental variation and its effects

In this section, we will consider the types of errors and deviations that NBESs make in the areas of word stress, rhythm, and intonation, these being the areas suggested by the majority of phonology authorities as having the greatest implications for intelligibility.

Word stress in ILT

Having dismissed the role of segmental errors, Daniels (ibid.) goes on to argue that 'the first and alas, often neglected priority should be to supply learners of English with 10 general and powerful stress rules, because it is at the level of word stress that the errors most damaging to comprehensibility occur'. But despite Daniels' fighting words, very little research appears to have been conducted on NBES word stress deviations and their effects on intelligibility, as compared with that in the other segmental and suprasegmental areas. Nevertheless, pronunciation teaching manuals make frequent reference to the need for correct word stress placement in order to preserve intelligibility. None that I am aware of, though, provides '10 powerful (word) stress rules'. This is probably because many of the rules have multiple exceptions and/or are far too complex for mental storage by students and teachers alike. This complexity is particularly true of the rules of so-called 'simple' word stress (cf. Roach 1991).

Nevertheless, English word stress is highly rule-governed, and learners have problems in acquiring these rules, particularly where the rules of the L1 are both different and less complex, and thus less 'marked' (cf. the discussion of Eckman's 1977 *Markedness Differential Hypothesis* in Chapter 5). This is the case for L1s such as Finnish, Polish, and Spanish, which all have fixed or relatively fixed word stress patterns (cf. Dalton and Seidlhofer 1994b: 38–9 for rules and examples). There is also a problem with cognates and false friends, where the L1 syllable and stress pattern is likely to be applied in the L2. For example, many European Portuguese speakers of English pronounce the word 'television' with five syllables, of which they stress the final one. This is a clear illustration of the differential effects of similarity on reading and listening comprehension, since receptively the similarity will be extremely helpful when the word is first encountered in a written text, but probably unintelligible when heard for the first time. At the level of production, the L1–L2 syllable and word stress difference may lead to serious intelligibility problems for both L1 and L2 receiver.

A further difficulty for NBESs with English word stress arises from the differing L1 cues with which it is signalled cross-linguistically. English tends to make rather greater use of vowel duration than do the majority of L1s, which tend to rely more on pitch change and loudness (although, as Dalton and Seidlhofer point out (1994b), loudness provides less of a guide for the receiver, as some sounds are intrinsically louder than others). The English stress system also involves far more weakening of unstressed syllables than most other L1s (except European Portuguese), with many L1s making only a small distinction here between stressed and unstressed syllables. Thus, although an NBES may place word stress correctly, it may not be perceived as such, especially by an L1 receiver, who will be accustomed to and therefore expect the acoustic cues of length and weakness in addition to that of pitch change.

The importance of correct word stress placement for L1 English receivers is borne out by recent research (cf. Kenworthy 1987; Brown 1990; Dalton and Seidlhofer 1994b), which suggests that these speakers from childhood onwards identify words in the first place through their stress patterns, and are therefore thrown badly off course in interpreting messages with misplaced stress. Brown illustrates this point with an example in which her 'instantly preferred interpretation was one that held the stress pattern that had been produced' (by an L2 speaker), i.e. 'anaemia' rather than one which made sense in the context of a discussion of *King Lear*, i.e. 'animism', pronounced /əˈnɪmɪzm/ (1990: 51). It is possible, however, that word stress errors made in context, and in the absence of other error types, are not automatically damaging for L1 listeners. Word stress patterns differ quite markedly among L1 varieties of English, most notably RP and GA, with no great subsequent loss of intelligibility (though admittedly, familiarity with these accents is likely to have a role in this). In addition, stress patterns may change over time with the dictates of fashion, while for a small group of words such as 'controversy' and 'kilometre', two distinct patterns are current and intelligible in British English use. All this suggests that L1 speakers are capable of a fair degree of flexibility in this area.

Some ILT word stress data

The effects of word stress deviations on NBES listeners are at present even less clear-cut. As was discussed in the previous section on segmental deviation, NBESs are far less likely than more competent speakers to bring contextual cues to bear on their interpretation of difficult pronunciations, and this no doubt extends to their attempts to interpret faulty word stress placement. However, in the present data, the majority of deviations that led to non- or mis-understanding in ILT occurred at the levels of sounds, syllable structure, nuclear placement, or various combinations of these. Only rarely did word stress deviations alone present difficulties, although they did sometimes compound the effects of other deviations, like the 'cartheft' example cited above (page 36). Interestingly, one of the few solely word stress errors to cause an intelligibility problem involved me, an L1 speaker, as listener, in an exchange which lacked any contextual information. A Turkish student, *à propos* of nothing that had preceded in the conversation, asked me for the opposite of the word 'mature', but pronounced it with the stress on the first syllable such that, assuming an approximation of the final /əʊ/ diphthong, I interpreted the word as 'macho'. The misunderstanding was only cleared up when the student wrote the word down. On the other hand, the ILT data contain no examples of word stress deviations alone leading to unintelligibity, even though many such forms occurred (for example, 'resort' and 'Korean' stressed on their first syllables), and there are even examples of such deviations being corrected by the NBES receiver (for example, 'sunshine' with stress on the second syllable).

The few word stress deviations that did lead to unintelligibility problems in the ILT data occurred in tandem with other types of deviation. For example, a French learner of English asked a Hungarian learner, 'How do you say hopeless in French?', but pronounced 'hopeless' with stress on the second syllable, deleting the word-initial /h/, and reducing the diphthong /əʊ/ to the short vowel /ɒ/. Likewise, in a conversation about ways of wasting time, an Italian-English speaker asked a Japanese student, 'Do you waste your time alone?', pronouncing 'alone' as /ˈelɒn/, with stress on the first syllable and two phonemic errors.

In these examples, it is difficult to assess the relative salience to the listener of the different types of deviation. I suspect, though, that in the first case, the misplaced word stress would not have caused a problem had there not also been segmental errors, since the syllable '-less' is familiar in isolation as well as in suffix form. On the other hand, in the second case, where a normally completely reduced syllable is given primary stress, and also because of the consequent misplacement of nuclear stress (see next page), the opposite may have obtained. Interestingly, in a third case, which occurred during a classroom exercise on connectives, the correctly pronounced word 'also' (by a Hindi-English speaker) was interpreted by a Brazilian student as 'although'. Presumably the reason was that he would have pronounced 'although' in this way as a result of L1 stress and sound transfer.

Generally more serious, however, were word stress deviations which occurred in combination with consonant deletions and which, in spite of contextual cues, rendered words totally unintelligible to all listeners. For example, the words 'product' and 'expenditure' were pronounced by a Taiwanese-English speaker in a conversation about advertising as [pɒˈdʌk] with stress on the second syllable, and [epeʔ ˈdɪʃɔ] with stress on the third syllable.

However, the most serious word stress deviations of all are probably those which also affect nuclear placement. The nucleus is the most prominent syllable in any group of words. It is the one which the speaker has chosen to highlight (by means of extra length and loudness, and a change in pitch level) as carrying the most salient part of his or her message, and thus the part on which he or she wishes to focus the listener's attention. This means that deviations in the placement of the nucleus have the potential to affect the listener's ability to process entire chunks of the speaker's message.

One such example was provided on the previous page, where the stress on the word 'alone' was wrongly placed on the first syllable. Because the second syllable of this word should have borne not only word stress but also nuclear stress, intelligibility was more problematic than would have been the case if the deviation had been one of word stress only. Another instance occurred when a Japanese-English speaker asked a multilingual group, 'Does anyone know where is Caribbean?', using the USA pronunciation of 'Caribbean', with stress on the second syllable. There was no response, because none of the students understood the question. The problem was not that they had not heard of the Caribbean, nor that they could not understand the incorrect grammar (they habitually made the same mistakes with embedded questions and article omission). The cause was the unfamiliar word stress, compounded by its co-occurrence with nuclear stress. Another example of this phenomenon occurred in an exchange between an Iranian and a Japanese student. The latter had been speaking about advertising, and the former asked him, 'Do you think the advertisers exaggerate subject about something that is unreal?', placing the stress in the final word on the syllable-initial '-un'. Although the question contained a number of grammatical errors, the listener understood the intended meaning once the stress on 'unreal' had been corrected. On a further occasion, in a lesson on idiomatic language, a Korean student defined the idiom 'to bite off more than you can chew' as 'to undertake more than you can fulfil', but pronouncing the final word as /ˈpʊlpɪl/. Thus, the nuclear syllable was not only misplaced, but the misplaced nucleus also contained a phonemic error. Although the Japanese receivers had this sentence written down on a worksheet, they were unable to identify it.

Rhythm and intonation

We now turn to the English rhythm and intonation system and consider first the concept of stress-timing. The original claim for the difference between so-called 'stress-timed' and 'syllable-timed' languages is now thought by many phonologists to be too strong, especially in relation to non-formal speech (see pages 149–50). Nevertheless, the English system of rhythm and intonation, with its alternation of strong and weak syllables and the extra prominence accorded to nuclear stress (common to all L1 varieties of English), operates regardless of the degree of formality of the speech situation, and acts as a 'guide to the structure of information in the spoken message' (Brown 1990: 43). The overall effect may thus be quite different from that of languages whose important content words are not highlighted or less important words reduced to the same extent.

This is borne out by Nelson's (1982) investigation of the differences between ('syllable-timed') Hindi-English and ('stress-timed') American English. Nelson finds that transfer of the former onto the latter leads to the placement of stress on a syllable next to the one where it would be expected by a 'native speaker', and a lack of unstressed vowel reduction. He concludes that rhythm is likely to have a significant effect on the intelligibility of 'non-native speaker' varieties of English. Wenk (1986) likewise observes the transfer of L1 rhythmic patterns of (French) learners of English on to their English L2. He suggests that learners only overcome such L1 influence at an advanced stage of proficiency, a view that is also expressed by Cruz-Ferreira, who refers to intonation as 'the last stronghold' of a foreign accent (1989: 24).

This latter claim is well supported in the present data, where advanced learners of English make frequent intonation errors, particularly with the placement of nuclear stress, whether unmarked (on the last content word of the word group) or contrastive (somewhere earlier). They tend to place it indiscriminately at or near the ends of sentences. For example, a Japanese student talking about the students in her previous class, said 'There were Spanish, German, French and I could tell the difference between THEM' (erroneous nuclear syllable in capital letters). Another Japanese student, discussing her new class, said 'They aren't all Japanese—we've got a lot of other STUDents'. The speakers in both of these examples had been studying English in the UK for well over a year.

Moving on to tones, although tone universals undoubtedly exist (see, for example, Brown and Levinson 1987, pages 104–6), it seems that the use of tones is also to a fairly large extent language-specific. Van Els and De Bot (1987) demonstrate this in an experiment where they find that the ability of listeners to identify the L1s of various 'non-native speakers' of English is significantly reduced when the latters' speech is monotonized. The avoidance of L1 tone transfer and the correct use of the English tone system is considered essential by many phonology experts and materials writers, and the literature abounds with references to the risk learners run of offending 'native speakers' (though not necessarily other L2 speakers), if they do not adhere to L2 politeness norms in their use of tones.

These writers are generally referring to what is often labelled the 'attitudinal' function of intonation. However, the use of tones by L1 speakers of English remains 'elusive' (Bradford 1982: 33–4) in relation to the expression of attitudes and, to a lesser extent, to the expression of grammar and discourse meaning,[4] and is almost always inseparable from speaker and context. Apart from the pitch direction in a number of intonational idioms such as 'You must be joking!' (Dalton and Seidlhofer 1994b: 45), it is therefore virtually impossible to provide cast-iron rules. This is evident even among experienced EFL teachers on in-service courses: agreement rarely results from tasks where, for example, some participants are asked to answer a question with the word 'yes', expressing (unknown to the other participants) for example, tentativeness, boredom, enthusiasm, and the like. There are generally almost as many different guesses of the attitudes being expressed as there are listeners.

Where tones are said to have a grammatical function (for example, a fall-rise for a *yes/no* question and a fall for a *wh-* question), on the other hand, there seems to be a higher level of (theoretical) agreement as to how these should be interpreted and also one or two cross-linguistic universals. Despite this, it is quite probable that intonation does not have a grammatical function at all (see Chapter 6, pages 151–2). Moreover, regardless of the issue of the function of particular tones, a surprising number of fluent speakers of English, teachers included, while able to identify the nuclear syllable itself, are unable to perceive consciously the direction in which its pitch moves. It is presumably for these reasons, and others which will be discussed in Chapter 6, that pitch direction was very rarely found to contribute towards unintelligibility and never to be the sole cause of it in the ILT data.

Although intonation universals undoubtedly exist because of the physiological constraints on the vocal apparatus, much intonation nevertheless consists of highly stereotyped patterns of which L1 speakers are not consciously aware (Nash 1969; Berkovits 1980). It is because intonation is both fleeting and operates at a subconscious level that NBESs are rarely aware of transferring their L1 patterns onto their English output. Meanwhile, although L1 speakers of English cannot articulate and explain intonation errors, they respond to their effects in interpreting meaning (Bradford 1988: 2), with the intonational message often taking precedence over the lexical (Nash 1969). The best-known example of this phenomenon is probably the one described by Gumperz (1982: 173). Recently hired Indian and Pakistani cafeteria staff working at a British airport were perceived as 'surly and uncooperative' purely on the basis of their intonation patterns. For instance, when offering gravy, they would say the word 'gravy' with a falling tone instead of the rising tone normally adopted by L1 speakers of English when making offers of this sort. This was interpreted by the cargo handlers they served as a statement of fact, and so redundant in the context, and indicative of indifference rather than the engagement involved in an offer.

It is the area of nuclear placement that seems to present the greatest suprasegmental threat to intelligibility in ILT, both in the placing of unmarked nuclear stress on the final content word in a word group and, more problematically, in the placing of marked or contrastive stress in an earlier position. One reason why NBESs fail to place nuclear stress correctly is very probably that they have problems in dividing the stream of speech into word groups (or 'tone units'). It then becomes impossible for them 'to single out the most important information within a group' (Kaltenboeck 1994: 17). By grouping words thus, fluent speakers of English indicate to their listeners which words should be interpreted together. This is achieved by structural means: the word group is normally bounded by pauses, contains (at least) one nuclear syllable[5] bearing what the speaker selects as the most important information, and is composed of an alternation of prominent and reduced syllables. Word groups also tend to coincide with syntactic boundaries, so that failure to divide the speech stream into these units can result in grammatical ambiguity or misinterpretation.

The claim for the word group as the primary structural component of English speech is supported by research into the use of formulaic expressions known variously as 'prefabricated routines and patterns' (Hakuta 1974), 'lexical sentence stems' (Pawley and Syder 1983), 'lexical phrases' (Nattinger and DeCarrico 1992), and by a host of other terms. This research, concisely summarized by Widdowson (1990: 92–6), demonstrates that a significant proportion of what 'native speakers' of English say is composed of ready-made, memorized chunks of language of varying degrees of fixedness. Although it is only relatively recently that firm links have been drawn between the word group and the lexical phrase (Seidlhofer and Dalton 1995), the usefulness of the lexical phrase for the teaching of intonation has previously been noted (Seidlhofer and Dalton 1993; Dalton and Seidlhofer 1994b; Kaltenboeck 1994).

The failure of NBESs to segment their speech into word groups results not only in problems with nuclear placement, but also in a lack of pause which, for the listener, creates a false sense of speed (Nash 1969; Van Els and De Bot 1987) and reduces the time available for the processing of information. Inevitably it poses more of a threat in ILT, where the less competent listener badly needs this 'pause' time for processing, while the less competent speaker needs it for planning. The absence of word-grouping is likely to result in non-fluent speech, with pauses occurring in unnatural places to facilitate the solving of linguistic problems rather than to serve the purpose of signalling information structure.

However, it is nuclear placement itself which causes the most serious suprasegmental problem for NBESs at the productive level. English has one of the most rigid word orders among the world's languages. This means that speakers of English, unlike speakers of many other languages, cannot rely on moving important words to salient positions such as the beginnings of phrases and clauses in order to emphasize them. Nor can they add inflections or particles to the endings of words to indicate their relative importance in relation to each other. To compensate for these restrictions, English allows free stress placement within the intonation group to an extent that other languages do not (Creider 1979). What this means in practice is that any word, regardless of its syntactic position, can be given nuclear stress if it is the one which the speaker wishes to make the focus of her or his message. (Though note that in words of more than one syllable, it is the stressed syllable rather than the whole word which bears nuclear stress.)

The unmarked position for the nucleus is on the stressed syllable of the last content word in the word group. But speakers regularly move the nucleus to earlier positions to indicate some sort of contrast. For example, the following is simply a statement of fact: 'My husband drinks a lot of BEER', in which 'beer' is the nucleus. However, if I say, 'My HUSband drinks a lot of beer', I have established a contrast between my husband and some third party known to both me and the listener. Although some L1s, for example, German and Russian, share with English the phenomenon of moving nuclear stress to signal contrastive information focus, many others achieve this purely by morphosyntactic means, such as word order, clefting, or topic markers, and retain a fixed position for the nucleus, with a tendency to prefer the final noun in the intonation group (Cruttenden 1986: 146–50).

A number of studies investigate the extent to which NBESs transfer L1 intonation patterns onto their English, and the effects this has on their ability to use English nuclear stress and, consequently, on the intelligibility of their speech. We will briefly consider three of these studies, which have particular relevance to the present discussion, before moving on to look at some ILT data. First, Wennerstrom (1994) examines the use made of pitch to signal meaningful contrasts among L1 speakers of Spanish, Japanese, Thai, and (American) English. She finds that while the L1 English speakers are consistent in their use of contrasts, all the L2 speakers tend to give equal prominence to items regardless of their importance in the information structure. They neither approach the degree of pitch increase produced by the L1 subjects on new or contrastive information, nor do they reduce pitch to the same extent on redundant words. She concludes that on the one hand, the thread of their speech would therefore be difficult for 'native speakers' to follow, while on the other hand, these 'non-native speakers' risk missing important aspects of 'native speaker' discourse structure.

In this study, the Thai subjects fare the least well and the Spanish subjects the best. Wennerstrom accounts for this result by the fact that Thai intonation functions the most differently of the three from English (Thai being a tonal language in which pitch is used to signal lexical rather than discourse meaning), while Spanish intonation has certain similarities to that of English. She also points to the part played by exposure to L1 intonation: the Thais had been in the USA for only two weeks, while the Spaniards had been there for over a month and, prior to their visit, had been exposed to American English via the media. Wennerstrom therefore recommends that longitudinal studies be conducted to investigate how 'non-native' intonation becomes more 'native-like' over time. However, as regards marked—and particularly contrastive—nuclear placement, it appears that exposure is more likely to benefit reception than production in the short term. Indeed, it seems to take well in excess of a year to filter through to the production of speakers of L1s intonationally distant from English, and only a little less for those who are closer. On the other hand, receptive competence in marked nuclear placement seems to be reasonably well acquired after a relatively short period of exposure (Bradford 1982; and see Chapter 6 below). This is plausible when one considers that the acquisition of productive intonation competence is a very lengthy process in L1 English (Cruttenden 1986: 173–4), whereas receptively it is acquired extremely quickly—in early babyhood or possibly even *in utero*. So while it may often (though not always) be the case that pronunciation reception precedes production, the gap between the two competences seems to be far greater for intonation than for other phonological areas, in both L1 and L2 English.

In the second study, Lanham (1990) investigates communication problems between speakers of South African Black English (SABE), whose mother tongue is one of the group of Bantu languages, and speakers of South African English (SAE). Bantu phonological rules, and particularly those governing intonation, are very different from those of SAE, and because many speakers of SABE are taught English by L2 speakers, there is inevitably a high degree of transfer. Lanham contrasts the heavy SAE exploitation of referring tones on nuclear syllables (Brazil et al. 1980; and see page 49 below) with the scant use of these tones made by SABE speakers, who reserve them for the ends of questions in spontaneous speech. This fact, along with a difference in the way the SABE speech stream is segmented into word groups (not necessarily coinciding with syntactic/semantic boundaries), the greater frequency and unselective placement of SABE prominent syllables, and the lack of distinction between SABE stressed and unstressed syllables, leads Lanham to propose that SABE intonation does not provide a discourse function for SAE speakers. The result, he argues, is the inability for speakers of the two groups to negotiate interactive discourse successfully.

In the oldest of the three studies, Nash (1969) investigates the use of contrastive stress of Spanish (Puerto-Rican) speakers of English and English speakers of Spanish at three different levels of L2 proficiency. She finds that the lowest level Spanish speakers of English use too little emphasis to signal contrasts, while the equivalent English speakers of Spanish use too much. The former therefore fail to give the necessary emphasis to make contrastive distinctions, while the latter apply more intensity than is appropriate in the context. Nash argues that accentual interference has wide-reaching repercussions on intelligibility because accent is concerned not only with the identification of meaning-bearing units, but with the identification of meanings themselves. To this extent, context provides less help (for the L1 receiver) than it does with segmental phonology, because the intonation pattern is, itself, part of that context. Nash also emphasizes the cumulative effect of such accentual interference, in which the hearer—unable to tune in to the speaker—cannot relate the meaning of one utterance to that of the next, with the result that the utterances become increasingly incoherent and, ultimately, either the speaker is judged as unintelligible or the message is misinterpreted.

Nash makes a number of points that are of interest in the context of ILT. Firstly, she finds that discrepancies between the most and least proficient Spanish speakers of English are not as great as those between the least proficient and those with a slight L1 accent. This is particularly true of the segmentation of the stream of speech into tone units, and seems to result from the fact that the Spanish speakers of English with a slight L1 accent exaggerate those features of English which they think will make them more intelligible, while the speakers with the heaviest and lightest accents do not. Presumably the former are not sufficiently competent in the L2 to attempt such reduction in the transfer of L1 intonation patterns, while the latter feel it unnecessary to exaggerate, since they are already easily intelligible. Secondly, Nash argues that, on the one hand, the requirements of intelligibility in the second language are reduced if both speakers share the same first language, while on the other hand, where both speakers come from different L1s, exposure to one another's imperfect speech will lead to the modifying of the perceptual apparatus and subsequently to increased intelligibility. Both these claims are supported by data produced in this book.

Nash's investigation is now around 30 years old. Somewhat surprisingly, considering the importance of the points she raises, there has been little progress in research or materials production in the area of nuclear stress in general and contrastive stress in particular. Instead, most intonation scholars have been attracted towards the work of Brazil and the study of discourse intonation (see the next paragraph). In Chapter 4, we will consider why the further investigation of nuclear stress (the old 'accentual' function of intonation) holds far more promise for intelligibility in ILT—

though not necessarily for 'native speaker'/'non-native speaker' inter-action—than does the investigation of discourse intonation.

From the 1970s until his death in 1995, David Brazil, together with his colleagues, worked on his theory of discourse intonation, developed from the work of Halliday and the Prague School (see Halliday 1970; Brazil et al. 1980; Coulthard and Montgomery 1982; and the posthumously published Brazil 1997). Discourse intonation essentially involves the placing of nuclear stress on the syllable within the tone group that the speaker sees as most salient in terms of the wider context of the utterance. In so doing, the speaker is said to select either a 'proclaiming' or a 'referring' tone, respectively a falling tone 'p' to signal that the information is in some way new from the listener's point of view, and a fall-rise 'r' to signal that the information is in some way shared, or 'given'. For example, the answer to the question 'When do you want to travel round the world?' could be the following:

(r) I want to travel round the world//(p) when I leave school

whereas the answer to the question 'What do you want to do when you leave school?' is more likely to be:

(r) When I leave school//(p) I want to travel round the world.
(Adapted from Dalton and Seidlhofer 1994a: 61).

Because of its relationship with parts of the utterance not in the immediate linguistic vicinity, a misplaced or mis-pitched nucleus may apparently affect meaning at the global level of the whole interaction. Such an error is undoubtedly the most difficult of all types of phonological error to identify and locate, because so much more than the immediate utterance is involved. For this reason, along with my strong conviction that discourse intonation 'errors' do not affect ILT intelligibility (see the study in Chapter 4), I do not present any data in the section that follows to exemplify errors in this area of intonation.

Some ILT intonation data

The intonation data consist of a number of errors in nuclear placement, both where the nucleus is automatically placed at the end of an intonation group (either on the last content word or indiscriminately on the last word whatever its status), and where an attempt to use contrastive stress misfires. Some of the errors involve nuclear placement alone, while the majority incorporate a mixture of segmental and/or word stress deviation and misplaced nuclear stress. As with the deviations described in previous sections, non- or misunderstanding was in each case the consequence, despite the presence of linguistic and/or extra-linguistic contextual information—though it could be argued that intonation is itself an essential part of the context (see the discussion of Nash 1969 above).

The first examples occurred during a (multilingual) classroom lesson at upper-intermediate level on idiomatic language connected with the body. In each case, the misplaced nucleus (indicated by capital letters) was the only error and resulted in non-understanding and a request for repetition:

1 'to put your foot in IT' (Japanese speaker)
2 'to pull your finger OUT' (Brazilian-Portuguese speaker)
3 'to be up to your neck in IT' (Brazilian-Portuguese speaker)

On the other hand, where the final item was a noun, resulting—probably by default—in correct unmarked nuclear placement, there were no problems in understanding, for example, 'to pull someone's LEG' (the same Japanese speaker), 'to have your heart in your MOUTH' (the same Brazilian-Portuguese speaker).

Further errors of this type, all made by Japanese speakers giving short classroom presentations, and causing non-understanding among the multilingual listeners, are:

4 'How exactly did you come BY this painting?'
5 '... a dirty tricks camPAIGN and allegations surrounding IT.'
6 'Richard Branson wants to expand his COMpanies, but recently he sold his record COMpany.'
7 'Before reading the books I opposed the jury SYStem, but now I am in favour of IT.'

Attempts to use contrastive stress, though encouraging as a sign that the system is beginning to penetrate, are fraught with potential intelligibility problems. This is illustrated by example 4. A further example occurred during an informal conversation which, although it took place in a classroom, was not part of the lesson. A group of students and I were making arrangements for a meal together in a local restaurant. A Spanish (Catalan) student asked me, 'Will you BOOK the table?' (making an unsuccessful attempt at placing contrastive stress). Until she rephrased it as 'YOU'RE going to book the table?', none of us understood her meaning.

The previous example also involved a phonetic deviation, since the words 'book' and 'table' were pronounced [βʊk] and [teɪβɬ]. The combination of misplaced nuclear stress and segmental deviation seems to be a particularly potent one for ILT unintelligibility. In a different conversation among four students, Brazilian, Swiss-French, Colombian, and Hungarian, as they sat together making posters for the classroom wall, the Hungarian student asked the other three: 'Have you got a blue VUN?' The three echoed the words 'blue vun' and 'vun' several times until the Hungarian student, holding up a blue pen, explained 'Blue vun like THIS', whereupon the whole group collapsed in laughter. The point here is that these students had been working and socializing together for three months and had therefore gained considerable exposure to each other's varieties of

English. In addition, the context of this exchange could have been expected to provide the listeners with clues to meaning, since they were sitting round a table with paper and coloured pens. I suspect that the segmental error alone would have presented them with little problem since it occurred on an unimportant word. Rather, it was the fact that nuclear stress was placed on this very word, thus presenting it as carrying the most salient information in the word group, along with the failure to use nuclear stress contrastively (the 'blue' one as opposed to the 'red' one), that combined to destroy the message.

Pirt provides a similar example where Italian speakers of English negotiate the position of a yellow pencil as contrasted with pencils of other colours. The yellow pencil is described by one of the speakers as a 'yellow PENcil', failing to use nuclear stress contrastively. Pirt points out, however, that the tendency to place the nucleus towards the end of the unit makes sense in the speaker's L1 Italian, where the corresponding phrase would be 'matita GIALla'. She therefore suggests that speakers, rather than simply transferring L1 intonation patterns, have 'difficulty in adjusting to a new linguistic paradigm', in that they fail to recognize the communicative value of prominence in English (1990: 151).

Similar non-understanding results where there are a number of segmental errors in conjunction with misplaced contrastive stress, even when the syllable wrongly presented as the nucleus is otherwise error-free. However, once the non-understanding has occurred, it is generally easier for interlocutors to clarify what was said if the segmental problem is restricted to a single word rather than occurring throughout the word group. An example of the latter—the combination of segmental errors and misplaced, though segmentally correct, nucleus within a word group—was overheard during a social conversation. A Taiwanese and Swiss-Italian (though trilingual) speaker of English, both at a reasonably advanced level of proficiency, having been banished to the garden as smoking was not permitted indoors, were inevitably discussing their smoking habit. During the course of the conversation, the Taiwanese speaker said to his Swiss interlocutor, 'I smoke more than you DO'. Not only did he fail to use nuclear stress contrastively and instead place it on a non-content word, but he also made segmental errors of both quantity and quality in the words 'smoke' and 'more', which he pronounced respectively as [zmɔk] and [mɔ]. After three repetitions had not clarified the meaning for his interlocutor, I 'translated' the sentence.

As has already been argued, the number of production errors that L2 speakers of English still make in relation to contrastive stress at a stage by which they are able to understand it if correctly produced (whether by L1 or L2 speaker), implies that receptive ability well precedes productive ability in this area. In Chapter 6, as we come to conclusions about what should be included in a phonological common core for ILT, I will substantiate this claim by outlining an experiment I carried out, which provides clear evidence of a receptive–productive mismatch in the use of contrastive stress. In the meantime, however, we will move on to examine the issue of intra-speaker variation and its implications for ILT.

Notes

1 This is not to suggest that L1 phonological transfer is itself a simplistic unitary process. On the contrary, it interacts with developmental and universal factors in complex ways, as discussed in detail in Chapter 5.

2 See for example, Cruttenden (1986); Kenworthy (1987); G. Brown (1990); A. Brown (1991); Dalton and Seidlhofer (1994a); Daniels (1995).

3 Though this was probably because the topic of this sentence had only a tenuous link with what had gone before, I was denied contextual help and, like the NBES students, was forced to rely on the acoustic signal alone.

4 The term 'discourse meaning' is used here to refer to the way speakers are said to distinguish between a nucleus bearing new information and one bearing shared or 'given' information, by means of a falling tone and a fall-rise respectively (see Brazil 1997, and page 49).

5 See Brown, Currie, and Kenworthy (1980) for evidence of tone units containing two nuclear syllables in informal speech.

3 The variation problem 2: Intra-speaker variation

'You have frequently seen the steps which lead up from
the hall to this room ... how many are there?'
'How many! I don't know.'
'Quite so!' said Sherlock. 'You have not observed.
And yet you have seen.'

A. Conan Doyle, 'A scandal in Bohemia' in *The Adventures
of Sherlock Holmes* 1894 (Penguin, 1981)

It was argued at the beginning of Chapter 2 that those who are aware of L2
intra-speaker variation generally interpret it merely as variation in
correctness. In terms of L2 spoken English, variation equals error, and the
entire EFL endeavour is, in a sense, directed towards the standardizing of
learners' speech to bring it in line with an imagined (see page 27) L1
standard. Not insignificantly, the verb 'standardize' is still very much in use
on teacher training courses. New teachers are trained first to elicit, present,
or introduce in some other more student-centred way, a new linguistic item,
be it grammatical or lexical, and then to 'standardize' it with each
individual student and/or chorally (i.e. with the whole class in unison). The
purpose of this is to bring the students' production—by which is chiefly
meant their pronunciation—as close as possible to that of a 'native
speaker'. Later on, whenever the student deviates from this standard pronunciation, the 'good' teacher will attempt to correct this 'error', whether
at the precise moment of its making (if the classroom focus at that point is
on accuracy) or later on (if the focus at that point is on fluency). Learners
expect this sort of remedial intervention from their teachers and regularly
complain if they do not receive what they consider to be enough error
correction.

All this presupposes, of course, that L2 learners of English should be
aiming for some sort of monochrome, monolithic English, completely free
of any intra-speaker variation in either style or grammatical correctness.
But L1 speakers of English vary their use of the language in both these
areas, however much the majority are unaware that they do so (see page 26

above). In fact, it was only with the publication in 1975 of Crystal and Davy's pioneering work, *Advanced Conversational English*, that even specialists in the field of ELT received their first hint that 'native speakers' sometimes speak ungrammatically in addition to employing extensive stylistic variation. The situation is further complicated in the sense that the so-called 'standard' from which these 'ungrammatical native speakers' are deviating is by no means a unitary one. Rather, the term 'standard English' represents an idealized abstraction far removed from the realities of 'the diversified and variable data of everyday interaction' (Milroy 1994: 156; and see also page 26 above). In real life, then, '"acceptable" English' is 'remarkably variable' (Brown et al. 1994: 153) and this is so particularly in speech, and still more particularly, at the phonological level.[1]

Given these facts of L1 use of English, Brown argues that 'we should not suppose that the second language learner is working towards some quite unattainable (and undesirable) goal—fixed and stable knowledge of the target language' (1996: 191). Far more useful to L2 learners of English is an ability to adjust their language in both style and level of accuracy (the two often being closely related in both L1 and L2 English) in response to the particular set of circumstances in which an interaction is taking place. And, because learners inevitably engage in intra-speaker variation, it makes far more sense for pedagogy to build overtly on this automatic process in order to give them more control over it, instead of trying (and failing) to eradicate variation from their ILs altogether.

It could be argued that intra-speaker variation is a matter of natural adjustment in use, as speakers converge towards or diverge from the speech of their interlocutors, and therefore that such accommodative processes cannot be taught—or at least do not need to be taught. However, I believe that in this respect, EIL is a special case. In international speech settings there will be an instinctive desire to converge as speakers bid for membership of the international community and simultaneously attempt to make their speech intelligible to interlocutors from a range of L1s. However, the means to converge in this way are unlikely to be within speakers' L2 repertoires unless there has been pedagogic help in this direction.

L1 and IL intra-speaker variation: a distinction

The concept of interlanguage as a linguistic system independent of both the native and target language has long been recognized. However, the original IL research (for example, Selinker 1972) took precisely the monolithic approach criticized in the previous section, failing to recognize, let alone attempting to explain, the potential of IL for internal variation. For ILs are natural languages and, like all natural languages, dynamic rather than static. They are thus subject to various influences which, in turn, lead to systematic language variation.

When such variation was first noticed, it was regarded by some scholars as an indication that ILs were not, after all, systematic and thus 'as an embarrassment for IL theory and its fundamental tenet that IL is a natural language' (Kasper 1989: 41). Nevertheless, early studies of IL phonological and morphological variation, such as those of the Dickersons (for example, L. Dickerson 1975; W. Dickerson 1976; Dickerson and Dickerson 1977) and Tarone (for example, 1978; 1979; 1980), were able to demonstrate IL systematicity, while Corder (1978) brought to the attention of SLA researchers the fact that first languages themselves vary systematically along sociological and situational parameters. The focus of IL research thence shifted to the study of its dynamic character.

Much of the literature on IL variation draws parallels with the sociolinguistic variation of L1 speakers, arguing that the same Labovian motivations of situation and linguistic context are concerned (for example, Ellis 1985, 1994; Sharwood Smith 1994). However, the similarity is to some extent one of process rather than of product (and even at the level of process there are a number of differences), since learners sometimes vary their language in ways not found in either the L1 or the L2 (Cook 1993: 82–92; and see the example of /dð/ given on page 31 above). In addition, IL variation at all but advanced levels of proficiency is characterized by more variability in the production of linguistic 'error' than by shifts between more and less colloquial styles; variability *per se* is also more prevalent in ILs than in L1s.

In view of their differences, Tarone distinguishes between L1 and IL variation by means of the terms 'style-shifting' and 'register-shifting': 'in interlanguage ... style-shifting should be viewed as distinct from the phenomenon of "register-shifting"—the sociolinguistic ability to speak casually in casual situations, or formally in formal situations'. She argues that 'the second-language learner may learn only one register of the target language, and still style-shift within that register in the sense of paying greater or lesser attention to speech' (1982: 73) and, presumably, speaking in a more grammatically or less grammatically acceptable way. Tarone (1983) accounts for this situation by claiming that most classroom second-language learners are likely to be exposed to only a single register.[2] Sato also draws attention to this area of difference between L1 and IL speakers, pointing out that learners 'do not have access to the second language norms about which linguistic forms are associated with which social parameters' (1985: 195).

Some qualification is called for here. While such differences between L1s and ILs undoubtedly do exist, for two reasons the situation seems to be less polarized than these writers suggest. Firstly, as I pointed out earlier, we have known for many years that educated L1 speakers of English make grammar 'errors' in their speech (far less so in their writing). In other words, their spoken language varies not just in style and register (in the conventional senses of these terms: see Note 2). It also varies in standardness, that is, in grammatical acceptability. Such speakers, even in relatively formal situations such as lectures, make grammatical slips in areas like subject/verb agreement. Secondly, for the past twenty years or so, second language classrooms and materials have begun to devote attention to concepts of formality and social appropriacy. As a result, many learners are nowadays likely to be exposed to more than one level of formality (i.e. style—or 'register' in Tarone's terms) and to the matching of linguistic forms with social parameters from a relatively early stage of learning.

It is all, then, a question of balance. L1 speakers employ variation in style and register extensively and also, though less so, variation in grammatical (including phonological) standardness. For IL speakers it is the reverse: while their speech does shift among different levels of formality, this sort of variation is not their most frequent. ILs are characterized by a far greater degree of variation in the form of grammatical error than are L1s. One contributing factor is the fact that ILs are susceptibile to permeation by both L1 (transfer) and aberrant L2 forms during—and, through fossilization, even beyond—the learning process. Another is that learners have different degrees of control over items according to the status of these items in their current IL: perhaps their knowledge of the item is incomplete; or perhaps they have not yet gained full control over the item and encounter problems of use when faced with a heavy processing load (see Sharwood Smith 1994: 111–2).

Phonological intra-speaker variation and its effects on interlanguage talk

In this section, we will examine some data collected as part of a study into phonological convergence in ILT to find out what actually happens when Non Bilingual English Speakers (NBESs) attempt to converge on one another's pronunciation. Because the subjects are not the L1 speakers or fluent bilinguals of most accommodation research, we cannot assume that, like the latter types of subjects, they will adjust their pronunciation in the direction of that of their interlocutors. One reason for this is the repertoire problem discussed in the previous section. Speakers from different L1 backgrounds frequently depart from target pronunciations in different ways. They are not necessarily able to produce the various phonological substitutions and conflations of their different-L1 interlocutors with the degree of facility and automaticity required in oral interaction, if at all. Another reason is that although in multilingual (but not monolingual) classes, students by definition receive exposure to other IL accents and over time become accustomed to them, these IL pronunciations are rarely, if ever, the subject (for reception) and never the goal (for production) of teaching. A third reason is the psychological (though largely unfounded) fear commonly found among students in multilingual classes of acquiring peer group pronunciation errors, and their consequent resistance to this outcome.

In an earlier pilot study (reported in Jenkins 1995) whose aim had been to establish that the intelligibility problem was greater in ILT than in other interactions involving NBESs, the majority of subjects had claimed to find it easiest to understand English speakers from their own L1 backgrounds and most difficult to understand those from unrelated L1 backgrounds. They had most frequently cited pronunciation (and hence, by implication, L1 phonological transfer) as the major source of the intelligibility problem. Where convergence occurs in ILT it is therefore likely to be similarly motivated to foreigner talk (FT), which is itself a form of convergence (see Chapter 7). One of the main motivations of FT is the 'native speaker's' desire to be understood by his 'non-native' interlocutor. Because he has difficulty in understanding the latter, with pronunciation being a prime factor, the 'native speaker' assumes the difficulty to be mutual and begins speaking more slowly, articulating more clearly, and so on. In ILT a similar (though two-way) process is likely, the main difference being that the adjustments operate in both directions, and on IL rather than L1.

For all these reasons, it was predicted that phonological convergence in ILT would take the form of replacement of problematic (for the receiver) transfer, with interlocutors attempting to converge largely on target-language forms, rather than on each other's pronunciation. This, in turn, would lead to variation in target and non-target forms, relating to the success or otherwise of the transfer replacement process. Such success was thought to be dependent on three main factors. Firstly, the type of transfer involved, with some phonological and phonetic areas being more taxing than others for speakers from particular L1s. For example, Japanese NBESs have great difficulty in producing the sound $/ɜː/$. Secondly, the amount of attention the speaker was able to give to replacing transfer rather than planning content. Thirdly, the salience of interlocutor comprehension at any given point in the interaction: in other words, was the intelligibility pay-off likely to be worth the cognitive effort involved? The latter, it was predicted, would depend on the type of task being performed. Thus, if crucial information was being exchanged, for example, then phonological intelligibility would be highly prioritized for the speaker.

Having said all this, however, it was not at all clear how the process would work in practice. Would transfer replacement affect all of a speaker's habitually-transferred forms or only certain forms thought, for some reason, to be 'high risk' (i.e. more likely to cause intelligibility problems for the interlocutor)? Or would it affect only those forms that the interlocutor also produced wrongly but differently from the speaker? Or would it perhaps affect only those forms that the interlocutor produced correctly (i.e. in the manner of the target language), thus implying convergence on the interlocutor's correct pronunciations? Were different combinations of these alternatives possible, perhaps depending on the state of play at any one point in the interaction, itself involving factors such as the linguistic environment of a potentially transferred item and the availability and type of contextual cues?

The data that follow are drawn from a study in which six learners of English, two Japanese, three Swiss-German, and one Swiss-French all of upper-intermediate/low-advanced level, were recorded completing various tasks as they practised for the Cambridge Certificate in Advanced English Speaking examination. They were recorded first in different-L1 pairs recorded on four separate occasions over a ten-week period, and also regrouped and recorded in same-L1 pairs (though not in the case of the single Swiss-French subject). The eight hours of recordings were transcribed, listened to again, and the transcriptions annotated phonetically wherever pronunciation deviated from an L1 target form. The annotated transcriptions were then examined for evidence of phonological convergence by means of suppression of L1 transfer errors, or a lack of it, depending on whether interlocutors shared one another's L1 or not. The phonological deviations that did occur were analysed qualitatively and then selected variables were subjected to statistical tests (Chi-square). The subjects also took part in interviews and completed questionnaires. Subsequent analyses, along with a replication using new subjects from a wide range of L1s (not engaged in examination practice this time), focused on phonological differences within the different-L1 dyads according to task type. (For a fuller account of the methodology, see Jenkins 1995.)

We will turn now to the data themselves. The first four extracts are typical of the data collected in order to compare pronunciation in same-L1 and different-L1 dyads. To enable valid cross-comparisons to be made, the following are all taken from the information exchange task (i.e. Task B) in each set of recordings. The speaker in Extracts 1 and 2 is one of the Swiss-German subjects, and that in Extracts 3 and 4 is one of the Japanese subjects. Full discussion of the implications of the data is provided after Extract 4. For the time being, the important point to notice is the far greater number of phonological deviations in the same-L1 dyad as contrasted with the different-L1 dyad in each pair of extracts.

Deviant pronunciations are indicated by means of the words containing them being transcribed into phonetics immediately beneath them. Word stress is indicated only where it is misplaced.

First study

Extract 1: SG1 (Swiss-German) in different-L1 dyad

(J) indicates that the Japanese interlocutor spoke briefly at this point.

Okay, it's a four storey house with two large balconies and one small
　　　　　　　　　　　　　　　　wɪv　　　　　　　　　　bælkɒnis　　　　　ænt

balcon, this the small balcon is on top-is the highest one (J) Balcon (J) I
　　　　　dɪs

think it's the right word. And in front of the house are is a is a yes it's a
　　　　　　　　　　　　　　　　　　ænt　　　　　　　　　dǝ

road, and on this road is a a lorry. And and in front of the house too there
ɹǝʊt　　　　　　　dɪs　　　　　　　　　　ænt　　　　　　　　dǝ

are is a parking a small parking space with let's say one, two, three, four,
　　　　　　　　　　　　　　　　　　　　　　wɪv

five, six, seven, eight parked cars and most of the cars are covered with
　　　　　　　　　　　　　　kɑːɹs　　　　　　　dǝ　　　　　　kǝʊwǝd

snow. And on the left side of the house there are there are four or five
　　　　　　　　　　　　　　　dǝ　　　　　　　　　　　　　deǝɹ

parked cars. Four are co-five are covered with snow and one is is, a red a
　　　　　　　　　　　　　　kǝʊvǝt　wɪv

red car is not covered with snow. In the back of the hou-of the house you
　　　　kǝʊvǝd　wɪv　　　　　　　　　　　　　　　　　　dǝ

can see, on the right side of the back of the house is you can see a mountain

with er covered with with trees and snow of course. And there are a f-few
wɪv　　　kɒvǝd　　wɪv　　　　　　　　　　　　　　　ænt

houses behind this main house I described to you.
　　　　bɪhaɪnt

Extract 2: SG1 in same-L1 dyad

(SG2) indicates that the Swiss-German interlocutor spoke briefly at this point.

All I can see is one square, it's (unintelligible) first with with two dia-dia-
　　　　　is　　　　　　　　　　　　　　　　　　　　wɪv　wɪv

diagonals I guess, this is the word, and now in every every corner of your
daɪægɒnæls　　　　　　　　w3ːɹt　　　　　　　　　　　　　　　　　ɒf

square is er, is another er, the square is yeah, a small square in every corners
skveǝɹ　　　　æŋdǝɹ

of your big square is a small one, and the length is about two, two-and-a-
　　　　　　　　　　　　　　　　　　　　　　dǝ　leŋgs

half, no three centimetres … (SG2) Yeah. So you have four small squares in
　　　　　　sentɪmitǝɹs　　　　　　　　　　　　hæf　　　　　　　skveǝɹs

the big square. Then you have the er a square with the same size in the
dǝ　　　　　den　　　　　　dǝ　　　skveǝɹ　wɪv　dǝ　　　　sais　　dǝ

middle where the two diagonals diagonals crosses each other, you have
　　　　　dǝ　　　　　　daɪægɒnæls　　　　　　　　　　　　　　hæf

another square. (SG2) Same size as the other (unintelligible) (SG2) Yes, you
　　　　　　　　　　ɒdǝɹ

have then (SG2) parallel to the the length of the big square … Okay, then
hæf　　　　　　　　　　　　dǝ　　leŋgs　　dǝ

you have, if you have drawn this er small one in the middle er the four
     hæf   dɹəʊn dɪs   zmɔːl   də
corners of this small square er hit the diagonals. (SG2) Then from there you
kɔːɹnəɹs   dɪs   skveəɹ   daɪæɒnæls   den   deəɹ
draw a line to the middle of the white, the length of the big square, so it
dɹəʊ   də   ɒf   də leŋgs   də   skveəɹ
gives you er (SG2) Four (SG2) Yeah, like arrows ... They all have the same
gɪfs   æɹəʊs   hæf
size ... should have the same size.
saɪs

Extract 3: J1 (Japanese) in different-L1 dyad

(SG1) indicates that the Swiss-German interlocutor spoke briefly at this point.

There is ah three sofas and one is one for three for four persons and other
                   səʊfɑːz

and the rest are for one person. And two cushions on the longer
                                          kʊsʃɔz

(unintelligible) and one cushion is on the right hand side of the sofa and ...
                                                              səʊfɑ

and about the middle orange (unintelligible) is on the table (SG1) Ah,

between mm between the sofa for one people-for one person, and also ahm
                              səʊfɑː
newspapers on the table, square or rectangle I don't know and the table is

made of wood and glass. Mm ... mm and ah a fruit basket on the cup
                                                       ɸruːt
cupboard and in the fruit basket I can see pine-pineapple and, grape ...

fruit? No, grape and maybe peach, and er there are three pictures on the
                                                                    sɹiː
wall. Mm on the picture I can see mm I don't know the name but all are of

flowers. Mm ...
fɹaʊwəz

Extract 4: J1 in same-L1 dyad

(J2) indicates that the Japanese interlocutor spoke briefly at this point.

I can see a man with his mouth widely open and also his eyes are wide um
                  mɑːn
circle. And mm he o-he opens his eyes wide wide widely and he is wearing

glasses ... and he is wearing hat and he has got whiskers, like, um whiskers
                                       hʌt   wɪskɑːz
(unintelligible) beard, beard beard here, whiskers on the cheek. (J2) Mm his
                   bɪɑːd   bɪɑːd   wɪsk3ːz
hands are, he he ... is rise-raise- he is rizing his hands. (J2) Ah, both, over
                                                                        əʊvɑː

over his head ... and he is wearing rings on every every fingers ... He is
əʊvɑː   fɪŋɡɜːz
wearing neck-er tie. (J2) This one ... and ... (J2) eh ... it's not round but

square, I think it's like drop, ah raindrop. (J2) It's like kind of hat (J2) Hat
skweɑː   ɹeɪndəɹɒp   hʌt
hunting hunter (unintelligible) (J2) Yes ... And um ... no, no, no, not beard,
                                                                        bɪɑːd
whiskers ... (J2) Whiskers on the cheek like hairs ... Ah also he is wearing
wɪskɑːz
watches on both wrist ... Um, I can see two strings from-hanging from
                                                  stəɹɪŋɡz   hæŋɡɪŋ
glasses. (J2) Until the side of head, what, I don't know what it is ... to hold

glasses. If when you take off glasses.

These two sets of extracts have been provided in full in order to exemplify
the contrast observed throughout the data in both amount and type of
phonological deviation between the different-L1 (DL1) and same-L1 (SL1)
condition respectively. Clearly, there is considerably more phonological
deviation in the latter than in the former. And this is all the more striking
when we consider that these particular DL1 data were recorded some six
weeks ahead of the SL1 data. If no other factors had been involved, we
would have expected phonological error to be more evident in the former
than in the latter, since phonological competence could be expected to have
improved during a six-week period of language learning. More importantly
in a qualitative sense, when we examine Extract 1 (DL1 dyad) more closely,
we find that the majority of SG1's deviations concern non-essential,
grammatical words such as 'and', 'with', and 'the', rather than lexical items
crucial to the information exchange task in hand (the subject's interlocutor
is trying to identify from six pictures which one is being described). In
addition, 'with' is always pronounced with a final /v/, which is acoustically
far closer to /ð/ than is /d/, making the word easier to interpret.

The three exceptions are 'balconies'/'balcon', 'road', and 'covered' (four
times). The L1 influence in the first can be explained by the fact that the
word is a cognate. The word 'road' is immediately repeated correctly.
Pronunciation of the third item, 'covered', however, appears to cause the
speaker some difficulty. Each time he repeats it, he gets a little closer to the
target sound, going from two relatively serious errors (of consonant
substitution and vowel quantity: see Chapter 6), which his interlocutor did
not understand (she later said that she had eventually guessed the meaning
because of the repetitions of the word 'snow') to one minor error (the
wrong short vowel). Interestingly, while the spelling continues to influence
his pronunciation until the fourth attempt, the subject removes his transfer
error (the substitution of /v/ with /w/, in fact an example of overcompensation) at the second. All this suggests strongly that he is attempting to replace

those non-target pronunciations which he thinks are likely to cause his partner comprehension problems, and thus that he has—whether consciously or subconsciously—identified 'high risk' categories.

Moving on to Extract 2, the same speaker in an SL1 dyad, the deviations from target are not only more frequent, but they also involve more content words crucial to the successful completion of the information exchange task ('square', 'diagonals', 'length', and 'centimetres') which involves the subject's interlocutor in trying to draw the diagram that is being described. In the feedback session after this interaction, the two Swiss-German subjects agreed that their pronunciation had seemed to be more accurate when they were paired with their Japanese partners, but pointed out that they had found one another very easy to understand, far easier in fact than they had found their respective Japanese interlocutors.

The next two extracts (3 and 4) come from the speech of one of the two Japanese subjects. These extracts, like those of the other Japanese speaker, contain noticeably fewer non-target forms than those of the Swiss-German subjects. However, this is not the result of higher phonological competence on the part of the Japanese subjects. Rather it reflects cultural differences in that they tend to say less, pause more frequently and for longer periods, speak more slowly, and probably think more carefully before they do so. This reflects the subjects' prior educational conditioning, in which making mistakes involved losing face and was to be avoided if possible (see Takahashi 1989 on these points). In the SL1 situation, this tendency is exaggerated: the Japanese subjects each say less in total than they generally do in their DL dyad recordings, they speak still more slowly, and pause more frequently and for longer. Convergence in the DL1 dyads is thus reflected in these extra-linguistic areas, as well as in the greater number of transferred forms which nevertheless occur.

Because the Japanese subjects monitor their output so rigorously, they considerably reduce the risk of automatic phonological transfer slipping through in the way that it does with the Swiss-German subjects, despite the latters' attempts to suppress transfer in DL1 dyads. Nevertheless, there are some phonological differences in the Japanese DL1 and SL1 data: not only are there rather more phonological transfer errors in the SL1 situation, but there are also differences in error type. In Extract 3, two of the deviations are phonetic rather than phonemic. Although phonetic problems may cause NBESs more problems than they do fluent speakers (see above, pages 36–7), they are in many cases still likely to be less serious for NBES comprehensibility than phonemic errors, such as the substitution of /r/ with /l/. This is true of the substitution of /fr/ with [ɸr] in the word 'fruit'. On the other hand, her pronunciation of 'cushion' contains one of the phonetic errors that will later be identified as a potential problem for intelligibility, namely the elision of word-final /n/ accompanied by nasalization of the preceding vowel. However, the subject repeats this word correctly a few seconds later.

In Extract 3, the pronunciation deviation potentially most threatening to intelligibility for her NBES interlocutor is the substitution of /l/ with /r/ in the word 'flowers'. The confusion between /r/ and /l/ is relatively rare in J1's speech and, in this instance, may, in fact, be a case of overcompensation. According to my Japanese informants, the single Japanese phoneme that is somewhere between these two English phonemes, and of which the latter are merely allophones, is actually closer to /l/ than /r/. Japanese speakers of English, I am told, therefore find this sound the easier of the two to produce. Early on, they tend to substitute /r/ with /l/ more often than vice versa. However, as they increase in proficiency, they become very conscious of the fact that they produce /r/ incorrectly and thence for a time err in the opposite direction, until they finally begin to distribute the two phonemes correctly. By comparison with her DL1 deviations, all those in this Japanese subject's SL1 extract (Extract 4) are phonemic. She repeats the same errors (in 'beard', 'whiskers', and 'over') three times without any apparent attempt to correct them. The problem that her SL1 interlocutor has with the word 'whiskers' (implied in the text and clarified in the follow-up interview) is because she does not actually know this (somewhat archaic) word.

The overall picture provided by the data of the first study is one of speakers making considerable effort to replace L1 phonological transfer when they are interacting in English with a speaker from another L1 as compared with a speaker from their own L1. This was confirmed by statistical tests very strongly in the case of the Swiss-German speakers, less so in the case of the Japanese speakers, largely because of the lower number of tokens (examples) obtained.

For various reasons which will be discussed later on when we consider the problematic issue of same-L1 interlocutors in dyads and groups (Chapter 6), and the role of context in intelligibility (Chapter 4), it was found that the SL1 data probably contained more transfer than these speakers would use in their unmodified vernacular. Thus the SL1 data do not offer the best possible base-line against which to measure the degree of replacement of potentially transferred phonological forms. In this connection, better data were found to be provided by the recordings of the subjects engaged in social conversation, which is probably as near as we can get to the subjects' vernaculars. Because of this, the data of the first study, along with those of the replication, were examined for evidence of contrasting amounts of phonological convergence in the social conversation and information exchange tasks, where the success of the task is dependent on the mutual intelligibility of the two DL1 interlocutors.

For the moment, we will look at extracts from one of the replication recordings, where a Taiwanese and a Korean interlocutor are engaged first in social conversation, and then in two different information gap activities. The reason for including these data at this point is to demonstrate that the type of convergence (by replacement of transfer) which we have claimed and identified in ILT really does involve the making of adjustments according to the needs of the receiver, and not merely an attempt at indiscriminate reduction in phonological (transfer) error. This can be clearly demonstrated where a subject increases the transfer of a particular L1 phonological feature in the information exchange task without affecting ILT intelligibility. We will look first at two extracts from a Taiwanese subject's speech and then at two from her Korean interlocutor.

Replication

Extract 5: Taiwanese subject, social interaction task

(K) indicates that the Korean interlocutor spoke briefly at this point.

Middle country, and here I I think I've been, I born there for a very long
mıdʊ   bɔ̃   lɔˀ
time, I've never moved to the big city or the other place. Yes, but I've fin-
taɪˀ   mʊv   də
I've just finished the senior high school and come to Britain ... London,
        fınıʃ   sınıɔ   skʊ   kʌ   bɹıtæ
when I first come here I don't-I didn't like London because first I don't like
        kʌ   dɔ̃   dıdə   lɔdɔ   dɔ̃
the food, yeah, it's quite terrible in here I think, you know in Taiwan
də   kwaıˀ   sıŋk
(unintelligible). (K) Then also I don't like the weather. (K) But now I'm used
                          æzəʊ   wezə   nəʊ   jʊz
to. (K)What do, what do you think? (K) But I think in your country there
                                sıŋk   deɹ
are lot(s) of sunshine. In your country it's warm. (K) It's a different way.
      lɔˀ   dıfə

Extract 6: Taiwanese subject, information exchange task

In my picture I think they're in a garden. The the house, be-er behind the
                      sıŋk   bıhaıˀ
house, they have the small garden. And there are one two three four five six,
                                          gɑːdə   sıs
six people in the garden. And I think they er have er one man and with his
                          gɑːdə   wız
wife and his mother I think, and they've got er three children, two boy, one
                      mʌdə   sıŋk
baby. And they are smiling, it seems quite happy and ... er, they're in the

garden and (unintelligible). I don't know what else I can say, but the
                                                                          kæ
woman, ah she hold a baby, and ... and, ah, the er old woman she sit
ʊmən   hʊd   ʊd
in the chair in the left my picture, left-hand, and the man sit on the right
                                                                          ɹaıˀ
side. And the other people they are standing. (K)
saıˀ

Extract 7: Korean subject, social interaction task

(T) indicates that the Taiwanese interlocutor spoke briefly at this point.

Yes, the capital of Korea is. Seoul and now, right now, I'm living in Seoul.
                           ɪzə

But actually I was born in the southern part of Korea but, I studied in Seoul
   æktʊæri   pʌt   bɒt

and after finish at the school and finishing my study I got a job at Seoul so-
  ɑːptə pɪnɪʃ   ætə   skʊ   gɒd

in Seoul, so I now live in Seoul (T) Ah my family. Yeah. Actually, right now
                                                æktʊæri

I'm living with my wife and my son, but … the concept of family is very
                 waɪp

different I think here and in my country. In my country when I, when we
                  sɪŋk

say about family, uh we think that we have father, I have my father and my
        pæmɪli   sɪŋk   pɑːdə

mother and my sisters and my brothers, all equally, and … uh I have three
mɒdə   sɪstəs   sɹiː

sisters and (T).

Extract 8: Korean subject, information exchange task

(unintelligible) tell you the six faces I've got. The first face I have is smiling
                                                            fɑːst

face (T) Yeah. Actually he's very happy and his mouth is very big. (T) Yeah.
feɪsə   ændə   maʊs   bɪgə

And his eyes is mm, almost closed. Can you imagine? (T) Yes … And the
                         kləʊzdə

other one I have is er maybe feel, she is very astonished, she is surprised. (T)
                                        əstɒnɪʃtə

and so her eyes is very large, big big. And the other one is oh, now he's very
                               lɑːdʒi   bɪgə

unhappy, so his eyebrush, eyebrow eyebrow is … shortened, eyebrow is
                      aɪbɹʌʃi   aɪbɹəʊ   aɪbɹəʊ   ʃɒtəndə

closed.

Both the Taiwanese and Korean languages show a strong preference for CV syllable structure, and speakers of both therefore have considerable difficulties in producing the many consonant clusters of English. The Taiwanese subject deals with the problem by means of consonant deletion, sometimes replacing the deleted consonants with a weak glottal stop (which at least indicates to the receiver that something is missing). This is, in fact, her most frequent type of phonological error. However, in those many areas where consonant deletion is not permitted according to L1 rules of English, it is potentially very damaging to intelligibility, because it makes recovery of the original form difficult, if not impossible. The Taiwanese subject seems to be aware of the problem—she has identified deletion as a high risk strategy for ILT intelligibility—but at this stage in her acquisition of English is only able to suppress deletion by the exertion of great cognitive effort. This she clearly does in Extract 6, the information exchange task, where words such as 'children' are pronounced without deletion—whereas she tended in her everyday vernacular classroom speech to produce it as [ʃʊɹe?] (see page 38).

On the other hand, the Korean subject's addition of paragoge to the ends of several words (usually schwa paragoge, sometimes [i], depending on the sound that precedes it) follows the opposite pattern. In the information exchange task, while reducing his other transfer errors, particularly the substitution of /p/ for /f/, he actually increases his use of the Korean IL strategy of paragoge. Although his current classroom vernacular IL contains little paragoge, as evidenced by its scarcity in Extract 7, he appears to regard it as an aid to intelligibility for his ILT interlocutor, and therefore uses it extensively in the information exchange task, particularly on key items such as 'closed', 'astonished', and 'shortened'.

Both subjects admitted reluctantly in follow-up interviews that there had been occasions when they had not understood one another, and that the main cause had been the other's pronunciation. Assuming that the chief motivation in ILT dyads, and especially those involving the exchange of crucial information, is communicative efficiency, the opposite behaviour of these two subjects in simplifying English syllable structure can be explained. Their mutual difficulty in interpreting one another's pronunciation can account for both the Taiwanese subject's *decrease* in consonant deletion and the Korean subject's *increase* in paragoge in the information exchange tasks as compared with the social conversation. This bears similarities to the motivation underlying foreigner talk (itself a manifestation of convergence), i.e. the speaker's difficulty in understanding an NBES interlocutor leading to an assumption that the latter will have corresponding difficulties in understanding him.

We will return to the implications of accommodation theory for ELT pedagogy in Chapter 7. For the time being, there is an important conclusion to be drawn relating to attitudes to L2 variation. This takes us back to the beginning of Chapter 2, where it was made clear that language variation away from 'the standard' is viewed by many people (including pedagogues) very negatively. However, we have since observed that L2 variation is very often the result of an attempt to produce pronunciation that is intelligible for the particular interlocutor—an attempt which can lead to both more and less target-like production, according to the interlocutor's pronunciation features involved. Phonological variation viewed in this light is a positive and not a negative characteristic of IL speech. Indeed, it appears from the data gathered in the first study that it is precisely the lack of such convergent behaviour which threatens successful communication in ILT.

The main implications for EIL pronunciation pedagogy that emerge from this chapter are therefore as follows. First, we need to get to grips with the nature of intelligibility as it relates to these specific L2 contexts, and this we attempt to do in the next chapter. Second, it will be important to identify contrived norms based on a subset of core EIL phonological features, which can then be learnt by all international speakers of English (including L1 speakers of English). This problem is tackled in Chapter 6. And third, we must devise methods for classroom pedagogy which build on the instinctive desire of NBESs to accommodate phonologically to their interlocutors in ILT speech situations. We return to this subject in Chapter 7.

Notes

1 In fact, with the rise of what I term the 'corpus syndrome', the pendulum has in one respect begun to swing the other way. Corpora without doubt have important uses, and one of their most salient disclosures for ELT has, to my mind, been the extent to which L1 speakers of English speak ungrammatically. This has serious implications for the correction of L2 English learners' errors though, regrettably, to date little has changed in this direction in classroom practice. On the other hand, the existence of the various corpora (British National Corpus, Collins COBUILD, and the like) has led to an obsession with 'real' English, and a feeling that in the classroom we must predominantly teach language that has been validated as 'real' or 'authentic' by virtue of its featuring in a 'native English speaker' corpus. For a fuller discussion of the issues at stake here, see Widdowson (1991).

2 Note that Tarone's interpretation of the terms 'style' and 'register' is not that generally employed by sociolinguists, who usually discuss 'style' with reference to level of formality, while reserving 'register' to describe the language specific to particular domains, such as occupational and interest groups.

4 Intelligibility in interlanguage talk

'Then you should say what you mean,' the March Hare
went on. 'I do,' Alice hastily replied; 'at least—I mean
what I say—that's the same thing, you know.'
'Not the same thing a bit!' said the Hatter. 'Why, you
might just as well say that "I see what I eat" is the
same thing as "I eat what I see!"'

Lewis Carroll, *Through the Looking Glass*, Chapter 1

What do we mean by intelligibility?

As far as the international intelligibility of English is concerned, the view
which once prevailed among applied linguists and ELT professionals was of
'a one-way process in which non-native speakers are striving to make
themselves understood by native speakers whose prerogative it was to
decide what is intelligible and what is not' (Bamgboṣe 1998: 10). This view,
although probably still widely held by the British and American general
public and even by many teachers of English, is no longer tenable. Not only
does it ignore the 'non-native' listener's perspective (a serious enough
omission in 'native–non-native speaker' interaction, a contradiction in
terms in 'non-native–non-native speaker' communication), but it also fails
to acknowledge any active role for the receiver. More recently, the focus of
research into intelligibility has tended to shift away from the speaker
towards the listener, and to consider the contribution of factors such as the
listener's background knowledge and processing skills. This, however, is
still to simplify matters, for there is as yet no broad agreement on a
definition of the term 'intelligibility': it can mean different things to
different people. So, before looking more closely at the intelligibility of
interlanguage talk, it would be as well to clarify how I interpret the term in
the context of communication between Non-Bilingual English Speakers
(NBESs). Let us begin by considering what others have said on the subject.

Bamgboṣe himself describes intelligibility as 'a complex of factors
comprising recognizing an expression, knowing its meaning, and knowing
what that meaning signifies in the sociocultural context' (ibid.: 11). He thus
uses 'intelligibility' as a blanket term to cover a range of speaker and

listener factors, arguing that in communication between a speaker and listener, both contribute to 'the speech act and its interpretation' (ibid.). Bamgboṣe's three aspects correspond closely, as he points out, to Smith and Nelson's terms 'intelligibility', 'comprehensibility', and 'interpretability'. The latter authors had earlier noted that in the literature on the subject of the international intelligibility of English, the three terms were often used interchangeably, with the result that 'the current state of the art in the study of the international intelligibility of English is one of confusion regarding these terms' (1985: 334). In order to clarify the situation, they suggested that the term 'intelligibility' be reserved for word and utterance recognition, with 'comprehensibility' being used to refer to word and utterance meaning (i.e. propositional content, or Austin's (1962) *locutionary force*), and 'interpretability' to refer to the grasping of the speaker's intention in producing the utterance (i.e. Austin's *illocutionary force*). The term 'interpretability' thus replaced for Nelson his previous use of the word 'intelligibility' to mean 'apprehension of the message in the sense intended by the speaker' (1982: 63). Intelligibility, as defined by Smith and Nelson, has something in common with Brown's term 'identification', by which she means the recognizing of items such as proper names and telephone numbers, and which she contrasts with 'understanding'—the grasping of the communicative content of utterances (1995: 10–11).

James, on the other hand, approaches the subject from the speaker's standpoint. He uses the word 'comprehensibility' 'as a cover term to refer to all aspects of the accessibility of the content—as opposed to the form— of utterances', with intelligibility being reserved for 'the accessibility of the basic, literal meaning, the propositional content encoded in an utterance' (1998: 212). Thus, James intends to convey by the term 'comprehensibility' the same meaning as Bamgboṣe's 'intelligibility', and by the term 'intelligibility' the same meaning as Smith and Nelson's 'comprehensibility'. James contrasts intelligibility with 'communicativity', which he describes as 'a more ambitious notion, involving access to pragmatic forces, implicatures and connotations'. Communicativity is 'a higher order achievement' involving the transmitting of 'the right social information' (ibid.: 216–7). Lanham (1990) had earlier pursued the same line of thought, though with a different allocation of the terminology, in his study of the intelligibility of 'errorful English spoken by second- or foreign-language users' by proposing a distinction between 'intelligibility' and 'comprehensibility'. The former he relates to the effect of errors on the recognition of linguistic form while the latter, he argues, is concerned with 'the communicative effect of error ... the consequences of error on the comprehensibility of contextualized discourse' (ibid.: 243). Brumfit, in a similar vein, though predating James, contrasts the 'intelligibility of world English *text*' with what he describes as the 'richer problem' of 'interpretability of world English *communication*' (1982: 95; emphasis in original).

It seems from this small sampling of the literature that there is still no general consensus in the use of the term 'intelligibility', whether viewed from a speaker or listener perspective. In other words, the terminological 'confusion', to which Smith and Nelson drew attention in 1985, is still with us. Nelson, in fact, a whole decade later, reiterates his view of the need for a division of 'general "intelligibility" or "understanding" into a three-level system of intelligibility, comprehensibility and interpretability' (1995: 274). What is clear, though, is the view, expressed or implicit, in most of the writings referred to above that, whatever the term actually used for the concept of formal recognition and recognizability of words and utterances, matters of form are considered by their writers to be of relatively minor relevance in spoken communication (and miscommunication) as compared with matters of meaning. We see this, for example, in James's (1998) contrast of 'intelligibility' with 'communicativity'; in Lanham's (1990) distinction between 'intelligibility' and 'comprehensibility'; and in Brumfit's (1982) claim for the 'interpretability of ... communication' as being 'a richer problem' than the 'intelligibility of ... text'.

The main research interest these days, it appears, is in higher-level concepts going by names such as 'interpretability', 'communicativity', and 'understanding'. The 'real' business of imparting and processing messages, it is frequently said, involves the top-down processing of contextual phenomena (background knowledge relating to personal and situational cues) rather than the bottom-up production and reception of linguistic form. As Brown argues, 'adequate communication' is regularly achieved, despite 'the pervasive underspecification of meanings of utterances'. This is because the sheer amount of shared background information enables interlocutors to establish 'a structure of mutual beliefs'. In other words, speakers are able to construct and interpret utterances in the light of beliefs about the other's state of knowledge, and to ascribe to each other the intentions which they 'would expect to experience themselves in uttering the utterance just heard in that particular context' (1995: 232–3). Of course, all this is only possible because, as Brown points out (quoting the sociologist Cicourel), there is a presumption that interlocutors are 'playing the same game' (ibid.). The interest is in discovering how this happens.

Although a number of writers (including Brown herself elsewhere) talk of more interactive models of speech perception, in which higher and lower level processes interact (see, for example, Flowerdew 1996), Brown is no doubt quite right about the role of shared belief systems in communication among fluent speakers of English (her comment was, in fact, made in the context of research into interaction between L1 speakers of English). For even leaving aside for one moment the role of extralinguistic contextual phenomena, there is another compelling reason why recognizability and recognition of form can play only a relatively minor part in the successful conveying and receiving of messages among fluent speakers. This relates to the quality and character of the speech produced and, in particular, to the way in which the individual speech sounds merge together in an 'acoustic blur' (Brown 1990: 11).

As many authorities have long pointed out (see, for example, Anderson and Lynch 1988; Brown 1990; Rost 1990), fluent speech perception involves rather more than the decoding of segments. This is because of the effects of both co-articulation and of the various assimilatory processes which take place in connected speech. Looking first at co-articulation, it is very difficult to isolate individual sounds in the speech stream—and even within one single word. Sounds change in different phonetic environments through the influence of neighbouring sounds. For example, in the words 'tea' and 'too', the /t/ in the first case will be coloured by the following /iː/, and in the second by the following /uː/. Thus, the former /t/ will be pronounced with spread lips and the latter with rounded lips. Because of the effects of co-articulation, it is usually difficult to identify where one sound ends and the next begins. This means that ideal phonemes are generally no more than 'reference templates' for fluent listeners (Rost 1990: 38).

Turning to assimilatory processes or what are more commonly referred to as the 'features of connected speech', we find that there is rarely a one-to-one match between words said in citation form (i.e. in isolation) and those uttered within a stream of speech. Assimilatory processes are used by fluent speakers to facilitate pronounceability by making articulation easier; that is, they are speaker-oriented. They include processes such as elision (the omission of sounds), catenation (the linking of sounds across words), and assimilation (the replacing of sounds to make them in some way closer to neighbouring sounds) (see Dalton and Seidlhofer 1994a: 24–31 for a fuller account). These contrast with dissimilatory processes, where speakers subordinate their speech strategies to their listeners' needs by articulating more clearly; that is, they are listener-oriented. Dissimilatory processes are marked. Fluent speakers of English do not normally use them, but reserve them for occasions when clarity is particularly salient, for example, when dictating an address over the telephone, or when conversing with an interlocutor who has hearing difficulties, or with one whose English proficiency is low (see note 3 and Chapter 7 on foreigner talk).

The use of co-articulation and of assimilatory processes of course presupposes a certain speed of speech, i.e. that of fluent speakers of English. According to David Crystal, this averages 350 syllables per minute, with everyday conversation tending towards a range of 400 to 450 syllables per minute, and with short stretches, such as sequences of auxiliary verbs, being uttered still faster. Slower speech made to incorporate features of connected speech, as Crystal has demonstrated, is reduced to gibberish.[1] The use of such features also assumes that we are dealing with fluent listeners. And in this connection, note that writers have a tendency to refer generically to 'the listener', as for example, in 'the ways in which *the listener* decodes utterances' (Rost 1990: 33; emphasis added). Thus they imply that processes of speech perception are pretty much the same regardless of an individual listener's level of proficiency. But as I will demonstrate in the following sections of this chapter, this is some way from the truth.

Defining intelligibility in interlanguage talk

The majority of the writings cited above relate either to interaction involving fluent (often L1) speakers of English or to that between 'native' and 'non-native' speakers of English. In fact, one of the problems in any discussion of listening in ILT is that the bulk of research on listening skills, and particularly on the role of context, has been carried out with L1 speakers. Few studies have been conducted from the perspective of L2 listeners, and even fewer with L2 listeners *and speakers*. Shifting from communication between fluent speakers of English to that between non-fluent speakers of English (i.e. NBESs), however, we are presented with a very different set of circumstances. These exert a strong influence on speaking and listening, particularly at the level of phonological form.

Communication between fluent speakers takes for granted a certain amount of shared knowledge. According to Hymes, this knowledge can be analysed in terms of four parameters:

1 Whether (and to what extent) something is formally *possible*.
2 Whether (and to what extent) something is *feasible*.
3 Whether (and to what extent) something is *appropriate* (adequate, happy, successful) in relation to a context in which it is used and evaluated.
4 Whether (and to what extent) something is in fact done, actually *performed*, and what its doing entails.
(Hymes 1972: 12; emphasis in original)

The third and fourth parameters are of particular relevance to the current discussion. As regards the third parameter or sociolinguistic competence, successful communication involves a substantial degree of shared socio-cultural knowledge. Either through the socialization processes of childhood (in the case of most L1 speakers)[2] or through prolonged contact with the target society (in the case of most L2 speakers in 'Foreign Language' situations), fluent speakers of a language have developed intuitive knowledge of what are and are not appropriate communicative behaviours in specific speech contexts, and interpret what is said to them accordingly.

Fluent speakers also have a high degree of linguistic knowledge (in the case of L1 English speakers, often purely subconscious) not only in the Chomskyan sense of grammatical competence—Hymes's first parameter—

but also in terms of attestedness, his fourth parameter. Their formal grammatical competence enables them to assess, for example, what can and cannot be a word and what syntactic and phonotactic permutations are possible. But they know far more than what is formally possible in an abstract, or idealized, sense. They know what other fluent speakers actually *do* in performance, and this knowledge involves a high degree of phonemic and phonetic intuition. As regards the former, such speakers are intuitively aware of the changes which often take place in connected speech (see page 72), and rarely—if ever—notice that words are not produced in full citation form even if they do not always make the correct grammatical link (for example, /wʊdəv/ is often written as 'would of' rather than 'would have'). For example, they have no problem in interpreting /weəjə gəʊɪn/ as 'Where are you going?'. In terms of the latter (phonetic) intuition, they are able both to perceive sounds categorially, i.e. to categorize a wide range of allophones as 'belonging' to one particular phoneme, and to make use of redundant phonetic cues. For example, they know instinctively that a /t/ or /p/ sound followed by aspiration nevertheless 'belong' respectively to the /t/ and /p/ phoneme, and that they are very unlikely to be word-final. Again, they know that the vowel sound /ɪ/ is slightly longer before a voiced consonant sound than before a voiceless one (for example, in 'pig' as opposed to 'pick'), and therefore which sort of sound they can expect to follow /ɪ/ in either case. Knowledge of this sort, along with the sociolinguistic competence mentioned in the previous paragraph, enables speakers to process the 'acoustic blur' of which much speech consists.

In EFL situations—interaction between 'native' and (non-bilingual) 'non-native' speakers of English—while the latters' intuitions about the formers' phonological and phonetic performance are likely to be undeveloped, the sociolinguistic characteristics described above may still obtain to some extent. Although there is not the same degree of shared socio-cultural background as exists between L1 interlocutors, English socio-cultural appropriacy is one of the subjects of learning and may even be its goal (for example, in British Cultural Studies). And outside pedagogic situations, 'non-natives' have plenty of access to British, American, Australian, etc. society and culture through the media. Some degree of shared socio-cultural background between L1 and L2 speakers of English can therefore be assumed.[3] On the other hand, when used as an international language, that is, between L2 speakers, English is not tied to any one cultural background[4] and thus, unlike EFL, no single English culture can—or should—be the goal of pedagogy. Culture learning is not part of EIL learning.

However, Davies questions whether 'a natural language without some cultural bias is possible' (1991: 157). Given that, for international purposes, a bias towards British, American, Australian, etc. culture is irrelevant, the only other possibility for General English (as opposed to ESP) classrooms, then, would be to introduce a wide range of L2 cultural backgrounds. In this regard, Kramsch (1998) discusses the pedagogic use of cross-cultural awareness-raising activities through which learners may develop into 'intercultural speakers'. Nevertheless, huge practical implications surface when one considers the possibility of reorganizing L2 English classrooms around the world to enable learners to compare and contrast their own L1 cultures with each other's and with those of L2 English speakers not represented among their number. Although the concept is attractive, it therefore remains at present largely an ideal rather than a pedagogic reality. The consequence for ILT is highlighted in multilingual classes, such as often feature in ENL (English as a Native Language) countries. It is learners in such classes who provide the data which will be presented later in this chapter. And, as we will see, even at these learners' relatively high level of English and after a period of exposure to each other's English, numerous miscommunications occur. Tarone asks:

> In a (*sic*) ESL classroom composed of 20 learners from seven different native-language backgrounds, can we really speak of speech communities and shared qualitative norms in the way we can speak of these for monolingual speakers? Can we expect learners from different native-language backgrounds to share the same perceptions of the social dimensions of English language use ...
> (1988: 118)

My answer is no, we cannot. Each multilingual ELT classroom is a microcosm of ILT as it occurs in the outside world. In each, we find people thrown together often in pursuit of common goals but without a common background to facilitate the achieving of these goals.

And herein lies the crux of the matter. To extend the paradigm of shared background context to ILT would, in effect, be to *deny* the role of context in ILT. Here, there is little if any shared background information available to interlocutors, be it social, cultural, linguistic, or otherwise. The primary contextual feature of ILT is, paradoxically, that there *are* no contextual features—at least in the sense of shared socio-cultural knowledge. And as Widdowson argues:

> People who have particular knowledge and experience in common, whose contextual realities, so to speak, are closely congruent, will manage to communicate by engaging relevant aspects of contexts with only sparing use of the linguistic resources at their disposal. Conversely, of course, those who have little in common have to place greater reliance on the language.
> (1990: 102)

In ILT, speakers 'have little in common' apart from their non-bilingual proficiency in the L2 and the mutual desire to achieve a particular goal in an interaction.

An illustration will help to demonstrate the point I am making about the role of shared L1 socio-cultural background. In a recent conversation with my teenage daughter, she was describing the newly built facilities in her school. She told me that there was a 'really big new I.T. complex' and then added what I heard as 'there's a new drummer complex too'. I was initially surprised (British secondary schools do not normally have such things and, in any case, this is a girls' school, where pupils tend to play flutes and violins rather than drums), but then searched my mental lexicon for an alternative to 'drummer' and soon located 'drama'. All this occurred in a matter of a couple of seconds, without the need for me even to articulate the initial miscommunication. My daughter had (apparently) substituted the short vowel sound /ʌ/ for the long vowel sound /ɑː/, but my extensive background knowledge of both the place and the person (my daughter is very interested in acting as opposed to, for example, sport), enabled me to deal with this 'high risk' core phonological error (see Chapter 6) instantly.

On the other hand, a similar type of phonological error was not so easily negotiated when the participants involved were an L1 speaker and a (fairly high level) NBES from Mexico. The interaction took place in a pub. The male L1 speaker (fluent in European Spanish) offered the female Mexican NBES a drink. She asked for what sounded like /saɪðə/. This time the listener was less able to rely on background knowledge to interpret meaning: although he was familiar with the range of beverages available in English pubs, he was uncertain of the alcoholic (or non-alcoholic) predilections of Mexican drinkers. However, he at least had the fluent English listener's advantage of knowing that 'sytha' is not an English word, let alone the name of a drink. Even so, and despite being well aware that Spanish speakers of all persuasions regularly transfer the pronunciation of inter-vocalic /d/ as /ð/ to their English, he had to ask for two repetitions before finally understanding the speaker's meaning as 'cider' (although the error in fact remained). This time, then, the relative lack of shared background meant that greater salience was attached to form and it was thus more difficult for the listener to interpret meaning when faced with a ('high risk' core) phonological error.

However, both these typical examples contrast with ILT, where there is neither shared socio-cultural knowledge nor a high level of linguistic knowledge such as that of the L1 listener in the previous interaction. Nor is there likely to be much familiarity with an interlocutor's accent of English. In Chapter 3 we looked at the types of phonological errors made by NBESs. Later in this chapter, we will consider a number of examples of miscommunication drawn from ILT, and will note how often it is the fact that these listeners are continually forced back on the language itself and, in particular, on the pronunciation, which leads to the miscommunication. We will see, furthermore, that miscommunication tends to remain as such, or to involve more than a couple of simple repetitions to be successfully resolved.

Of course, it is not only in the lack of shared background knowledge between interlocutors that ILT differs from interaction between fluent speakers of English. I mentioned earlier the effects of co-articulation and assimilatory processes on pronunciation and made the point that it is the speed of speech which motivates these processes. Because NBESs speak far more slowly than fluent speakers of English, they make little use of co-articulation and connected speech processes. They acquire some of these features automatically as their linguistic competence increases beyond that of NBESs and their speech becomes faster. Other features—notoriously weak forms—are never acquired for regular use by the majority of L2 speakers, even BESs (see Chapters 2 and 6). What this means then is that listeners in ILT are receiving speech sounds that are much closer to their citation form, and thus more amenable to bottom-up processing than the sound remnants in fluent English speech.

Another difference between fluent interaction and ILT is that NBESs seem to have an instinctive reluctance to signal non-comprehension. In 'NS–NNS' interaction this reluctance is probably the result of the NBES listener's desire not to lose face. In ILT, listeners are concerned also about the face-loss of their non-fluent interlocutors, for the signalling of non-comprehension of an NBES interlocutor's speech may serve to draw attention to the latter's inaccuracies of phonological form, in other words, to their 'poor' English accent. This was a response that my questionnaires elicited not infrequently, and particularly from Far Eastern subjects. In fact, some of the latter were not even prepared to commit comments about their interlocutors' pronunciation to paper, but instead came to tell me privately.

At the level of phonological form, fluent speakers are generally able to say what they mean with great regularity and automaticity, while when a fluent speaker interacts with an NBES, only one of the two interlocutors is not positioned to do so. In ILT, on the other hand, both interlocutors have difficulties with phonological form which prevent them from saying what they mean even though, like Alice, they probably mean what they are trying to say. In addition, both interlocutors have receptive processing problems as described above and in the next section, which phonological L1 transfers (such as the example on page 76) can only exacerbate. A central dilemma for ILT, then, is that while in this speech context, probably more than in any other, successful communication depends to some considerable extent on the ability of speakers to compensate (particularly at the level of phonological form) for listeners' linguistic and extralinguistic inadequacies, speakers are not well equipped to do so.

And so, finally, to my interpretation of the term 'intelligibility'. The reader will be aware from the previous discussion that I attach considerable importance to the phonomenon of recognition of phonological form in ILT. Like Smith and Nelson, I believe that it is important to standardize the use of the term 'intelligibility', and I have no problem with their restriction of its use to word and utterance recognition. Unlike them, however, I do not believe that 'the most serious misunderstandings occur at the level of comprehensibility and interpretability' (1985: 335) where ILT is concerned. This view is not by any means intended to imply that I consider misunderstandings of a more pragmatic nature to be completely irrelevant to ILT: 'comprehensibility' (recognition of word and utterance meaning) and 'interpretability' (recognition of speaker intention) both have their place. Rather, it is borne of the conviction, backed by hard evidence (see examples of miscommunication in the ILT data provided later in this chapter, pages 84–8), that in ILT such higher-level misunderstandings are relatively rare because of the regularity with which phonological problems 'get in the way', mainly as a result of NBESs' contextual processing difficulties. Less able to draw on knowledge of the appropriate and the attested in order to interpret messages, speakers engaged in ILT have to focus their attention on meanings inscribed in form to a far greater extent than do those familiar with the English language and its customary use.

In fact, there is evidence that phonological problems regularly get in the way of successful communication not only in *inter*national contexts, but in *intra*national ones also. For example, Bansal (1990) describes how English is used within India as a lingua franca among speakers from different L1 Indian backgrounds. He argues that the differences in their varieties of English are 'much greater in respect of phonological and phonetic patterns' than in lexis and grammar (ibid.: 219), and goes on to pinpoint a number of phonetic features as 'likely to affect the intelligibility of spoken English within India' (ibid.: 229), citing in particular the following: lack of clear articulation, accent on the wrong syllable, and vowel or consonant substitution. Similarly, in his discussion of the use of English as a common language among speakers of the roughly 400 indigenous languages of Nigeria, Ufomata relates mutual intelligibility specifically to accent and argues that it is important to 'study the varieties which have emerged in second language situations' in order to 'identify areas which cause in-telligibility failures within these accents' (1990: 216).

My own use of the term 'intelligibility' is thus, unashamedly, that of Smith and Nelson (1985), but it is approached more in the spirit of writers such as Bansal and Ufomata. It concerns the production and recognition of the formal properties of words and utterances and, in particular, the ability to produce and receive phonological form, but regards the latter as a prerequisite (though not a guarantee) of ILT success at the locutionary and illocutionary level.

This is not to say that the recognition of phonological form is a straightforward, unilateral matter. It is a commonplace to talk of the negotiation of meaning as a pragmatic process, but even with such an apparently limited interpretation of intelligibility, we are still concerned with negotiation, with a two-way process involving both speaker and listener at every stage of the interaction. The negotiation of intelligibility consists of 'the establishment and maintenance' of the necessary conditions to achieve understanding (Widdowson 1984: 115). In ILT the 'necessary conditions' are, probably above all, mutually intelligible pronunciation, for even 'high adequacy in lexis and grammar can be negated by incompetence in the signalling phase' (Gimson 1994: 270). Speakers assess moment by moment the extent to which their phonological output appears to be comprehensible to their interlocutor(s), and make adjustments and corrections as they judge necessary, and *insofar as they are able to*. Meanwhile, listeners are as responsible as speakers and, as Bamgboṣe (1998) argues, part of a listener's contribution to intelligibility is in the making of allowances for an interlocutor's accent, i.e. in converging receptively (see Chapter 7 for a fuller description and discussion of the accommodative process of convergence). Thus, even at the level of pronunciation, intelligibility is dynamically negotiable between speaker and listener, rather than statically inherent in a speaker's linguistic forms, even though participants find the process of negotiation more problematic than do fluent speakers.

Lynch provides a number of good examples of this sort of negotiation in progress. In the following extract, four learners are engaged in a jigsaw speaking activity. In this type of task, a text is cut up into single sentences, one sentence is given to each member of a group, they each memorize their own sentence and hand it back, and the group then work out the original order by a process of negotiation. In this interaction, A and E are from Japan, H is from Spain, and J from the Faroe Islands.

E   yes + the Queen + Queen Elizabeth
H   Queen Elizabeth
E   is the largest passenger + largest passenger
J   the Queen is the largest passenger?
H   passenger?
E   the Queen Elizabeth second
A   hm?
E   sorry + I mistook + Queen Elizabeth the second
A   hmhm
H   it's the second?
E   is the largest passenger in the
H   in the?
E   in the world
A   yeah in the
H   in the?
J   in the boat?
E   in the world
H   in the bar?
E   world

J   in the w-o-r-l-d *(stretching the vowel)*
E   in the world yes
H   oh w-o-r-l-d
(Lynch 1996: 114)

The main obstacle to successful communication here seems to be E's typical Japanese rendering of the vowel sound /ɜː/ in 'world' as /ɑː/, as shown by H's interpretation of 'world' as 'bar'; though the fact that H and J both consider words beginning with /b/ as possibilities suggests a problem with the /w/ also. On the other hand, as we would expect, following the discussion of same-L1 dyads in Chapter 3, the Japanese interlocutor clearly has no problems with this phonological transfer ('yeah in the'). Thus the negotiation in this interaction essentially entails the querying and correcting of an item of L1 phonological transfer.

The point of all this, then, has been to emphasize a number of crucial distinctions between ILT and oral communication either between fluent speakers of English or between a fluent speaker of English and an NBES. For, in a number of important ways, the negotiation of intelligibility in ILT cannot be considered typical of such negotiation in interaction where one or both interlocutors are fluent speakers of English, not least when it comes to the controversial issue of the relative roles of bottom-up and top-down processing in NBESs' speech perception, which we turn to next.

Bottom-up and top-down processing

A bottom-up model of speech perception assumes that 'we perceive speech by building up an interpretation in a series of separate stages, beginning with the lowest level units (the phonemic segments of words, for example, /b/, /ɒ/, /g/) and gradually working up to the larger units such as the utterance, from which we then derive our interpretation of the speaker's meaning' (Anderson and Lynch 1988: 22). This contrasts with top-down processing 'which uses knowledge and expectancies to guess, predict, or fill in the perceived event or message' (Pinker 1994: 474).

Psycholinguists have tended, for the past decade or so, to favour more interactive models of speech perception rather than purely top-down models (see, for example, Anderson and Lynch 1988; Flowerdew 1996; Lynch 1996 for further discussion). Nevertheless, it will be clear from the previous section that I am suggesting that NBESs, even at relatively high levels of competence, still process speech using a predominance of bottom-up strategies. As listeners they seem to find it difficult to make much use at all of the context underlying and surrounding the speech they receive, at both linguistic and extralinguistic levels. This is not to claim that learners cannot be taught to apply some (but not, in my view, all) of the contextual inferencing strategies they undoubtedly employ in their L1; but simply that at present they rarely do so (but see, for example, Anderson and Lynch 1988; Field 1998 for a different opinion).

I have already spoken at length about the way in which NBESs' mutual lack of shared socio-cultural background forces them into a far greater reliance on the acoustic signal—on what they actually hear—than is generally the case between fluent speakers of the language. However, shared socio-cultural background does not comprise the only type of accompanying information available to interlocutors. Not only may information be provided by features of the extralinguistic context, but also by the co-text, and each of these types of information may or may not be accessible to interlocutors.

Contextual and co-textual features comprise elements which are in some way present in, respectively, the extralinguistic and linguistic speech event. They are thus available to listeners to interact with the speech signal and compensate for its limitations and deficiencies by confirming or denying what is unconfidently heard, filling gaps, correcting mishearings and productive errors, and so on. NBESs' failure to make use of these features in processing messages is far more of a threat to successful communication in ILT than it is in 'native/non-native' interaction. This is because, as we have already noted, in ILT the speech signal received by the listener is likely to contain considerable L1 phonological transfer, whereas in 'native–non-native' interaction, the speech received by the 'non-native' by definition cannot transfer from an L1.

A couple of examples from my data will serve to illustrate this point (see Chapter 3 for a full account of the methodology). The two instances of miscommunication which follow occurred despite the fact that contextual information was available to guide the listener to more likely meanings than those of the acoustic signals that he had received.

In the first extract, a Japanese subject (B) was describing an alpine scene to her Swiss-German interlocutor (A). He had the same set of six pictures, although in a different order. His task was to identify in his set the picture being described. He had problems in completing the task successfully because the speaker had told him that in her picture there were 'three [led] cars'. This was confirmed by the following (tape-recorded) exchange which took place between them immediately afterwards:

A I didn't understand the let cars.
   What do you mean with this?
B Let [let] cars? Three red [red] cars *(very slowly)*.
A Ah, red.
B Red.
A Now I understand. I understood car to hire,
   to let. Ah, red, yeah I see.

This breakdown in communication occurred even though only one of the six pictures contained any cars, these cars were red, and there was no evidence to suggest that they were for hire. As Tench, in his discussion of my data, puts it, 'The Japanese phonological filter had produced [led] for /red/ and the Swiss-German filter had perceived the [led] as [let]' (1997: 33).

Four weeks later, the same two subjects were engaged in a similar task. Again, the Japanese speaker was describing a scene which her Swiss-German interlocutor had to select from a set of six pictures.

B   And second picture, the bottom of the bottom
      of the picture there's mm gley [gleɪ] house,
A   *(frowns)*
B   *(registers A's frown)* grey [gɹeɪ] and small house,
      it's very s-old?
A   Yeah, there's a grey house, yeah.
B   Mm, okay.

So four weeks after the previous interaction, the Japanese subject was still having problems with /r/, albeit less frequently. She was more aware of the problem and quicker to correct and usually to [ɹ], rather than to her earlier use of the flapped approximation [ɾ]. In the follow-up discussion, her interlocutor said that he, too, had become aware of her problem in this area and always listened for it. Nevertheless—and despite the fact that one of his pictures clearly contained a grey house—he trusted the acoustic information. Influenced also by his Swiss-German filter, 'perceiving the [g] as the Swiss-German unaspirated [k]' (Tench 1997: 34), he said he had initially understood his interlocutor to have said 'clay'. And it was only when his interlocutor corrected her phonological error that he understood which picture she was describing.

It seems then that in ILT speakers have very limited access to context to compensate for the inadequacies of speech perception and production. Nor do they fare much better in relation to co-text. Compared with fluent speakers, NBESs are 'less sure of the forms of the language, the typical syntactic structures, and the conventional vocabulary' used in the discussion of a particular topic (Brown 1990: 60). When something seems not to make sense, they are unable to decide whether the speaker has used a word with which they are unfamiliar, whether they have misheard, or whether the speaker has, in fact, made an error. This situation is especially problematic when the cause of non-sense is speaker error, and thus in ILT for, as Olsson (1978) points out, a listener needs to know that he has heard an error before he can begin to seek an alternative meaning. The failure of NBESs to exploit contextual and co-textual information and, hence, their dependency on phonological form, may be either because it is unknown, and so *unavailable*, or because it is known but *inaccessible* for some reason (for example, the pressure of on-line processing).

What happens in ILT seems to be a circular process. The lack of shared socio-cultural background between interlocutors, coupled with their mutual lack of access to aspects of the linguistic context, throws them back onto a focus on the acoustic signal. This in turn diverts cognitive resources away from features of the context, which are thence not available to compensate for any limitations in speech perception or production. And because ILT is characterized by so much L1 phonological transfer, pronunciation is often a first-base obstacle to communication beyond which the interaction is unable to proceed in a satisfactory manner. In this scheme of things, there is little scope for the higher level pragmatic factors, which are so often the culprits where communication fails between fluent speakers, to enter the equation.

To observe how this happens in practice, we might consider the sentence: 'It's very hot in this room'. This may be a simple statement of fact; it could, on the other hand, be an oblique request for someone to open a window. If the latter message is intended but only the propositional content of the sentence is perceived, the result is pragmatic failure. However, a French NBES is likely to have a problem with the consonant sound /h/ and the vowel sound /ɒ/: he may omit the /h/ altogether and pronounce the /ɒ/ as /ʌ/. Thus, the word 'hot' /hɒt/, pragmatically the most crucial one in the utterance, may well sound more like 'ut' /ʌt/. For the reasons already discussed, an NBES receiver from another L1 will probably not be able to make use of the available linguistic and extralinguistic cues to compensate for this mispronunciation. He will therefore be unable to interpret even the basic propositional meaning of the sentence, let alone its probable illocutionary force. Instead, he will either let the breakdown in communication pass without comment, or will signal non-comprehension and request clarification. If he opts for the latter course, there may well follow an exchange involving several moves, during the course of which the first speaker will reformulate and, most likely, express his original request more transparently. Whatever the outcome, the effect of the phonological deviation is to pre-empt the possibility of the emergence of pragmatic failure: unable to recognize the word 'hot', the listener is never in the position of being able to ponder the speaker's underlying intention.

It is inconceiveable that pronunciation is a major cause of problematic communication in interaction between fluent speakers of English and even, perhaps, between 'native' and 'non-native' speakers. But in ILT, given speakers' frequent inability to 'say what (they) mean' pronunciation-wise, which is compounded by listeners' seemingly ubiquitous use of bottom-up processing strategies, pronunciation is possibly the greatest single barrier to successful communication. And this seems to be the case well beyond the beginner and elementary learner levels mooted by most of those who write on speech perception in L2 English (for example, Anderson and Lynch 1988; Rost 1990, 1996). As we will see in the next section, it is still much in evidence when learners are at upper-intermediate level and beyond.

The role of phonology in ILT: miscommunication in the ILT data

In order to demonstrate the extent of the phonological barrier to successful communication in ILT and thus substantiate the claim made in the previous paragraph, I will now describe and discuss all the communication breakdowns that occurred in one of my studies (see Chapter 3 for the methodology). In a sense, these breakdowns demonstrate what happens when the process of convergence, discussed briefly in the last chapter, does not, for whatever reason, come into play.

Altogether there were forty occasions on which a receiver was unable to understand the intended meaning of his or her interlocutor. Each one occurred during interaction in the different-L1 dyads: there was not a single example of such communication breakdown in the same-L1 interactions. This does not necessarily mean that the latter interactions contained absolutely no misunderstandings at the pragmatic level. The occasional pragmatic failure may have occurred but passed unnoticed or without comment by the interlocutors, both at the time and during the subsequent playback of the recordings. However, because of the nature of the interactions taking place, I can say with confidence that if there were any such instances of pragmatic failure, they neither disturbed the flow of the conversation nor affected the final outcome of the task.

I have divided the forty instances of communication breakdown, which occurred in the different-L1 data in this study, into the following categories:

1 Pronunciation
2 Lexis
3 Grammar
4 World knowledge
5 Ambiguous/miscellaneous cause.

In the data and discussion which follow, the subjects and task types are coded in the following manner:

J1, J2	Japanese subjects 1 and 2
SG1, SG2, SG3	Swiss-German subjects 1, 2, and 3
SF	Swiss-French subject
(A)	social conversation task
(B)	information-exchange task
(C)	joint problem-solving task

The numbers 1–4 before (A), (B), or (C) refer to the specific interaction (the four separate interactions having taken place regularly over a 10-week period). The item responsible for each instance of communication breakdown is shown in bold, regardless of whether or not it was uttered correctly (or, in other words, whether the problem was receptive only or, as was more common, productive and receptive). Where the cause is pronunciation, a phonetic transcript (within square brackets) is provided.

Following each token of breakdown cause, the communicative outcome is indicated in parentheses.[5]

1 *Pronunciation (Total: 27)*

1 (1B) SG1:   **wood** pronounced [wʊt] (J1 hears 'water'.)

2 (1B) SF: **toys** as [taɪz] (SG3 does not understand until SF repeats correctly.)

3 (1B) SG3:   **wool** as [wəʊ] (SF does not understand at all but says nothing.)

4 (1A) J2:   **football match** as ['ɸuːtəbɔl 'mætʃ] (SG1 does not understand until J2 repeats correctly.)

5 (1A) J2:   **soccer club** as ['sʌkɑː klʌv] (again SG1 does not understand until J2 repeats correctly.)

6 (1A) SG2:   **hobbies** as ['hɒbɪs] (J2 is initially not sure what SG2 means, and asks ['hɒvɪz] with rising intonation. He says 'yeah' at which point J2 understands and the interaction continues.)

7 (1B) J2:   **wood chair** [w] pronounced [ɷ]. (SG2 understands 'chair' and ignores the word 'wood'; see page 89 for discussion of this example.)

8 (2A) J2:   'You **want** work in England?' as [wəʊnt] (SG2 does not understand until J2 repeats the question correctly.)

9 (2A) J2:   'after I return to **Japan**' as [dʒæ'pæ] (SG2 asks 'after what?'—J2 repeats with same pronunciation but adds 'from England' and SG2 understands.)

10 (2B) J2:   'three **red** cars' as [led] (SG2 does not understand and assumes she means 'let cars', that is to say, 'cars to let'.)

11 (2B) SG2:   'table is surrounded by **chairs**' as [tʃeəs] (Assumes J2's problem is 'surrounded' and rephrases, but in fact she is not sure whether he means 'chairs' or 'chess'.)

12 (2B) SG1:   **balcony** as ['bælkən] (J1 does not understand but says nothing.)

13 (2B) SG1:   **covered** as ['kəʊwəd] ['kəʊvəd] ['kəʊvət] and ['kɒvəd] (J1 eventually guesses from her picture and SG1's three repetitions of the word 'snow'.)

14 (2B) J1:   **cushions** as ['kʊʃɔ̃] (SG1 does not understand until J1 repeats correctly.)

15 (2B) J1:   **scissors** as ['sɪzɑːz] (SG1 does not understand until J1 repeats correctly.)

16 (2C) J2:   'it looks more **sad**, much **sadder**' as [sæt] and ['sætə] (SG2 does not understand until J2 repeats correctly.)

17 (3A) J1:   'Japanese **animation** films' with final syllable as [ʃɔ̃] (SG1 understands only Japanese films and does not pursue

the word 'animation'.)

18 (3A) J1:   **mall** as [mɑːl] (SG1 does not understand but says nothing.)

19 (3A) J2:   'are they **English**?' as ['ɪŋgrɪʃ] (SG2 asks 'Are?' but then grasps it before J2 repeats.)

20 (3B) SG3:   **hat** as [hɒt] (SF only understands after SG3 reformulates his sentence, though he does not actually improve his pronunciation of 'hat'.)

21 (3B) J1:   **zipper** as ['dʒiːpɑː] (SG1 does not understand at all but says nothing.)

22 (3B) SG1:   **hat** as [hɒt] (J2 assumes he said 'hot', infers 'warm clothes', and draws a sweater. She is not aware that he has mentioned a 'hat'.)

23 (3C) J2:   'I'd take the **bird**' as [bɑːd] (SG2 asks 'You'll take?' and understands when she repeats correctly.)

24 (4B) J1:   **man** as [mɑːn] twice (SG1 does not understand until J1 repeats it a third time correctly.)

25 (4B) J2:   '**grey** house' as [gleɪ] (SG2 initially looks for a 'clay house'. J2 registers his frown, corrects her pronunciation almost immediately and SG2 understands.)

26 (4B) J2   **curtain** as ['kɑːɹtən] (SG2 does not know at first, but guesses from the word 'blind', although he later claims not to have been very confident about his guess.)

27 (4C) SG1:   'The weather is even **worse** [vɜːɹs] there than here' (J1 does not understand until SG1 repeats with correct pronunciation.)

2 Lexis (Total: 8)

28 (1B) J1:   **mantelpiece** (SG1 does not know this word.)

29 (1B) J1:   **vase** (SG1 does not know this word.)

30 (1C) J2:   **couch potato** (SG2 does not know the term—J2 explains.)

31 (2B) SG3:   **booklets** instead of 'magazines' (SF does not understand what he means.)

32 (2B) SF: **ashtray** (SG3 knows the word but could not place it at that moment.)

33 (3B) J1:   **chest long** to describe hair length (SG1 understands when she rephrases as 'up to her chest'.)

34 (4B) SG1:   substitutes the word **furniture** for 'kitchen units' (J1 does not understand.)

35 (4B) SG1:   substitutes the word **plate** for 'kitchen surface' (Again J1 does not understand.)

3 Grammar (Total: 1)

36 (2C) SG1: 'to use children as the cover is not the **baddest** idea' (J1 does not understand 'baddest'.)

4 World knowledge (Total: 1)

37 (2A) J1: **flower arranging** (SG1 knows the words but not that the course is available in the school and assumes J1 has made a mistake.)

5 Ambiguous/miscellaneous cause (Total: 3)

38 (1A) SF: '**What is your work?**' spoken very fast. (SG3 does not understand until repeated more slowly.)

39 (1B) SG1: **oven** pronounced [əʊfən] then [əʊvən]; wrong word—he means 'fireplace' (J1 does not understand at all.)

40 (2A) SF: '**You need English a lot?**' quietly and with falling intonation although intended as a question. (SG3 understands when repeated correctly.)

The above comprise all the examples of communication breakdown (non-understanding or, less often, misunderstanding) in the different-L1 interactions that were either apparent when they occurred, or were not apparent at the time, but were acknowledged by the subjects during the follow-up interviews. Although there may have been other instances of non-comprehension, this was unlikely as the pairs of subjects and I listened in detail to the tapes together, pausing frequently to check whether what had been meant was what had actually been inferred. And although learners are often reticent about signalling non-comprehension (see page 77 above), these subjects appeared comfortable with the idea of doing so in the follow-up stage, if not always during the task itself. This was, I believe, because of the non-threatening manner in which the follow-up discussion was conducted, the goal being not to criticize either speaker or listener, but to help them to identify together the ways in which they could mutually improve their performance for the forthcoming CAE Speaking examination.

The most noteworthy feature of the list is obviously the high proportion of instances of communication breakdown caused by pronunciation errors. Of the 40 samples, one is the result of speed of delivery; another is the result of the lack of world knowledge; one is the result of grammatical error (two if the 'ambiguous cause' number 40 is included); eight relate to lexis (nine if number 39, the ambiguous 'oven', is included), either the speaker's misuse or the receiver's lack of lexical knowledge). But a remarkable 27 of the breakdowns were the result of pronunciation (29 if we include the two 'ambiguous causes' 39 and 40, which involve pronunciation), and all 27 were caused by the transfer of L1 sounds. Thus L1 sound transfer is responsible for more than twice the other causes added together. This finding is well supported by convictions expressed not only by the six subjects themselves, but also by many other EFL students who have experience of ILT, with whom I have spoken. By contrast, it does not fit in comfortably with current experts' claims for suprasegmental phonology as the prime cause, pronunciation-wise, of learners' lack of intelligibility (see Chapters 2 and 6, and Jenkins 1996a). I suspect, however, that the latter view reflects the fact that many of these people work in EFL and (American) 'ESL' rather than ILT situations, and towards a pedagogic goal of intelligibility for listeners who are 'native speakers' of English.

These examples also provide evidence of the minor role of grammar errors in ILT miscommunication. For, despite countless such errors in the data, only once did a problem occur (or twice if the lack of inversion in the final 'ambiguous cause' compounded the faulty intonation pattern). The fact that learners seem to grasp what is intended when their ILT peers make errors in grammar is probably at least partly a function of the developmental factor in the acquisition of L2 grammar (see Chapter 5 and Ellis 1994, Chapter 3). Although learners from different L1s acquire their L2 English grammar at different rates, taking differential periods of time to pass through the various developmental stages according to their L1 grammar, they nevertheless pass broadly through the same stages. The likelihood then is that learners will be able to interpret the grammar errors of their peers even when their own interlanguage has moved beyond the developmental phase of which those errors are characteristic. This is paralleled in L1 use, where adults rarely have problems in understanding the deviant grammar of young children (*Mummy gone* and *He's tooken it* being typical English examples).[6]

In fact, it seems that in L1 English interaction, syntactic effects have a very limited role by contrast with lexical effects in the decoding of words. Rost (1990) notes that in experiments on lexical effects, subjects 'tended to identify sounds as English words as long as there was some phonological evidence that a word could be identified'. On the other hand, 'data on syntactic processing suggests that **syntactic context plays a very limited role in constraining word recognition**' in English which, Rost points out, is not surprising, 'since it is only rarely possible to predict with certainty the form class of any given lexical item because each syntactic constituent in English has optional members' (ibid.: 48–50; emphasis in original). In other words, the syntactic context in English does not provide many cues to facilitate the prediction of what is to come or the decoding of what has gone before —what Rost refers to as 'look-ahead and look-behind assessments of language as it is heard' (ibid.). ILT thus has much in common with fluent/L1 interaction in terms of the role of syntactic (as opposed to phonological and lexical) context in intelligibility in speech perception.

Turning back to the ILT data above, one other area calls for particular comment. This is the large number of L1 pronunciation transfers which are processed bottom-up and result in some sort of communication breakdown, when top-down listening strategies would probably have avoided this outcome. In many of the breakdowns where the source can be traced back to the speaker's pronunciation, there was extensive extralinguistic contextual information available. In examples 10, 12, 16, 23, 25, and 27, the listener had a picture showing this information visually (and remember that in the case of task C, the two interlocutors were looking at the *same* picture). In examples 2, 11, 14, 24, and 26, the listener did not know for certain they had the item in question in their picture, but they knew at least (because they had been told at the beginning of the interaction) that their task B picture showed a very similar physical setting to that of their partner, with any differences being in the fine detail. Yet in example 11, for instance, the listener opts for 'chess' rather than 'chairs' ('Table is surrounded by chess') despite the fact that the former would be extremely unlikely in either the linguistic or extralinguistic context. In examples 20, 21, and 22, the listeners were attempting to draw a person from the speakers' descriptions. They could therefore be expected to have established a schema which included words such as 'hat' and 'zipper', especially considering that in example 20, the speaker said 'She wears a hat *on her head*', and the 'zipper' in example 21 is mentioned in the context of a raincoat. In examples 4 and 5, although there was no visual information, the subject of football was already under discussion and, once again, one could have expected a football match schema to have compensated for pronunciation problems.

Notwithstanding what has just been said, there are signs in the data of occasional attempts to use top-down, context-based strategies when difficulties arise. However, not only are these strategies very rare, but the subjects—despite being of upper-intermediate to low-advanced proficiency levels—do not seem to use them with any great degree of confidence. In fact, only in three of these 27 instances did a listener appear to be making much use of top-down strategies. In example 7, the Japanese speaker described a wooden chair as a 'wood chair', pronouncing 'wood' with [ɷ] rather than [w]. Even though the deviation is only a slight one, the Swiss-German listener did not understand the word at all. However, after two (still inaccurate) repetitions, he decided to ignore it and, latching on instead to the word 'chair', managed to identify the picture being described. In example 13, the Swiss-German speaker repeated the word 'covered' four times, each time with a further small improvement in the pronunciation, but never pronouncing it in such a way as to be identifiable to his Japanese interlocutor. In the follow-up discussion, she admitted that she had eventually realized what he meant because she had guessed from her own set of pictures and several repetitions of the word 'snow'. Again, in example 26, the Swiss-German listener realized that a 'carton' was unlikely in the context of a window and used this knowledge along with the linguistic information (the word 'blind' co-occurred) to guess 'curtain'. Nevertheless, after the Japanese subject had finished her description, he asked: 'I'm not sure if I understood it the right way the the window, there's no there are no curtains?', and admitted in the later discussion to having been unconfident about his guess.

We noted in the previous chapter that in ILT speakers tend to minimize the use of L1 phonological transfer when they are able to do so and when intelligibility for an interlocutor is particularly salient. However, there appears to be something of a tension between the desire to minimize difficulty for the listener and the desire to minimize difficulty for self. The avoiding of phonological transfer by summoning up and 'adding' the target form (see Chapter 8 on the concept of 'accent addition'), demands a considerable degree of cognitive effort on the part of the speaker, so it stands to reason that they will not attempt to do so if they do not consider it to be absolutely essential. This is where context comes into play. When deciding how much cognitive effort to invest in replacing transfer with a more target-like pronunciation, speakers may (either consciously or subconsciously) weigh up the risks involved for their NBES interlocutors. If clear contextual cues are available, they may assume that it is safe to relax their 'controls' on pronunciation, and thus those sounds which have not yet become automatically target-like will emerge with L1 transfer. In other words, like fluent speakers of English in their use of assimilatory features (see above pages 72–3), they will opt for the easiest route to speech production if they think they can 'get away with it'. One explanation for the phonological transfers in the ILT data may therefore relate to speaker/listener differences in orientation to context.

In L2, this preference for ease of articulation is particularly true of sounds in certain phonological environments as compared with others. Some L2 phonological processes and sound combinations are clearly more difficult than others for L2 speakers of English, depending on the interaction of their L1 phonology with phonological and physiological universals (see Chapter 5). Where such 'difficult' processes and sounds are involved, and in the presence of contextual information, speakers seem less likely to make the necessary cognitive effort to replace L1 transfer. A tentative example of this phenomenon is number 25 above (also discussed on page 82), involving a Japanese speaker's substitution of /r/ with /l/. The former sound is more marked than the latter, in that if a language contains /r/ it will also contain /l/, but not vice versa. In addition, although about 75 per cent of languages contain some type of /r/ phoneme, it is most commonly a variety of trill rather than the (British) English approximant [ɹ] (Ladefoged and Maddieson 1996), a sound which L1 (British) English children have difficulty in acquiring. The implication is, then, that it is universally easier to articulate /l/ than (the (British) English form of) /r/, and particularly for speakers such as the Japanese, whose first language has only a single flapped sound somewhere between the two English sounds. Clusters involving /r/ are even more difficult for them. In fact, clusters with /r/ are difficult for all speakers (Macken and Ferguson 1981)—even L1 speakers of English have articulatory problems with /tr/ and /dr/, which they tend to pronounce respectively as /tʃr/ and /dʒr/.[7]

The interplay between context and phonological environment may thus account for forms such as 'gley' for 'grey' in example 25. The /gl/ combination is easier to produce than /gr/, particularly for those such as Japanese speakers of English. So on this occasion, because of the presence of the visual cue, the speaker at first does not make the necessary effort to select (a cognitive process) and produce (an articulatory process) a [ɹ]. However, the fact that the context does not clarify her meaning for her interlocutor suggests that speakers and listeners have different agendas in relation to context and, perhaps oddly, that in the role of speakers they are not able to keep in mind the difficulties that they have as listeners in dealing with contextual information.

Even for fluent listeners, language is a guide to context which, itself, cannot be activated until the utterance has been heard. Listeners have to select from an 'explosion of potentially relevant information' (Brown et al. 1994: 35), whereas a speaker, in referring to features of the context, has by definition already selected these features. This means, as Brown points out, that from a listener's perspective, 'context alone may not illuminate language use unless language is first deliberately used to guide listeners to identifying those features of context which will be relevant to the interpretation of language' (1989: 97). But in ILT, the potential for this to happen is heavily constrained. For here, we are presented with a unique situation: a combination of the inability of language to 'guide' reliably because of speakers' phonological difficulties and the inability of listeners to be guided because of their top-down processing difficulties. The pity is that, because of the sheer amount of phonological transfer in the speech of NBESs, an ability to make use of contextual information would be doubly helpful to NBES listeners. In my view, however, this is not a likely outcome for the majority, and we should focus the EIL pedagogic effort above all on enabling learners, in the words of the Mad Hatter, to 'say what (they) mean'. This will best be done, on the one hand, by establishing a core of intelligible pronunciation which can be made available to all learners regardless of their L1 and, on the other, by developing learners' accommodative skills so that they are able to improve their intelligibility for specific listeners. These are the subjects respectively of Chapters 6 and 7, where we move on to consider pedagogic priorities.

Intelligibility and the spread of English

No discussion of intelligibility in ILT would be complete without some comment on the concerns which continue to be voiced over the possibility that English will ultimately fragment, like Latin, into a number of mutually *unintelligible* languages (see, for example, Maley 1985; Quirk 1985; Crystal 1997; and McArthur 1998 for discussion of this issue). Crystal points out that 'prophets have been predicting such doom for some time'. He cites Henry Sweet's inaccurate prophecy of 1877 that 'England, America, and Australia will be speaking mutually unintelligible languages, owing to their independent changes of pronunciation', and a similar one, made still one century earlier, by Noah Webster with regard to British and American English (1997: 134). Although both Crystal and McArthur stress that 'this whole topic is so recent that it is difficult to make predictions with much confidence' (Crystal ibid.: 135), they remain positive: 'despite all the diversity and because of all the recent technological innovations the centre will after all probably hold' (McArthur 1998: 183).

McArthur, in fact, takes the argument one stage further in his conclusion that the issue can be viewed from three perspectives: the 'pessimistic', the 'optimistic', and the 'neutral'/'pragmatic'. The pessimists, i.e. those people for whom Latin 'offers a suitably dire analogue of mutually unintelligible 'post-English' languages', he argues, 'are usually conservatives in the Wyldian tradition,[8] asserting a 'Received Standard' to which all should adhere or aspire, and which is for them the true English language' (ibid.: 181–2). This view, however, is not as thinly spread as McArthur implies. Not only is it relatively common among the 'NS' lay population (see Chapter 2), but it is also prevalent among teachers in ELT schools, particularly (though not exclusively) 'NS' teachers in the UK and USA, and is implicit in the bulk of teaching materials produced by publishers in the 'NS centre'. And such teachers and publishers are not generally people who consider themselves to be 'conservative' in the Wyldian or any other tradition. Widdowson, taking a rather more pragmatic (and realistic) position, argues that standards of intelligibility in EIL are sustainable, but in relation to specific purposes rather than to some vague global intelligibility: 'English as an international language is English for Specific Purposes. Otherwise it would not have spread, otherwise it would not regulate itself as an effective means of global communication. And otherwise there would, for most people, be little point in learning it at school or university' (1997: 144).

Any reference to unintelligibility of course begs the question 'unintelligible to whom?' Evidently the many L1 speakers of English, teachers or otherwise, who still regard their role as that of privileged 'native speakers' of the language, mean unintelligible to themselves. In this connection, we notice that even in the most recent communicative speaking examinations such as the CAE—which stipulates the examining of candidates in pairs and minimal input from the two (usually 'NS') examiners—judgements of intelligibility are based on whether these two examiners understand the candidates, rather than on whether the latter understand one another. And these judgements are themselves influenced above all by the perceived closeness or distance of candidates' L2 accents from those of the examiners. (See Chapter 8 for a discussion of the testing of pronunciation in communicative exams.)

The scenario described in the previous paragraph is unlikely to change, however, while most of the pronunciation teaching which takes place around the world remains heavily-biased towards 'NS' accents. Willis (1996), though referring to grammar, describes the outcome of this sort of bias as 'conformity' rather than 'accuracy': conformity to 'NS' norms rather than accuracy in the establishing of a relationship between form and meaning in the context of the particular interaction. This implies a focus on acceptability for L1 speakers of English rather than on intelligibility for NBESs.

In terms of pronunciation, however, interlocutors engaged in ILT, of necessity, resort to accurate perception of phonological form because they are unable to access other sources of information in the level-switching process (from sound to word to co-text to context) which characterizes fluency. Accuracy is thus critical in Brumfit's (1984) sense (i.e. as opposed to fluency). Nevertheless, phonological accuracy in EIL is quite a different matter from conformity to the norms of L1 speakers. The phonological core (see Chapter 6) both includes features that would not be considered acceptable by the latter and omits a number that they would consider crucial. In this regard, then, I find Willis's accuracy/conformity distinction a very useful one, and will take it up again in Chapter 6. Pushing learners to acquire authentic 'NS' norms of course is, and always has been, an oxymoron in both senses. L2 speakers of English, however high their level of proficiency, by definition never engage in authentic 'NS–NS' interaction. And even in 'NS–NNS' (EFL) conversation, the 'NNS' interlocutor is not receiving authentic 'NS' discourse from his addressee because, as Riley points out, 'exolinguistic discourse is never a matter of one Native Speaker discourse plus one Non-Native Speaker discourse, with one speaker behaving 'normally', the other speaking 'like a foreigner'. Observation has shown … that both participants modify their discourse and that this is a discursive situation *sui generis*' (1989: 122).

As far as EIL is concerned, however, we are interested not in intelligibility for 'native-speaker' receivers but for participants in interlanguage talk, i.e. NBESs. And here, the prospect of mutual unintelligibility does need to be taken seriously. Above I quoted Crystal's comment about the recency of EIL and the consequent difficulty of making sound predictions about mutual intelligibility. The general consensus, nevertheless, appears to be that mutual intelligibility in EIL will probably be safeguarded by virtue of international technology and telecommunications. However, it seems to me that this view reflects something of an inner circle perspective. While I agree in general terms that English is unlikely to fragment into the modern-day equivalents of Italian, Spanish, French, and so on, I do not believe that this outcome will happen of itself as if by some sort of linguistic magic. Because EIL is so very different from both EFL and ESL, people will need to work at it; and they will need pedagogic support to facilitate their efforts.

The starting point of EIL is, of course, that it involves L2 English speakers from myriad first languages. If we set aside the minority of fluent speakers of English (whether BES or MES) who engage in EIL, English is always—and often to some considerable degree—characterized by phonological transfer from its speakers' first languages. Indeed, pronunciation, as we have already noted, is the linguistic level which most distinguishes one (educated) variety of English from another, whereas the different L1 groups, even at NBES level, maintain far more common ground in their grammar and lexis, particularly in written English. We saw earlier in this chapter the difficulties that result from L1 pronunciation transfer, not only because of the transfer problem *per se*, but also on account of listener factors relating exclusively to interlanguage talk. EIL is therefore at far greater risk of succumbing to mutual (phonological) unintelligibility than has ever been the case for EFL or ESL.

Clearly, we need far more EIL-based information than is currently available as to whose accents are (un)intelligible to whom and, more specifically, as to precisely which pronunciation features lead to loss of intelligibility. Most of the small amount of research on the intelligibility of different L2 accents of English has approached the issue mainly or entirely from the perspective of 'NS' listeners (for example, Nelson 1982 and Bansal 1990 on the intelligibility of Indian English; Lanham 1990 on the intelligibility of South African Black English; Ufomata 1990 and Tiffen 1992 on the intelligibility of Nigerian English).

Noteworthy exceptions which consider intelligibility from the point of view of both 'NNS' and 'NS' listeners are Lane (1963); Smith and Rafiqzad (1979); Smith and Bisazza (1982); and Smith (1992).[9] Lane (1963) looked at the effects of noise on the intelligibility of foreign accent for both 'NS' and 'NNS' listeners. He found, predictably, that 'NNS' listeners suffered to a greater extent than 'NSs' (63 per cent loss as compared with 55 per cent). The next two studies compared the intelligibility of different accents of English for 'NS' and 'NNS' listeners. Smith and Rafiqzad (1979) found that the intelligibility of the different accents was consistent for all listeners; that only two of the eleven groups of listeners rated their own countrymen as the most intelligible; and that the 'NS' was always one of the least intelligible. Smith and Bisazza (1982) found that the intelligibility of an accent was strongly linked to the listeners' familiarity with that accent, i.e. to the amount of prior exposure they had had to it. Smith (1992) had similar concerns to those of the previous two studies. He came to similar conclusions in relation to 'native speakers' of English (they appeared to be neither the most easily understood nor the best able to understand different varieties of the language) and the importance of familiarity with a range of English varieties across cultures. To my knowledge, no other research has considered phonological intelligibility within a 'non-native/non-native' framework until my own work in the 1990s, which focuses on this interaction type exclusively, and which attempts to identify both which phonological features impede intelligibility and which are of no consequence in ILT.[10]

We noted in Chapter 1 that RP is not necessarily the most easily understood accent of English, even for L1 speakers who speak other varieties of English. The studies of Smith, Smith, and Rafiqzad, and Smith and Bisazza (and see also Smith and Nelson 1985) provide further evidence that a 'native speaker' of a standard variety of English is not necessarily either the most intelligible or the best judge of intelligibility in EIL. Their evidence, along with the distinction between accuracy· and conformity mentioned above, and the findings of my own ILT research, indicates a pressing need for us to redefine phonological error and correctness within the context of EIL rather than within the framework of a standard language ideology. In the process of doing so, we will be able to redress the balance between intelligibility and acceptability by giving far more weight to intelligibility for NBESs and far less to acceptability and appropriacy for L1 speakers. This, in turn, will ensure that judgements of error and correctness are acceptable and appropriate to EIL.

Conclusion

In terms of pronunciation, what the discussion in this chapter indicates is the need for some sort of international core for phonological intelligibility: a set of unifying features which, at the very least, has the potential to guarantee that pronunciation will not impede successful communication in EIL settings. This core will be contrived to the extent that its features are not identical with those of any one L1 or L2 variety of English. As we will see in Chapter 6, a phonological core of this kind already exists among all L1 speakers of English, whatever their variety. A core of sorts also exists among L2 speakers, insofar as speakers of all languages share certain phonological features and processes. However, this shared element is limited. Indeed, were it not so, there would be no reason for me to write this book: L2 speakers of English from different parts of the world would understand each other's pronunciation with relatively little difficulty. Thus, while we can build on what L2 speakers already have in common phonologically, we must take the argument one very large step further by identifying what they *need* to have in common and contriving a pedagogic core that focuses on this need. However, such a core, while necessary, will not alone be sufficient to achieve the goal of preventing pronunciation from impeding communication. Bamgboṣe makes the obvious yet frequently missed point that 'it is people, not language codes, that understand one another' (1998: 11). Participants in EIL will also need to be able tune into each other's accents and adjust both their own phonological output and their receptive expectations accordingly.

In Chapters 6 and 7 we will look more closely at these two approaches to EIL communication and consider their pedagogic implications. Chapter 6 is both a discussion of the complex issues involved in the establishing of a core of phonological intelligibility for EIL, and a presentation of the core which I am proposing. Then, in Chapter 7, we move on to a consideration of how best to both promote learners' productive and receptive use of this core, and to encourage the development of speaker/listener accommodative processes which will facilitate mutual intelligibility in EIL. But first, in the following chapter, we will consider in detail the relationship between L1 phonological transfer and EIL intelligibility.

Notes

1 Lecture at International House London, 4 December 1992 and again at the 33rd TESOL Convention, New York, 11 March 1999; and see Chapter 6 page 149 for an example of this phenomenon.

2 This also applies to those in intranational Second Language situations, most notably—though not exclusively—ESL.

3 In addition, the 'non-native' in such speech situations may be addressed in foreigner talk. In particular, the 'native's' speech will be more slowly and clearly articulated than normal, to compensate for any gaps in shared background and linguistic knowledge, which would undermine the 'non-native's' ability to process the 'acoustic blur' (see also Chapter 7).

4 Though EIL is associated with cultural background to the extent that interlocutors share cultures of specialized knowledge and expertise within specific ESP genres, and these can—and should—be dealt with in ESP classrooms.

5 Some of the non- and misunderstandings did not become evident until the recording of an interaction was played back to the subjects.

6 Asterisks are used to indicate that a grammatically incorrect item is non-attested.

7 Though I once had a colleague who regularly pronounced the word 'children' with an epenthetic (added) schwa sound between the /d/ and the /r/.

8 This refers to Henry Cecil Wylde, the originator of the early 20th Century term 'Received Standard English' (the standard language spoken with a public school accent). Wylde described this accent as 'neither provincial nor vulgar, a type which most people would willingly speak if they could, and desire to speak if they do not' (1934, quoted by McArthur 1998: 125).

9 A major difference between these studies and my own, however, is that the listener subjects in the former were in the position of 'eavesdroppers' whereas those in my studies were also participants in the discourse.

10 Although not being concerned specifically with accent, Lynch 1996 discusses learner–learner interaction and provides some illuminating examples of phonological problems and their negotiation (see, for instance, the example taken from Lynch's data on pages 79–80).

5 The role of transfer in determining the phonological core

Is the research in L2 phonology leading us in the direction of developing effective methods for teaching accent-free speech to adults?

G. Ioup and S. H. Weinberger 1987, *Interlanguage Phonology*, page xiii

L'accent du pays où l'on est né demeure dans l'esprit et dans le coeur comme dans le langage.[1]

Duc de la Rochefoucauld 1678, *Réflexions ou Sentences et Maximes Morales*, page 342

In the previous chapter, we established the central role of the phonological signal in intelligibility among Non-Bilingual English Speakers (NBESs). We noted, though, that this signal is of its very nature unstable, with speakers of different first languages varying their pronunciation under the influence of their L1 phonology. If we are to identify a phonological core on which speakers can rely, we cannot disregard these natural processes of transfer, but must take account of them. Our proposal must be based on an understanding of the process of phonological transfer and its effects, and the extent to which it is realistic to expect speakers to replace transferred items with other forms.

In this chapter, we will prepare the ground for the proposal of the phonological core which follows in Chapter 6, by establishing both what is involved in phonological transfer and the links between this and intelligibility and teachability.

The complex process of L1 phonological transfer

In the 1950s, L1 transfer was thought to involve, in a relatively straightforward way, the 'interference' of old (i.e. L1) habits in the acquiring of new (i.e. L2) habits, in those cases where contrastive analysis showed the two languages to differ. According to the Contrastive Analysis Hypothesis, or CAH (Lado 1957), while L1–L2 similarity equates with simplicity in L2 acquisition, L1–L2 difference equates with difficulty. L2 acquisition was thus regarded at that time as the 'getting rid' of old habits (a view still held by many pronunciation teachers today, as indicated by the use—actual or implicit—of the term 'accent reduction'). Owing to its behaviourist connections, the notion of transfer as an important process in adult L2 acquisition lost credibility with SLA researchers (if not with teachers) for several years. Subsequently it has been welcomed back into mainstream SLA theory, and is now acknowledged as having a major role in adult L2 acquisition—though in far more complex ways than those proposed by its earlier advocates.

Because our interest in L1 phonological transfer is primarily in its relevance to the establishing of a phonological core of intelligibility for EIL, we will not be examining its complexities in fine detail. Any reader who is interested in studying these complexities is directed to Ioup and Weinberger (1987), a collection of authoritative articles on interlanguage phonology. Nevertheless, some awareness of the origins of L1 phonological transfer and its consequent implications for adult L2 pronunciation is important, in order that readers understand the rationale underlying a phonological core whose goals are universal teachability and international intelligibility. The complex nature of phonological transfer derives from its interactions with a number of other processes and factors. We will consider briefly those which have been found to exert the greatest influence on the transfer process. They are, respectively: universal processes, developmental processes, stylistic and contextual factors, habit formation and automaticity, cognitive factors, and notions of ambiguity.

Transfer plus universal processes

Much of the research done in the 1960s and 1970s into children's acquisition of L1 phonology was influenced by the universalist theories of Jakobson, Smith, and Stampe. These theories predicted orders of acquisition (Jakobson); identified universal tendencies, such as consonant and vowel harmony and cluster simplification (Smith); and emphasized innate processes which derive from human perceptual and articulatory forces, some of which have to be 'unlearnt' because they do not apply to the child's particular L1 (Stampe). (For accounts of these theories, see, for instance, Jakobson 1968; Stampe 1969; and Smith 1973.) Although subsequent research has uncovered other important contributory factors such as the child L1 learner's cognitive abilities, this earlier work demonstrates the universal influence on phonological acquisition of 'the purely linguistic constraints imposed by the nature of human language and human articulatory and perceptual systems' (Macken and Ferguson 1981: 7).

Since they are universal, such linguistic constraints can be expected to play an important part in the acquisition of L2 phonology, and subsequent research into interlanguage phonology has duly revealed tendencies similar to those operating in L1 acquisition. For EIL, an important case in point is that of consonant cluster simplification. There is in L1 child acquisition a tendency to simplify consonant clusters by means of consonant deletion, so that a child will probably go through a stage of pronouncing, for example, the word 'crisp' as /kɪp/. Such is the strength of the universal desire to avoid consonant clusters that it continues in fully developed L1 speech as the acceptable and often expected process of 'elision', albeit in a rather more restricted, L1-rule-bound manner. In English, it occurs both within words (for example, 'scripts' frequently becomes /skrɪps/) and between words (for example, 'walked by' becomes /wɔːk baɪ/), but is never permitted word-initially. In L2 acquisition, the same preference for cluster simplification may, depending on the learner's L1, be reflected in the use of consonant deletion in a manner similar to that of L1-child acquisition. Alternatively, it may result in epenthesis (vowel addition). For example, an Arabic learner of English may pronounce 'film' as /fɪləm/ because of an L1-related difficulty in producing the cluster /lm/.

The desire to avoid clusters has been traced to a universal preference for the CV (consonant-vowel) syllable, which itself is probably 'a universal articulatory and perceptual unit such that the articulators tend to operate in basic CV programs in all languages', but that 'different languages elaborate on this basic program in various ways, adding different combinations of permissible initial and/or final consonants' (Tarone 1978: 78). The problem for EIL, then, is that the specific learner's L1 means for realizing the universal preference for CV syllables may result in an L2 simplification which conforms not to the rules of English elision but to the rules of their own L1. And because L1s differ widely in their permissible syllable structures and, thus, in their speakers' routes to cluster simplification, international English intelligibility is likely to be jeopardized. This contrasts with another universally difficult feature of English, the pair of dental fricatives /θ/ and /ð/. These are commonly substituted in L2 by a limited set of alternatives—/t/ and /d/, /s/ and /z/ or, less commonly, /f/ and /v/—and, thus, the universal difficulty is likely to be solved by an L1 transfer which will not impair intelligibility (even if it is at present stigmatized by educated L1 speakers of English).

Two other interlanguage processes, schwa paragoge—the addition of schwa to word-final obstruents (plosives, fricatives, and affricates)—and terminal devoicing—the loss of voice on certain word-final consonant sounds—have been shown to be motivated by constraints that relate to phonological universals. The use of schwa paragoge is thought, like that of consonant deletion, to be related to the universal preference for open CV syllables discussed above, although the precise resolution of this preference appears, as with consonant deletion, to be influenced by the structure of the particular speaker's L1. For example, Mandarin permits only vowels and sonorant consonants (approximants, liquids, and nasals) in word-final position. Mandarin speakers of English may, therefore, tend to add schwa to words which end in obstruents, for example, the word 'tag' may be pronounced /tægə/.

However, a rule of schwa paragoge is a more difficult one for Mandarin learners to internalize than a rule of consonant deletion, since they have to internalize with it the word-final obstruents to which the schwa is added, and which do not exist in their L1. On the other hand, it results in pronunciation which is more intelligible, since deletion would produce forms such as /tæ/—thus removing the distinction between 'tag', 'tab', and 'tad' (see Eckman 1981a for full details and many more examples). It may be, then, that where the rules of the first language are conducive to schwa paragoge, this process, rather than consonant deletion, is selected by sufficiently proficient learners of English—probably subconsciously—as being more likely to promote the intelligibility of their speech. Though as far as teachability is concerned, it will probably be easier to encourage schwa paragoge over consonant deletion where the structure of learners' L1s facilitates its use.

While the process of schwa paragoge is found only in interlanguages, terminal devoicing is motivated for the grammars of a number of first languages such as German, Polish, and Russian. For example, German permits only voiceless obstruents word-finally. Thus, the German word for 'day', which is pronounced /tagə/ in its plural form *Tage*, becomes /tak/ in the singular *Tag* (see Eckman 1981a).

The process of terminal devoicing also features in L1 English. But because voicing contrasts are permitted word-finally in English (i.e. some words end in voiceless and others in voiced sounds), the process operates only at an allophonic level, involving a small reduction in voice rather than its complete loss. It affects words ending in voiced plosives, for example, 'bed' and 'rib', which become [beḓ] and [rɪḇ] respectively. Full-scale terminal devoicing in English, on the other hand, would result in the production of a contrastive sound, i.e. a completely different sound from the original (voiced) phoneme, and potentially a different word altogether (for example, 'bed' and 'rib' would become respectively 'bet' and 'rip'). Intelligibility is thus likely to be compromised in interlanguage talk in such cases, not only because of the resulting ambiguity, but because this is compounded by NBESs' inability to make use of contextual cues (see the previous chapter for discussion of this phenomenon).

So far, we have only considered terminal devoicing in relation to those L2 speakers of English for whom L1 transfer is involved. However, it seems that the existence of terminal devoicing in a speaker's first language is not a precondition for it to operate in a second language: the process occurs also in the English of speakers of languages such as Cantonese, Spanish, and Hungarian, for whom it is not a native-language process. For example, Cantonese speakers of English tend to pronounce the word 'pig' as /pɪk/ (Eckman 1981b), while Hungarian speakers of English have been shown to devoice final consonants even where the following word begins with a voiced consonant (Altenberg and Vago 1983).

Eckman accounts for the apparent universal tendency towards terminal devoicing in L2 by recourse to the notion of relative degree of difficulty which, in turn, he bases on the concept of typological markedness. He defines the latter thus: 'A phenomenon A in some language is more marked relative to some other phenomenon B if, cross-linguistically, the presence of A in a language necessarily implies the presence of B, but the presence of B does not necessarily imply the presence of A' (1981a: 140). In terms of voicing contrasts, the relative difficulty of final as opposed to medial, and medial as opposed to initial position, is thus predicated on the grounds that all languages which contain final voicing contrasts also contain medial and initial contrasts, but the same is not true in reverse. In other words, a language like English, which allows both voiced and voiceless consonants in word-final position, also allows them in word-medial and word-initial position. On the other hand, a language like German, which does not allow voiced consonants in word-final position, but does allow them in word-medial position, also allows them in word-initial position. And there are no languages which operate in the opposite fashion, by allowing voicing contrasts later but not earlier in words.

Eckman encapsulates this principle of difficulty-related-to-markedness in the Markedness Differential Hypothesis (MDH). Because of its central influence on recent work on language transfer, it will be stated here in full:

> The areas of difficulty that a language learner will have can be predicted on the basis of a systematic comparison of the grammars of the native language, the target language and the markedness relations stated in universal grammar, such that,
> (a) Those areas of the target language which differ from the native language and are more marked than the native language will be difficult.
> (b) The relative degree of difficulty of the areas of the target language which are more marked than the native language will correspond to the relative degree of markedness.
> (c) Those areas of the target language which are different from the native language, but are not more marked than the native language will not be difficult.
> (Eckman 1977: 61)

The MDH therefore takes transfer one stage further, by predicting an area of difficulty as arising from a difference between the native and target languages only where the target language is relatively more marked than the native language, thus predicting the direction of difficulty. This would explain why Eckman is able to provide evidence that German learners of English, for example, seem to have considerably greater difficulty with the voicing of final voiced consonants than do English learners of German with the devoicing of all final consonants (even though the latter have also to contend with the distractions of spelling).

The MDH, in its ability to predict the direction of difficulty, has therefore contributed to the refining of the CAH, and a number of studies attest to the decisive role played by markedness in phonological transfer (for example, Anderson 1983; Broselow 1983, 1984). However, the MDH is not as yet able to provide a complete account, since it cannot predict the resolution of difficulty (for example, the specific sound which will replace /θ/) any more than can the CAH.

One final point, before we leave the subject of universals: we should not lose sight of the fact that transfer does not only interact with universal processes, but is itself a universal process. Much research has demonstrated the facilitative effects of perceived similarity on SLA, in terms of both reduction in errors and rate of learning. Some of this research draws specific links with schema theory, which concerns the activating of prior knowledge structures, or *schemata*, in new contexts. Schachter, for example, includes in the language learner's previous knowledge both the L1 and the imperfect knowledge of, and expectations about, the L2 (1983: 104).

As far as pronunciation in SLA is concerned, L1 knowledge is the inevitable starting point, operating a stronger influence than it does in the case of either grammar or lexis. This is because of the greater ease and automaticity with which we are able to apply our knowledge of the L1 phonological and phonetic inventory. Grammar and lexis may differ enormously from one language to another, at times making interlingual identifications difficult, if not impossible. On the other hand, many features of the L2 phonology, while different from those of the L1, particularly at the phonetic level, are instinctively categorizable within the L1 system and possible to approximate in varying degrees of closeness to the L2. The fact that learners do not necessarily meet with success when they transfer their L1 pronunciation knowledge to L2 will not prevent them from making the attempt, whether conscious or subconscious.

Pedagogically, then, it is crucial to accept L1 phonological transfer as a universal, a fact of life and, for the purposes of EIL, to respond to it selectively, as it interacts with intelligibility and teachability. The critical questions for pronunciation teachers are: in which phonological and phonetic areas does the transfer of L1 pronunciation militate against EIL intelligibility, and to what extent is it feasible to teach learners to replace their L1 forms with L2 forms in these areas? These are far more important—and potentially beneficial—considerations than attempts to 'rid' learners of as much pronunciation transfer as possible—attempts which work against, rather than with, learners and natural universal processes.

Transfer plus developmental processes

Studies of the interaction of transfer and developmental factors in interlanguage phonology have generally pursued two main lines of inquiry. The first of these is the *L1 = L2 hypothesis*, in which parallels are drawn between L1 and L2 phonology acquisition. The second line of inquiry concerns the similarities that have been noted in the development of L2 phonology among learners from different L1 backgrounds.

A fact which should be borne in mind as we look more closely at the *L1 = L2 hypothesis* is that it is not always possible to make a clear-cut distinction between developmental processes and the universals of the previous section. One area of overlap involves terminal devoicing, which was described above as a universal process, since it appears in the interlanguages of learners of English for whom it is not a native language characteristic. However, terminal devoicing has also been found to occur in L1 acquisition. For example, Edwards (1979, cited in Hecht and Mulford 1982) reports the terminal devoicing of fricatives in L1 children's acquisition of English. The appearance of this process in interlanguage can therefore be considered a developmental as well as a universal feature.

On the other hand, we also have less ambiguous evidence of developmental processes at work in L2 phonological acquisition. Hecht and Mulford (1982), for example, find such evidence in the acquisition of fricatives and affricates. Having compared the order of difficulty of these phonemes for L1 and L2 learners of English, they conclude that while transfer is the most salient factor in determining the difficulty of any of these sounds, it is developmental processes which determine the way in which a particular difficulty is resolved. That is, developmental processes determine which specific sound will be substituted for the target sound. Hecht and Mulford suggest that the substitutions which are most likely to remain in a learner's interlanguage are those which result from both transfer and developmental processes.

Schmidt (1977) also studies fricatives, in this case the interdentals /θ/ and /ð/. Some of his Egyptian Arabic subjects have been exposed to Classical Arabic, which itself possesses these fricatives in its repertoire. For this reason, Schmidt considers the possibility that his subjects' problems may derive in part from the same kinds of developmental sources that affect the L1 acquisition of these sounds. In this connection, he cites a study (by Moscowitz) of the phonology of a two-year-old American girl, which suggests that problems with interdental fricatives are due to a lack of sufficient motor control. Schmidt also points out that /θ/ and /ð/ are well documented as 'the sounds mastered last and substituted most frequently by English native speakers' (ibid.: 367). This may explain why L2 learners from virtually all L1 backgrounds have problems with these two sounds: transfer processes are compounded by the developmental difficulty experienced by child L1 learners in making and maintaining the fine adjustments to their articulators that are needed to produce these sounds. It may be that features of L2 English which do not occur in a second language learner's L1, *and* are late (or even never) acquired by its L1 speakers, are unteachable for that learner (in the sense that no amount of teaching will result in automatic production). The evidence certainly points to this being the case for /θ/ and /ð/. (Though see below, page 109, for evidence that these sounds also vary with the stylistic context.)

We turn now to the second line of inquiry, the parallels in acquisition among learners from different L1s, rather than between L1 and L2 learners. As De Bot points out, the concept of 'the *L2*-developmental error' is well justified by the fact that 'numerous observations have shown that certain types of error are made by nearly all learners of a given language, irrespective of their mother-tongue', and that it would be 'too simplistic to claim that such developmental errors merely reflect acquisitional sequences in the L1' (1986: 113; emphasis added). Major draws attention to the fact that while 'there is no fundamental difference in the mechanism of substitutions in children acquiring L1 and adults acquiring L2', there is a difference in the starting points of the two categories of learners. For child L1 learners this is 'the native pre-language system', whereas for adult learners it is the native language system (1987: 105), since the latter learners, by definition, start the L2 process having already mastered a first phonology. This suggests that if we are able to identify specific areas of English pronunciation which are difficult for both L1 children and the majority of those whose starting point is a different L1 phonological system, then we have a further case of developmental processes interacting with and compounding the effect of transfer processes. These items may then be further candidates for unteachable phonological features, in the sense that the vast majority of L2 learners are unlikely to proceed to the developmental stage at which the items are fully acquired.

Within the field of interlanguage phonology (though not necessarily grammar or lexis) there is general agreement that transfer errors manifest themselves at earlier stages and developmental errors later on. For example, a study by Wenk (mentioned above, page 43) of the acquisition of English speech rhythms by French learners demonstrates that 'beginners do transfer rhythmic features of the L1 and that advanced learners can and do succeed in overcoming mother-tongue influence' (1986: 125). An explanation for this ordering of processes is provided by Major's Ontogeny Model (1987). According to the model, interference processes predominate in the early stages when learners—who rely on previous cognitive experience in order to learn new information—have recourse to little else (see the previous section on transfer and universal processes).[2] Transfer processes thus prevent developmental processes from surfacing in early L2 acquisition. But with the decrease of interference over time, developmental processes come to the fore and, themselves, gradually decrease.

But regardless of the ordering of transfer and developmental processes, the vast majority of adult L2 learners experience difficulty, irrespective of L1 background, in the acquisition of a native-like accent. Leaving aside for now the role of L1 identity in this phenomenon, and the argument that such a goal is not, in any case, an appropriate one for an international language, we will look at evidence to suggest that even if it were appropriate, it is not realistic. This is because some aspects of the L2 phonology appear to be unteachable. Here, we will consider two studies, the first by Neufeld (1978) and the second by Ioup and Tansomboon (1987). The first examines the problem of adult as compared with child acquisition of pronunciation in general; the second looks at the problem of L2 intonation patterns in particular.

Neufeld's aims were firstly to test Lenneberg's 'critical period for language learning' hypothesis at the phonological level and, secondly, to find out whether learners can acquire a native-like accent without reference to grammar or meaning. After being given extensive exposure to a series of L2 (Japanese and Chinese) utterances, during which they were instructed to remain silent, the L1 English-speaking subjects were asked to reproduce the sounds that they had heard. Their performance was then judged by native Japanese- and Chinese-speaking judges and, in the majority of cases, was considered to be either native or near-native, thus suggesting that a native-like accent is, after all, a feasible goal at least for the second languages involved in Neufeld's study.

However, Ioup and Tansomboon explain Neufeld's findings very differently. Pointing out that 'the subjects were quite likely approaching the input stimuli as melodic contours rather than linguistic data' and that 'they would therefore be utilizing Gestalt cognitive strategies associated with the right hemisphere' (1987: 345), they account for Neufeld's results in terms of 'the mode of information processing employed'. They argue convincingly that completely different results would have been obtained had the subjects approached the L2 data from a linguistic perspective. In other words, it is by no means certain that Neufeld's subjects would have produced native-like pronunciation if meaning had been introduced. But even in the unlikely event of their having done so, the most interesting implication of Neufeld's findings for our purposes is their support for the view that some aspects of L2 pronunciation (and hence native-like pronunciation) can only be acquired through extensive (probably non-pedagogic) exposure to the second language. In other words, they are not teachable.

Ioup and Tansomboom's own study lends support to their interpretation of Neufeld's results. Like Neufeld, they examined the question of age differences in second language acquisition, though exclusively in relation to the acquisition of tone. They used data elicited from Thai learners of various ages, including taped conversations and a humming task, where subjects were asked to imitate sentences by humming the intonation contour and ignoring segmental information. Their results indicate that 'tone is one of the earliest aspects of Thai to be acquired by children, regardless of whether the language is their first or second, and one of the latest to be acquired by adults'. They argue that such a difference seems 'likely to be a function of the types of cognitive processes involved', with adults processing tone as they do all aspects of a second language system, via the left hemisphere, and children, who have not yet developed the necessary cognitive framework to process linguistic data in this way, via the right (*ibid.*: 341–4). This claim is supported by the authors' humming data, which demonstrated that when an intonation contour was divorced from other aspects of the linguistic system, it presented no problem to the adult subjects. As in Neufeld's study, then, it appears that the adult subjects in Ioup and Tansomboom's study were processing the humming task using holistic strategies associated with the right hemisphere such as children utilize, rather than analytic strategies associated with the left hemisphere which they normally rely on for all aspects of language learning.

There is much evidence to support the view that pitch movement is the earliest speech feature experienced in all first languages, probably from as early as 26 weeks *in utero* (see Locke 1993). On the other hand, it is well known among teachers of adult L2 learners that pitch movement is the most difficult aspect of the language to teach, either receptively or productively. Indeed, my own view is, like that of others such as Taylor (1991) and Dalton and Seidlhofer (1994a), that it is not teachable to adults. Rather, that it is one of those pronunciation features referred to above which is only acquirable through extensive non-pedagogic exposure.

Ioup and Tansomboom's findings in relation to Thai provide support for this claim, and their explanation highlights a basic contradiction in attempts to teach pitch movement to adults: we cannot expect adult L2 learners to be able or willing to eschew all other linguistic levels as a long-term strategy in the pursuit of L2 pitch movement. And even if they were able and willing, the only good reason for learning pitch movement is for its contribution to meaning, so it is difficult to see how it could be taught for meaningful use unless it is taught in association with meaning and, thus, with other linguistic levels. For the purposes of EIL, given that the interaction of transfer and developmental processes seems to militate against the classroom learning of this aspect of L2 intonation, we need instead to consider the extent to which pitch movement, in fact, contributes to EIL intelligibility. If it does so in important ways, we should find ways of encouraging learners to notice it during non-pedagogic exposure to the language; if it does so only minimally, we should not waste learners' time on something which has relevance only for L1 speakers of English.

Developmental processes, like universal factors, thus interact with language transfer in important ways in interlanguage phonology. And, as has already been suggested, those substitutions that are predicted by both developmental and transfer processes tend to remain in interlanguage the longest, sometimes as permanent fixtures. A number of other factors have also been found to interact with transfer, and it is to these which we turn in the following section.

Transfer processes plus stylistic and contextual factors

As far as style (degree of formality) is concerned, it appears that phonological transfer decreases in formal speech contexts and increases in informal ones. This is because speakers pay greater attention to form in formal contexts and, as a result, are more aware of their potential for transfer, and better positioned to replace it with more target-like pronunciations. On the other hand, attention to content predominates in more casual settings and so the potential for transfer of formal features is less salient. In his study of Arabic speakers of English, Schmidt (1977) shows how his subjects' pronunciation of /θ/ and /ð/ undergoes variation, with transfer of /s/ and /z/ occurring in colloquial but not in formal speech. Similarly, in a study of Brazilian Portuguese speakers of English, Major (1987) finds less L1 transfer for the phenomena investigated—the pronunciation of /r/ and final consonant clusters and obstruents—in formal than in casual speech.

Thus, it seems that L2 speakers will instinctively attempt to replace L1 phonological transfer with more target-like forms in more formal speech contexts. This may be largely a function of the salience (to speakers) of intelligibility for their receivers. For in such contexts there is less scope for repetition or clarification, and a greater likelihood of embarrassment— whether of speaker or listener—resulting from unintelligible pronunciation. This phenomenon is closely connected with task type. Tarone (1988) describes interlanguage as a continuum which ranges from a vernacular to a careful style, depending on the degree of attention to speech which, in turn, depends on the formality of the task. Tarone's interlanguage continuum paradigm has found support in research such as that of L. Dickerson and Sato. In a study of Japanese-English pronunciation in different task situations, L. Dickerson shows how the most target-like variants occurred in the most formal task (reported in Dickerson and Dickerson 1977). Sato (1985) demonstrates similarly systematic task variation for word-final consonant clusters in the interlanguage of a Vietnamese learner of English.

Stylistic variation in the degree of transfer in interlanguage phonology may also occur as a function of variability in the model(s) heard by the learner. In their study of the English of Steinar, their Icelandic subject, Hecht and Mulford suggest that much of Steinar's phonological variation may result from the range of target language models he is exposed to, including the L1 speech of his school friends, schoolteacher, the adult investigator, and the Icelandic-accented L2 English of his parents. Discussing Steinar's 54 per cent devoicing of final /z/, which would be predicted by both transfer and developmental positions (Icelandic has only the voiceless counterpart /s/, while final devoicing is also common among children acquiring English as their first language), Hecht and Mulford suggest the L1 model he encounters as a third factor in Steinar's high rate of devoicing of this phoneme. This factor is one which may help to explain why the devoicing does not improve over the course of the fourteen weeks, for 'it is an acceptable American English pronunciation in some phonetic contexts and speech styles (for example, in rapid speech and sentence final position)' (1982: 223).

Phonological transfer also interacts with variation due to the linguistic context. According to Tarone, 'some variables ... whether phonological, morphological, or syntactic, can be shown to vary in form depending upon those linguistic forms immediately adjacent. Some environments seem to have a 'facilitating' effect, correlating highly with an increased number of target-like variants; other environments seem to be "debilitating", correlating with an increased number of non-target-like variants' (1988: 60).

The earliest studies (L. Dickerson 1975; W. Dickerson 1976; Dickerson and Dickerson 1977) provide evidence both for a systematic relationship between accuracy and phonological context, and for change over time, spreading systematically from one phonological context to another. Gatbonton's 'gradual diffusion model' (1978) also documents a relationship between diachronic variation and phonological context. However, whereas the Dickersons suggest that the acquisition process may involve variation from the start, Gatbonton proposes that in the first phase of acquisition, a learner first uses one incorrect phonological form in all contexts, and then introduces another form, which is used in free variation with the first, while in the second phase, each form is gradually restricted to its own context. Either way, the consequence of the interaction between transfer and linguistic context is that difficult target items will sometimes be more difficult and thus more susceptible to transfer in some phonological contexts as opposed to others. Where this is found to be the case, and where the items are crucial to EIL intelligibility, it would make good sense for teaching to focus on the problematic phonological contexts rather than—as so often happens—on the difficult item alone.

Before we leave the subject of 'transfer plus', two other factors should be mentioned because of their implications for the phonological core. The first of these is the cross-linguistic frequency of phonological items. Odlin is critical of the fact that many contrastive analyses fail to take into account the cross-linguistic frequency of sounds. As he points out, some phonemes, for example, [m], are very common among the world's phonological systems, while others, for example, German [x], are relatively rare, and 'there seems to be a rough correlation between the frequency of a sound and its difficulty for adults learning a second language' (1989: 120).

Since the aim of the phonological core is to identify those features which are crucial to safeguard phonological intelligibility in EIL, the relative frequency or infrequency in the world's languages and often, by implication, the relative ease or difficulty of different L2 items for the majority of learners, is an important consideration. For where an item is more or less universally difficult, whether this difficulty derives from the interaction of transfer with developmental or with universal phonological processes, it is unlikely to result in unintelligibility in EIL. A case in point is the pair of interdental fricatives /θ/ and /ð/, which we considered earlier. The fact that these sounds are so infrequent among the world's languages supports their exclusion from the EIL phonological core on the grounds that classroom time will not be wasted on difficult items whose omission does not jeopardize EIL intelligibility.

The other factor which we will consider here is avoidance. We cannot assume that because a learner does not appear to have a problem with a particular item known to be difficult for speakers from their L1, that no problem, in fact, exists. The learner may, because of the difficulty involved, or because of embarrassment at producing a particular feature of the L2, simply be avoiding the item altogether.

Schachter and others have investigated this phenomenon, although mainly in relation to syntax and lexis (for example, Schachter 1974 on the avoidance of relative clauses by Chinese and Japanese speakers of English). The lack of avoidance data for phonology may reflect a very real difficulty that learners have in employing this strategy at the phonological level, for while they may not find it difficult to avoid certain L2 structures or lexical items, the avoidance of phonological features would involve forward planning and quick thinking of a kind unlikely to be within the grasp of all but the most advanced learners. In addition, the majority of learners will probably not have within their repertoire sufficient alternative ways of expressing themselves in order to avoid specific pronunciation problems. The result would therefore be such a degree of hesitation and general dysfluency that learners probably opt for L1 phonological transfer rather than avoiding the target phoneme altogether.

Nevertheless, there is one study of interest. Celce-Murcia (1977) describes the process of avoidance at the phonological level in the speech of her daughter, as she learns English and French simultaneously. Physiologically problematic forms are found to be systematically avoided.

For example, the child finds the fricative /f/ difficult to articulate and therefore consistently prefers the French word 'couteau' to the English 'knife', and creates a new word 'piedball' in order to avoid the word 'football'. Where such phonological avoidance does occur among adult L2 speakers, it may be motivated not only by articulatory difficulty, but also by embarrassment. This may result when a feature, for example, a particular sound, both does not figure in the L1 system and is one which for speakers of that L1 system is a stereotype of the L2: in other words, it is a feature which is used when speakers of that L1 mimic speakers of the L2, whether for comic effect or worse.

Habit formation and automaticity

Describing the common problem that English speakers of German have with uvular [ʀ], which results from lack of use of the uvula in the native language, Odlin points out that although it is misleading to equate transfer with old habits, the English problems with uvulars 'suggest that a theory of habit formation may be applicable to certain types of phonetic transfer' (1989: 116).

It is widely agreed that habit formation in language transfer figures more extensively at the phonological level than at either the syntactic or lexical levels. As regards positive transfer, there is a major difference between the acquisition of phonology as compared with that of syntax: 'if a sound or process in L1 also occurs in L2 the learner will automatically transfer it to L2 without having to go through any intermediate stages ... This contrasts with the acquisition of syntax and morphology, where developmental processes often operate even when transfer would produce the correct utterance in L2' (Major 1987: 106). In other words, where a phonological item in the L1 is perceived by learners as being the same as an item in the L2 (even if they are mistaken: see the next section), there will be no constraints on its transfer from L1 to L2. On the other hand, such constraints may operate to inhibit transfer in comparable lexical and grammatical situations.

The influence of L1 phonological habits in second language acquisition is due largely to the nature of the speech process itself. Once the neurolinguistic phase (which involves the central nervous system, and determines the lexico-grammatical structure of the utterance) is completed, the process thence consists of motor commands flowing out through motor nerves to muscles in the speech organs. These muscles in turn act upon the air contained within the vocal tract to generate sound waves, and proceed through proprioceptive feedback loops. To this extent, the production of speech sounds is unlike that of lexis and syntax, since it does not involve passing messages through the brain, but rather the development of highly automatized motor skills and, consequently, over time, the formation of L1 speech habits which are not easily de-automatized in L2.

It is, then, not surprising that a strong automatic element is noted in the transfer of phonology as distinct from that of syntax. Faerch and Kasper point out that 'transfer may occur at the articulatory level only, all other levels being processed according to the IL system'. They cite the example of even advanced Danish learners of English, who 'in unattended speech, use voiced stop consonants in medial position in words like *bitter, rapid, litre*, automatically transferring Danish phonological structure'. They explain this process as 'a result of a Danish phonological plan, controlling the articulation of word-medial stop consonants, and competing with the corresponding English plan, according to which medial stop consonants are either voiced or voiceless' (1986: 60).

The role of habit formation in L2 transfer and, in particular, the fact that the highly automatized L1 phonological system 'is not changed or modified for actual productive use without considerable controlled effort' (Ringbom 1987: 60), has implications for the selection and subsequent teaching of the phonological core. There will be little purpose in attempting to encourage learners to modify the phonological habits of a lifetime, unless *not* to do so would threaten international intelligibility. Indeed, EIL speakers are likely to resist such attempts if they do not themselves perceive the need for them. And where changes to L1 phonological habits are required, the method-ology used will have to be directed towards enabling learners to replace one automatic response with another. This means that the practice of drilling, which has in recent years been much maligned, will assume an important role in the ELT classroom once again.

Cognitive factors: perceptions of L1–L2 similarity

Despite the automaticity involved in phonological transfer, there is also a cognitive element—something we touched on in the discussion of transfer and universal processes. The facilitating effects of L1–L2 similarity in the early stages of second language acquisition, when learners rely more heavily on previous cognitive experience in order to process new language information, are well documented. Learners make interlingual identifications (that is, they perceive resemblances across certain features of the L1 and L2), and are then tempted to produce the L2 feature in the same way as the L1 version. Selinker argues that the making of interlingual identifications is 'a basic, if not *the* basic, SLA learning strategy' (1992: 260; emphasis in original). It seems that 'crucial similarity measures have to be met before speakers draw on the various elements of their L1 repertoire to cope with the L2 targets' (Wode 1986: 179), and pronunciation is particularly amenable in this respect because of the categorical manner in which we perceive sounds.

However, this is not to claim that similarity necessarily facilitates ultimate acquisition. There has been a considerable reinterpretation of the influence of similarity on language transfer in recent years, one which has been most revealing at the phonemic–phonetic level. No longer is L1–L2 similarity simplistically equated with ease of acquisition and difference with difficulty. In fact, the reverse is now thought to obtain as far as target-like pronunciation is concerned. It seems that fossilization occurs precisely because of L1–L2 similarity judgements which are, themselves, a function of learners' categorical perceptions.

The problem with categorical sound perception is that phonemic equivalence does not necessarily imply allophonic equivalence. But it seems that 'judging acoustically different phones to be members of the same category is a fundamental aspect of human speech perception' (Flege and Hillenbrand 1984: 177). For example, English bilabial /m/ is articulated as labiodental /ɱ/ before /f/ and /v/ (for example, in 'comfort') but is perceived as belonging to the same phonemic category. It is more difficult to learn sounds similar to those in the L1 precisely because learners analyse them as identical. Flege and Hillenbrand's study of the acquisition of French [y] and [u] by native English speakers demonstrates that sounds which are new are likely to be acquired more accurately than those which have a counterpart in the L1 because they escape 'the limiting effect of previous phonetic experience' (ibid.: 198). So while similarity may facilitate the acquisition of L2 lexis and syntax and receptive pronunciation, it may well be a handicap in that of L2 productive pronunciation.

A related problem arises with the learning of new uses for old sounds, where sounds which are distinguished only allophonically in the L1 are phonemically distinct in the L2. The example which immediately springs to mind is that of Japanese and Korean /l/ and /r/, which are allophones of one sound (somewhere between the two) in the L1, but separate phonemes of English. And Selinker describes anecdotally a Thai student who consistently referred to his field of study, philosophy, as [kwəlasokwi] because [kw] and [f] are variants of the same phoneme in his L1 (1992: 34–5).

A further distinction has been made between the influence of similarity on L2 perception and on production. It seems that 'crosslanguage influences in speech reception should … be considered in a totally different light from such influences in speech production' because there is clear evidence of the facilitating effect of L1–L2 similarity on the former (Sajavaara 1986: 67): it 'makes certain aspects of the learning of a second language comprehensible' (Broselow *et al.* 1987: 351).

In their study of the role of transfer in the perception of tone by English learners of Chinese, Broselow et al. note that the fourth Mandarin tone, a falling tone, is perceived significantly better in final position in the sentence than elsewhere. They account for their findings in terms of the ease of hearing 'a familiar item in a familiar position' (final being the unmarked position for falling tone in the learners' L1, English) as a result of positive transfer, while the difficulty of hearing the tone elswhere in the sentence results from the negative transfer of an unfamiliar item.[3] And in a study of my own, which will be discussed in the following chapter, a group of learners of English from different L1s are shown to have varying degrees of ease or difficulty in identifying patterns of contrastive stress as a function of similarity and difference in the signalling of focus between the L1 and L2. A similar effect has been demonstrated in a study of syllable structure transfer, with strings of Egyptian Arabic being factored into words by American English learners according to the syllable and word boundary rules of their first language as the result of negative perceptual transfer (Broselow 1984).

What all this indicates as regards the intelligibility of pronunciation in EIL is, firstly, the need for more phonetic (as opposed to phonemic) productive classroom work and, secondly, the need for a greater pedagogic distinction between the ways learners are encouraged to make use of their L1 knowledge in production and in reception. In terms of the first indication, the categorizing of an L2 sound in terms of the L1 system may result in the omission of essential phonetic information. For example, while it is not necessary for EIL intelligibility that learners distinguish all English sounds according to the English phonemic system, it is crucial that they do acquire certain target-like phonetic features such as the aspiration of word-initial voiceless stops, to prevent words such as 'pack' sounding more like 'back' (see Chapter 6 for details).

In addition, certain phonetic realizations that learners transfer from their L1 as a result of categorical perception may be perceived by speakers from other L1s as 'belonging' to a completely different phoneme from that intended. Such phonetic realizations will thus threaten the intelligibility of their pronunciation in EIL, and should be replaced by more target-like production. For example, in Spanish, the bilabial fricative [β] is used for both 'b' and 'v', while the allophonic distribution of the phonemes /m/, /n/, and /ŋ/ is such that /m/ tends to be replaced by /n/ or /ŋ/ at the ends of words. Transferred to English, words like 'boat' and 'dream' may be pronounced respectively 'vote' and 'drean', or 'dreang'. And, as was discussed in the previous chapter, where the result is a non-word, the problem is not diminished for NBES receivers, as they are less confident than fluent speakers of English as to what is and is not a 'legitimate' lexical item.

Teachers of EIL would thus advance their learners' cause if they were to spend less time working on the English phonemic system *in toto*, and more on a smaller number of—sometimes allophonic—features. They would also enable learners to make more effective use of the support provided by L1–L2 similarity if they differentiated more clearly between productive and receptive uses and, in particular, emphasized how knowledge of the L1 pronunciation system can help learners understand what they *hear* in the L2. In the latter respect, teaching could focus on pronunciation universals as well as on specific L1–L2 similarities and include extensive exposure to a wide range of L2 English accents in order to highlight the similarities among them.

Notions of ambiguity

According to the philosopher Grice (1975), participants engaged in conversation share a 'cooperative principle', the purpose of which is to ensure that the activity is beneficial to both speaker and listener(s) in terms of mutual understanding. The 'cooperative principle' involves four maxims, those of quantity, quality, relevance, and manner, often referred to as 'Grice's maxims'. Of these, the maxim of manner, which directs speakers to avoid obscurity and ambiguity, is of particular interest here, since this is what appears to underlie various phonological transfer choices in interlanguage talk.

The demands for clarity of expression are greater in interlanguage talk than in 'NS' interaction, since the potential for miscommunication increases when participants lack a shared background and the medium of communication is a foreign language (Varonis and Gass 1985b). As we have already noted, at the phonological level in particular, the fact that NBESs tend to deviate in very different ways from the L2 system (Bradford 1982) can lead to serious intelligibility problems for listeners. However, it seems that NBESs are, themselves, aware of the scale of the problem, and that they endeavour as speakers to take steps to minimize it. This is evident in some of the transfer choices they make, where, in line with Grice's maxim of manner, the prime motivation for their choice often appears to be their assessment of the degree of potential ambiguity of the phonological form.[4] It may also account for whatever truth there is in the claim that 'NSs teaching the language appear to be far more tolerant of learners' errors than NNSs who command the TL as an FL' (Selinker 1992: 121), at least as far as pronunciation is concerned, since the latter have first-hand experience of the intelligibility problem for the NBES listener engaged in interlanguage talk.

In a study which has much relevance here on account of its explanation for the motivation underlying learners' phonological adjustments, Weinberger (1987) first examines the conflicting results that different studies have obtained for word-final syllable simplification. He notes that the two strategies found variously in these studies, namely consonant deletion and epenthesis (termed 'schwa paragoge' where it occurs word-finally), serve the same function despite producing completely different outputs. For example, the word 'big' would become /bɪ/ by consonant deletion, but /bɪgə/ by schwa paragoge. However, as Weinberger points out, only simplification by means of the latter strategy provides an unambiguous form, since /bɪ/ could be the surface representation of other words such as 'bid'. (See also the discussion of consonant deletion and epenthesis/addition earlier in this chapter.)

Weinberger argues that 'it is safe to assume that all natural languages contain a constraint against rampant ambiguity, particularly that resulting from homonymy of underlyingly distinct phonological forms' and that the notion of recoverability, defined as 'the ability to work backward from the surface form through a derivation to obtain the unique underlying representation' is highly valued by the grammars of natural languages (ibid.: 404). Since interlanguages are natural languages, he concludes that interlanguage phonology must, too, respect the notion of recoverability and include a constraint against ambiguity.

Weinberger goes on to consider the presence of glottal stops in two other studies. The first is Tarone (1980), where glottal stops occur in preference to linking across word boundaries. For example, a Cantonese subject renders 'she wanted to eat' as [ʃiwʌntətuʔit] and Korean subject renders 'a sandwich and' as [əsæmiʔæn]. In both cases, where one word ends with a vowel and the next begins with one, the glottal stop changes the syllable structure to a CV pattern. The second study is Broselow (1984), where glottal stops are preferred to cross-word syllabification. For example, instead of linking the final /s/ to the word-initial vowel in 'this ink', an Egyptian speaker of English is more likely to insert a glottal stop at the beginning of 'ink'. Tarone accounts for the glottal stops in her study by means of a universal preference for CV syllables, while Broselow argues that cross-word syllabification is more marked than glottal stops. However, Weinberger invokes the motivation of recoverability in both cases, since the presence of the glottal stops results in recoverable derivations and the reduction of ambiguity.

If Weinberger's analysis is correct, logically epenthesis and schwa paragoge should predominate over consonant deletion for precisely the same motivations. But on closer inspection, he notes that the differential use of these strategies found in the studies is also a function of linguistic context relating to task type. Informal tasks such as spontaneous speech, he argues, have sufficient redundancy built into them to counteract ambiguity, whereas formal tasks such as word-list reading lack such contextual cues and therefore require unambiguous phonological strategies. Weinberger incorporates this proposal into his Syllable Simplification Strategy Hypothesis, the second part of which states that 'the degree of overall syllable simplification will increase as the task formality decreases', and the third part that the percentage proportion of epenthesis to deletion 'should be greater in tasks without linguistic context than in tasks with linguistic context' (1987: 408).

Support for part two of Weinberger's hypothesis is provided by Major in his study of Portuguese-English speakers' pronunciation of word-final consonant clusters: 'schwa insertion ... would be expected more frequently in a more formal style than would consonant cluster simplification ... This is because schwa insertion is a fortition process that *insures* that the final consonants are perceived, whereas consonant cluster simplification is a lenition process' (1987: 108; emphasis in original). Similarly, the data which Weinberger collects in his own study of the word-final syllable simplification of Mandarin Chinese speakers of English supports the third part of his Syllable Simplification Strategy Hypothesis: the proportion of epenthesis to that of deletion is found to be considerably greater in the word-list task than in the paragraph-reading and story-telling tasks.

These studies demonstrate that when speakers are particularly concerned with the phonological intelligibility of their speech, they avoid using assimilatory strategies such as deletion and prefer instead to use strategies such as addition, because of the effect on the recoverability of their words for the listener. Where there is less available context and co-text, the argument goes, the speaker compensates with less ambiguous pronunciation. However, the informal tasks in Weinberger's and Major's studies differ from interlanguage talk in one crucial way: the *receivers* are L1 speakers of English. Context and co-text could thus be expected to compensate for any non-recoverability of pronunciation. But as we saw in Chapter 4, NBES receivers are less able to make use of context and co-text in this way. When intelligibility is highly salient, then, we can predict that speakers will react as Weinberger's subjects did in the absence of context and co-text. That is, they will attempt to ensure that their use of L1 transfer does not impede recoverability for their NBES interlocutors.

Weinberger also considers the strategies of epenthesis and deletion in terms of phonological rule-ordering, demonstrating that there appears to be a clear ordering relation between them. Deletion is likely to occur first, he argues, because it requires a word boundary or consonant after the deleted item, and epenthesis would remove this environment. For example, in the case of the word 'and', epenthesis would produce /ændə/, rendering deletion obselete, whereas deletion would produce /æn/, which could then become /ænə/ by epenthesis. Weinberger concludes, then, that deletion predates epenthesis in developmental sequence.

Weinberger therefore suggests that the notion of recoverability is acquired developmentally. He points out that children simplifying by means of the strategy of deletion have not yet acquired the notion, but that by the time they do so, they also possess a high level of phonetic accuracy. They therefore no longer need to simplify to this extent, and epenthesis thus becomes obsolete before the stage at which it would be utilized. On the other hand, he argues that adult learners of second languages acquire the notion of recoverability considerably in advance of their attainment of second language phonetic accuracy, which is in any case most likely to fossilize at some point short of BES competence, and therefore, unlike children, they 'are better equipped to abide by ambiguity constraints' (ibid.: 413).

Weinberger suggests that within a second language, awareness of potential ambiguity may increase with proficiency. This would explain the conflicting results obtained in some of the previous studies of epenthesis and deletion, with the more proficient speakers being more likely to employ the strategy of epenthesis. Thus, we have a possible explanation for the glottal stops that frequently replace deleted consonants in the speech of less proficient Cantonese, Mandarin, and (some) Korean speakers of English: they are intended to compensate for the consonant deletion where speakers have not yet 'acquired' epenthesis, but have begun to recognize the potential ambiguity.

This study has been discussed at some length because the notions of recoverability and ambiguity avoidance are highly relevant to the EIL phonological core of intelligibility which will be proposed in the next chapter. The source of this core is EIL (interlanguage talk) interaction data, in which we find NBESs making precisely the kinds of adjustments described in Weinberger's study (for example, epenthesis rather than deletion) when interlocutor intelligibility is highly salient, in order to ensure that their words are recoverable by an NBES from a different L1, for whom co-text and context do not compensate for phonological non-recoverability. The notions help to account for which habitual L1 transfers (for example, most consonant sounds) learners attempt to replace with more target-like forms in such situations and, on the other hand, which features of the L2 target (for example, weak forms) they avoid.

Conclusions: transfer, intelligibility, and teachability

In this discussion of L1 transfer, we have considered a number of issues relating to the intelligibility and teachability of L2 English pronunciation in EIL. Most importantly, we have examined the complicated combination of factors involved in transfer and, as a result of this, the immense degree of effort involved in replacing a transferred form with an L2 form. Phonological transfer is deep-rooted and can be of benefit to learners; it is not—and should not—be abandoned easily or willingly, unless there is very good reason to do so. Indeed, where the difficulty with an L2 English pronunciation feature is universal, or is known to pursue a certain developmental path, we are looking at an item that may well be unteachable, in the sense that learning will not follow classroom teaching. In such cases, it is not realistic to expect learners to forego their L1 variants readily, and the best we can probably do is to draw their attention to the item, in the hope that if they continue to be exposed to the L2, they will acquire it over time and when they are ready to do so. This is the 'realistic' argument, according to which there are features of the L2 which are unteachable (see Taylor 1993) and, this being so, there is little point in teaching them for production.

However, there is also a 'relevance' argument which, for the most part, renders the 'realistic' argument unproblematic. This is the phenomenon of

EIL intelligibility, which is not necessarily threatened by L1 transfer. Where learners do not perceive that their continued use of a particular phonological transfer causes their pronunciation to be unintelligible to their EIL interlocutors, they are unlikely to be motivated to make the effort of replacing it simply in order to approximate more closely the accent of an absent 'native speaker'. Nor should they feel an obligation to do so.

It seems that there is a one-to-one correspondence between teachability and intelligibility in EIL. Items may be 'difficult' for universal or developmental reasons, or because learners regard their replacements as causing ambiguity (as is potentially the case with certain features of English connected speech for listeners not easily able to disambiguate by using contextual cues).[5] Where there is a universal difficulty, such as the production of consonant clusters, or a developmental difficulty, such as the articulation of /θ/ and /ð/, I suggest that the outcome depends on whether the item is needed in order to preserve intelligibility. In the rare instances where this is the case, motivation enters the equation, and an item which might otherwise have remained unteachable (for example, word-initial consonant clusters) becomes teachable. On the other hand, where it is not the case and transfer does not threaten EIL intelligibility (for example, /θ/ and /ð/), the item is rarely learnt, regardless of the time spent on it in the classroom. Such items are not relevant to EIL intelligibility, so learners are unlikely to be motivated to make the substantial effort required to master them. These are all issues which we will take up again in the following chapter, in discussing the proposed phonological core.

As this chapter has demonstrated, the language transfer process in all its complexity plays a crucial role in interlanguage phonology. Ioup has argued against 'a new trend in the study of interlanguage phonology which suggests that transfer plays only a minimal role', adding that 'it is the opinion of this author that transfer is *the* major influence on interlanguage phonology' (1984: 13; emphasis in original). This being so, it is possible that, whatever the extent of the research into L2 phonology, the vast majority of adult learners will not acquire L1-accent-free speech. It is possible that the Duc de Rochefoucauld had greater insight into the matter of 'the accent of our birthplace' more than 300 years ago than we do today, with all the research instruments at our disposal. In the light of this discussion of the role of transfer, we move on in Chapter 6 to the detailing of the Lingua Franca Core and the redefining of phonological error in EIL.

Notes

1 The accent of our birthplace remains in our minds and hearts as it does in our speech.

2 For those who have learnt other second languages in adulthood, such languages also form part of their previous cognitive experience and may influence the language currently being learnt.

3 Though it should be noted that this is not only in the ear of the hearer: the fourth tone is realized much more strongly in final position.

4 For example, Japanese learners of English put considerable effort into eradicating /r/–/l/ confusion.

5 For example, the phrase 'the right pair' spoken quickly could be produced as /ðə raɪp peə/ with assimilation of the final /t/ of 'right' to the initial /p/ of 'pair'. The phrase could then be heard as 'the ripe pear'.

6 Pedagogic priorities 1: Identifying the phonological core

The Heart of the Matter

Graham Greene

The purpose of this chapter is to propose to the reader a pedagogical core of phonological intelligibility for speakers of EIL, the 'Lingua Franca Core'. This has been established by means of prioritizing those pronunciation features identified in my interlanguage talk (ILT) data (two studies, an experiment, and a corpus of field observations) as impeding mutual intelligibility. As we noted earlier (Chapter 2), the phonological features which, throughout the various data, regularly cause unintelligibility are those which involve interspeaker variation and, more specifically, some kind of L1 transfer. The main issue at stake, then, is the extent to which the abundance of transferred items typical of much NBES speech needs to be replaced with closer approximations to the L2 target in order to safeguard phonological intelligibility.

It emerged from the discussion of phonological transfer in Chapter 5 how deeply rooted and far reaching are the factors and motivations involved in what, on the surface, appears simply to entail the use of an 'incorrect' L1 phonological form in place of the relevant target form. We concluded that it is both unrealistic and unreasonable to expect learners to relinquish (or 'reduce', as it is often expressed) such transfer to the extent encouraged by most pronunciation manuals and teachers. The account of transfer, on the contrary, provides an explanation as to why such attempts to rid learners of the total sum of their L1 phonological transfer tend to fail miserably.

My phonological core, on the other hand, is an attempt—with EIL primarily in mind—to scale down the phonological task for the majority of learners, by leaving to the individual learner's discretion and to later acquisition outside the classroom the learning of peripheral details, and focusing pedagogic attention on those items which are essential in terms of intelligible pronunciation. This kind of prioritizing seems to me not only to be far more relevant to EIL communication, but also to be far more realistic in its likelihood of meeting with classroom success.

Establishing the Lingua Franca Core

In this chapter, we will consider the extent to which it is necessary for international speakers of English to replace phonological transfer with other forms—those of the Lingua Franca Core (LFC)—and the extent to which it is feasible for them to retain their L1 varieties of English. What follows also holds good for speakers of English from both inner and outer circles when they operate internationally, though, of course, we are not in these cases talking about transfer from L1 to L2, but from an intranational variety of English (ENL or ESL) to an international one (EIL).

While the LFC is concerned, above all, with international intelligibility, clearly it cannot escape the need to achieve acceptability also. But we are no longer concerned with the acceptability of 'non-native' speakers to 'native' hearers, rather with that of 'non-native speakers' to each other. And equally importantly in international contexts, the acceptability criterion must include the needs of speakers as well as hearers. In other words, what is it acceptable to demand of *speakers* of EIL? Any answer to this question involves both the psycholinguistic angle (what is realistic?) and the sociolinguistic angle (what is reasonable?). Despite the problem of linguistic insecurity (see pages 211–12), many EIL hearers respond less negatively to the L2 accents of their 'NNS' interlocutors than do 'NS' hearers. Acceptability is a more salient issue for production than it is for reception in EIL contexts. Here, it relates both to the notion of identity and to context of use: to what extent is it acceptable to encourage learners of an international language to 'reduce' their L1 accents, given that these accents are closely bound up with their speakers' L1 identities and with non-L1 English contexts of use? These are questions which we have already touched on, and which we will take up in greater detail later on. But for the moment, and with the criterion of intelligibility in mind, we will consider core approaches in general, the LFC in particular and, finally, assess the latter's implications for the definition of phonological error.

Other phonological core approaches

The main problem to beset anyone attempting to establish a phonological core of EIL intelligibility is the lack of data on which to base it. As Graddol (1997: 13) points out, there has to date been little research into 'NNS–NNS' interaction in general. This, in turn, means that there is little information available as to which phonological and phonetic features lead to intelligibility loss in EIL contexts. 'What is required', argues James, with both 'NNS–NNS' and 'NNS–NS' interaction in mind, 'is information concerning which phonological characteristics of particular ILs (especially those of the emergent New Englishes) precipitate most intelligibility loss when distorted by foreign accent' (1998: 213). The questionable implications of James' use of the word 'distorted' notwithstanding, it is undoubtedly the case—as we began to see in Chapter 4—that certain L2 phonological features relative to others cause intelligibility problems for receivers from different L1s, and that we need to know what these features are in order to establish an EIL core of intelligibility and thence redefine phonological error in EIL.

In establishing the EIL phonological core of intelligibility, there are two possible but opposing approaches: either the identification of the core as common EIL features discovered across varieties, or the specification of the core as an invention drawn, but not derived, from common features. The 'extracted' vs 'constructed' opposition is one which has a long history, though more often with regard to lexis and grammar than to phonology. For example, West's *General Service List of English Words* (1953) adopts the first, empirical approach in looking to find the simple essentials of English lexis by reference to word frequency. Ogden's (1930) *Basic English*, by contrast, specifies these essentials as a conceptual construct. Before examining the way in which the LFC reconciles the two positions, we will consider the few previous attempts to establish a phonological core and the problems associated with both empirical and artificial approaches.

The first to broach the establishing of a phonological common core grounded in mutual intelligibility was the American linguist Hockett (1958), who proposed the existence of a common core based on what is mutually intelligible among the L1 dialects of English. This is a proposal which the sociolinguist Bell finds intuitively appealing: 'in spite of the variability of speech, the high degree of mutual intelligibility between different varieties of mother tongue English ... seems to imply the existence of some underlying shared system' (1976: 45). Hockett's proposal, however, was motivated not by a wish to facilitate pronunciation teaching, but rather to provide support for a structuralist theory of language, by means of identifying a strong element of homogeneity among 'NS' varieties of English. His interest thus lay purely in 'NS–NS' communication, and at the level of description rather than prescription.

Some thirty years later, the phonetician Bryan Jenner, now with pedagogy very much in mind, echoed Hockett's empirical approach by advocating the need 'to establish what *all* native speakers of *all* varieties have in common which enables them to communicate effectively with native speakers of varieties other than their own' (1989: 2; emphasis in original). Jenner's core was motivated specifically by the desire to provide a list of pronunciation teaching priorities for 'NNS' learners of English, which 'would offer the learner a guarantee of intelligibility and acceptability anywhere in the world' (ibid.). His priorities were as follows:

1   The consonantal inventory.
2   Vowel quantity: i.e. long and short.
3   Syllabic structure: i.e. closed with clusters.

4   Syllabic values: strong, weak, reduced.
5   Rhythmic patterning: 'stress-timing'.
6   Prominence and tonicity: i.e. location of pitch features.
7   Tones: *some* binary opposition, such as fall vs. fall-rise.
8   Articulatory setting: laxity and lack of movement.
9   Vowel quality: all vowels should be drawled. The details of shape then follow.
10   Pitch levels: high, mid and low.
(11   Voice quality, if the learner's native habits are disturbingly different from those of native varieties of English.)
     (*ibid.*: 4; emphasis in original)

This was Jenner's position in the late 1980s and one from which he has subsequently moved on. At the time, he was one of the first to argue that many learners neither want nor need to sound 'native-like', and that we should be thinking instead of a certain minimum level which would render them intelligible and acceptable to 'native speakers'. This was an important position to take at the time, and one which has subsequently been very influential. It provided several people—myself included—with the impetus to adopt a core approach and prioritize pronunciation teaching in an informed way, rather than continuing either to 'select' arbitrarily, or to fuss over every last inconsequential detail of pronunciation. However, in claiming that his common core would provide the learner with 'a guarantee of intelligibility' throughout the world, Jenner somewhat overstated his case. For as we saw in the previous chapter, intelligibility is an elusive and complex phenomenon, and one that cannot be guaranteed by pronunciation alone.

More problematic for EIL, though, is Jenner's appeal to the 'native speaker' as both producer and receiver of intelligible pronunciation. This was a reasonable stance to adopt when English was still being learnt in the expanding circle for communication mainly with its native speakers, i.e. EFL—though it was never a reasonable stance either philosophically or practically for English in the outer circle, i.e. ESL. But given that the situation in the expanding circle has altered so dramatically over the past few years (see Chapter 1), it is no longer realistic to approach NBES pronunciation production primarily in terms of its intelligibility for 'native speakers' of English, or NBES reception primarily in terms of the ability to interpret native speech. For the next 50 years at least, assuming that David Graddol (1997) is correct in his predictions, any core approach to pronunciation teaching in the expanding circle will need to be based on mutual intelligibility between NBESs, or it will not be relevant to the prevailing pattern of cross-cultural communication, EIL.

One possible empirical way forward may be to identify what all L2 varieties of English have in common, in other words, an 'International English', and to build on that. Indeed, the identification of International

English is the approach which Jenner has recently begun working on. This will require a substantial corpus to be gathered from all the main varieties of English around the world, but will then have the advantage of representing virtually all the world's varieties of English, regardless of their origin. Jenner uses the label 'International English' intentionally because he believes 'that there is, at some level, a single underlying phonological system governing all the many varieties of English used around the world. This system is used, or referred to, as much in interactions between native speakers of different varieties as in those between non-native users from different backgrounds' (1997a: 10). Jenner clearly believes that this shared L2 phonological system is different from any L1 system, as he later on argues that because of the sheer number of L2 speakers involved, 'it is more likely that native varieties will shift under the weight of this influence than that these users of English will move closer to the phonology of one or other native variety' (*ibid.*: 13).

Until his extensive research programme has been carried out, Jenner is unable to say for certain what the International English (IE) core consists of. For the time being, however, he has some hunches about vowels: 'It seems likely ... that the vowel system of the international norm will be based on a set of about 13 vowels, consisting of five economically spaced peripheral positions, and three true diphthongs. Length, as in ScE [Scottish English], will be an optional realizational feature for some speakers, and central vowels will be entirely lacking' (*ibid.*: 14). In other words, the IE vowel system, if Jenner is correct, contains around 13 vowels as compared with the 20 of RP or 16 of GA, and does not contain schwa.

However, to serve any pedagogic purpose, an IE phonological core will not be sufficient as it stands. Even assuming that one can be identified and that it is substantial enough to warrant serious attention (for it may be very small as compared with Jenner's phonological core of L1 varieties), we cannot avoid the fact that if such a core already exists, it has not to date resulted in mutual international intelligibility among speakers of English. And nor should we expect it to when we consider that the inevitably larger phonological core of L1 varieties does not necessarily guarantee mutual phonological intelligibility between, for example, a speaker from Glasgow and one from New York. What is *not* shared is just as important a factor for intelligibility as what *is* shared. The quantity and quality of the non-shared features may be such that even a relatively large shared element is unable to compensate.

An IE core, then, may be an interesting phenomenon for phonologists at the descriptive level, but it will require some sort of mediation if it is to be useful pedagogically at the prescriptive level. In particular, it must take into account not only what speakers actually produce, but also—just as importantly—how listeners process linguistic signals. And once we begin to adjust the parameters of this IE core in various ways, it will no longer be

'International English' in the sense of representing what *all* speakers of English do. It will include features that many speakers of English (including L1 speakers) have to acquire if they are to achieve international intelligibility: in other words, we are back with 'English as an International Language'.

This is not to suggest that I disagree completely with Jenner. It is entirely plausible that there is a shared element among L2 varieties of English. In fact, it is unthinkable that one does not exist. L2 speakers with NBES status from different phonological backgrounds sometimes understand one another's pronunciation with relatively little difficulty and this cannot be purely the result of exposure to one another's varieties of English. But it is unlikely, by the same token, to be purely the result of shared phonological features. Rather, it is most probably the sum total of the shared element, an acquired phonological element and an acquired ability to make phonological adjustments (both productive and receptive) in the context of the individual interaction. In effect, the already extant shared element is the foundation on which we can build; the starting-point rather than the end-point as far as pedagogy is concerned. This has for some time been recognized by members of the outer circle. For example, Ufomata has argued that although we should retain RP as 'the basis of an international accent', we should identify the various standards that have emerged in L2 situations, the areas where accent causes intelligibility failures, the ways in which these accents differ from RP, and what they have in common, so that 'what would emerge would be forms which share a common ground for intelligibility and which would be very similar to what can be described as "basic RP"' (1990: 216).

Bhatia, like Ufomata, claims a role for the L2 (institutionalized) varieties and the need to build on these in the formation of 'international English': 'it is necessary to recognize nativized norms for intranational functions within specific speech communities, and then to build a norm for international use on such models'. In his view, we should regard IE as 'a kind of superstructure rather than an entirely new concept', one that 'can be added ... by making the learner aware of cross-cultural variations in the use of English and by maximizing his or her ability to negotiate, accommodate and accept plurality of norms' (1997: 317–8). This implies that while there may be a core IE based on L2 varieties, it is equally important—perhaps even more so—for learners to be able to tolerate variation across varieties, to accept 'a polymodel concept rather than a static monomodel approach' (ibid.; and see Kachru 1992: 66 on a 'Monomodel vs. Polymodel Approach').[1] Varieties of English would nevertheless have to be referrable to a common core, since tolerance of such variety is dependent on establishing a centre to ensure mutual intelligibility. It is only in areas designated non-core—where mutual intelligibility is not an issue—that we have a situation in which 'anything goes'.

Bamgboṣe similarly favours a '*pluricentric* view of English'. Discussing lexis and syntax as well as pronunciation, he argues that it is not possible to impose closeness among the different varieties of English, 'since the emergence of separate national norms presupposes a certain degree of divergence between varieties', but that 'unifying norms are provided by the fact of common origin, and in the case of non-native varieties, universals of language learning strategies, and institutional context of language acquisition' (1998: 11–2; emphasis in original). Like Jenner, then, Bamgboṣe believes that the 'non-native' varieties of English already have some common ground, but he goes further by locating the origin of this shared element in certain factors involved in the L2 learning process.

Bamgboṣe also shares with Jenner the belief that should an IE ultimately arise, it will not be based on L1 varieties of English: 'If an international standard does emerge, it will not be identical with any national variety, native or non-native, because all the varieties would, in varying degrees, have contributed to it' (ibid.). Thus, Bamgboṣe seems to be suggesting that IE, if it materializes, will be some sort of amalgam of all varieties of English. This may be what Crystal has in mind to some extent in his prediction of the emergence of a 'World Standard Spoken English' (WSSE). Although he believes that US (and not UK) English will be influential in the development of an international variety, he argues that 'the situation will be complicated by the emergence on the world scene of new linguistic features derived from the L2 varieties ... as the balance of speakers changes, there is no reason for L2 features not to become part of WSSE' (1997: 138).

Gimson argues that an international standard of this kind will not develop of its own accord but will have to be artificially contrived: 'if there is to be an acceptable international pronunciation of English in the foreseeable future, it seems likely that it will have to be artificially formulated and disseminated ... a type of hybrid English pronunciation' (1994: 271). However, he points out that there are 'formidable difficulties which beset the acceptance of a solution of this kind, not least of which is the native speaker's inability to use a type of hybrid English pronunciation which only partially resembles his own' (ibid.).

Despite these difficulties, Gimson has himself attempted to establish an artificial phonological core by means of simplifying the RP phonemic inventory. His 'rudimentary international pronunciation (RIP)' (1978) was based on the premise that a new category of L2 speakers of English has emerged. These are speakers who need to use English as a lingua franca only in their work 'as a technical aid to communication', who 'deal with mainly predictable concepts in a restricted situation (such as in air traffic control)' and can thus 'be expected to operate with more rudimentary forms of English syntax, lexis and pronunciation than exist in any natural model' (1978: 47). Gimson argues that an artificial model of this kind has three prerequisites:

1   the model should be as easy to learn as any natural model, and, if possible, easier;
2   it should be readily intelligible to most native speakers of English;
3   the learner of such a model should thereby possess a base for understanding the major natural varieties of English.
    (ibid.)

Gimson clearly has 'NS–NNS' rather than 'NNS–NNS' communication in mind: 'a reduced framework of this kind is likely to provide a high level of intelligiblity amongst native listeners and foreign learners who have acquired the system' (ibid.: 51). This is not surprising given that his artificial core dates back to the late 1970s, a time when very few scholars had begun to consider the international use of English. Nevertheless, his RIP is relevant to our present purposes in that it provides exemplification of an artificial route to establishing a core phonology.

In his RIP, Gimson reduced the phonemic inventory of RP (i.e. 24 consonant sounds and 20 vowel sounds) to 14 and 15 respectively. The following is a typical example of the result:

'tɛns 'fɒk 'naʊ 'kəfərs θə 'hoːl əf 'səθərn 'ɪnklənt, wɪθ
fɪsə'pɪlətɪ ət ə 'maksɪməm əf 'eːtɪ 'miːtərs. θɪ 'eːrpoːts əf
'iːθ'roː, ənt 'kætwɪk ər ən'laɪkli tə rə'siːf 'ɪnkəmɪn 'flaɪts
əntɪl ə'prɒksɪmətlɪ ɪ'lɛfən 'əntrət 'aʊərs. 'eːrkraft ər 'piːɪn
taɪ'fəːrtɪtə tə 'mantʃəstər, 'prɛstwɪk oːr 'parɪs.
(ibid.)[2]

The most noticeable differences between this contrived pronunciation and RP are firstly the loss of the lenis consonant phoneme in each of the eight fortis-lenis (voiceless-voiced) pairs p–b, f–v, θ–ð, t–d, s–z, ʃ–ʒ, tʃ–dʒ, k–g; secondly, the reduction of many short vowels to schwa; and thirdly, the loss of all but two of the eight diphthongs and their substitution with long monophthongs. Despite Gimson's claim that this sort of thing should be intelligible to both 'NS's and learners of English, this was not the case when I presented the extract to an international audience.[3] Although there were a number of phonologists and phoneticians present, the only person able to interpret the words with little difficulty was the professor of phonetics, Peter Roach.

But the problem with an artificially reduced approach goes deeper than this. Even if we were able to identify a completely intelligible core of this kind, it would be extremely difficult to impose such constraints on speakers of English. We could force them neither to acquire these forms in the first place, nor to maintain them without elaboration in their subsequent interactions. Influences such as the media, local norms, and group identity would undoubtedly intervene, a conclusion that Gimson himself seems to have reached, judging by his comment on page 129 above. The difficulty may have some connection with the manner in which artificial cores have hitherto been devised. Gimson's RIP shares with Quirk's Nuclear English (1982) and even Ogden's Basic English (1930) the fact that it is not firmly rooted in actual speech behaviour but relies more on 'native-speaker' intuition (i.e. Gimson's own) as to what receivers are likely to find intelligible. Gimson also takes functional load into account: hence the retention of the voiceless rather than the voiced consonants in each pair, since the latter carry a lighter load (i.e. distinguish fewer words). But this tells us no more about what English speakers, L1 or L2, find intelligible— let alone psycholinguistically salient—than does Ogden's selection of 850 everyday words for Basic English or Quirk's systematic elimination of grammatical and lexical redundancy for Nuclear English. Nor does it take into account phenomena such as markedness (see page 103) or the teachability–learnability distinction (see pages 132–3).

The origin of the Lingua Franca Core

In devising the Lingua Franca Core I attempted to avoid the problems of previous approaches by reconciling the two opposing positions that variously underpin them. That is, on the one hand, my proposals are—in the tradition of West—empirically based, focusing on genuine interactional speech data. On the other hand, they are also based on the evidence of how people actually respond, so correcting the assumption that intelligibility is a function of relative frequency in naturally occurring speech. To the extent that the empirical work reveals how people process linguistic signals, it deals with the conceptual salience of different features, so taking into account considerations in the tradition of Ogden.

The consequence of reconciling the two traditions is that although the LFC is grounded in RP and GA, this is only to the extent that features of these varieties are shown in the data to be crucial to intelligibility among L2 (NBES) speakers of English. Some RP/GA features clearly have the opposite effect while others appear to be inconsequential for international intelligibility. In the latter two situations, the core is modified in the direction of L2 varieties. In addition, although the LFC, like Gimson's 'rudimentary international pronunciation', attempts to impose certain phonological forms on learners, to a large extent it leaves them free to make choices, and use L1 varietal features if preferred. In this sense, although I prefer not to describe my approach in terms of 'model' at all but rather in terms of a range of EIL varieties, it has much in common with Bhatia's (1997) 'polymodel concept' and Bamgboṣe's (1998) 'pluricentric view'.

Because of the dearth of research into phonology in EIL contexts, the LFC is based entirely on my own data. Before I began collecting the data, however, I carried out an exploratory study, followed by a more formal pilot study, to ascertain whether, in principle, speakers of English from different L1 backgrounds did indeed find one another's accents difficult to understand. Both studies were conclusive. Of the 48 respondents in the pilot study, the majority concurred in finding the English of speakers from unrelated L1s the hardest to understand, followed by those from related L1s and 'NSs' of English, with those from their own L1s by far the easiest. The figures involved were found to be statistically significant,[4] and all but one respondent mentioned at least one aspect of L2 pronunciation as a major source of difficulty in understanding an EIL interlocutor (see Jenkins 1995: 7–9 for details).

The ILT data, on which I based the phonological core, was collected over several years and by a number of different means—an arduous and time-consuming task, but crucial because of the lack of EIL research as yet in the public domain. Once I had established that the phonological problem of which I had been aware informally for some time did indeed have a firm basis in reality, data collection began in earnest. Firstly, field observation: examples of miscommunication and communication breakdown in both multilingual classrooms and multilingual social contexts. Secondly, recordings of different-L1 pairs and groups of students engaged in communication tasks. Thirdly, an investigation into NBES production and reception of nuclear stress. Throughout, attention was focused on the causes of any problematic discourse that occurred: the extent to which these causes were phonological, and where so, which phonological features were most recurrent and, in each case, the relative contribution of speaker and hearer(s) to the problem.

The most important areas for the preservation of mutual phonological intelligibility in ILT to emerge from the data were the following:

1 Most consonant sounds
2 Appropriate consonant cluster simplification
3 Vowel length distinctions
4 Nuclear stress.

However, when fine-tuning the LFC, I took two other phenomena into account: firstly the teachability–learnability distinction, and secondly the role of phonological universals. We will consider these in turn.

The teachability–learnability distinction relates to the fact that—as Allwright observed long ago in an article aptly titled 'Why don't learners learn what teachers teach?' (1984b)—classroom teaching does not necessarily bring about classroom learning. For phonology, perhaps more than for the other linguistic levels, we need to draw a distinction between learning which may result from teaching and that which may only occur outside the classroom through exposure to the language. Dalton and Seidlhofer suggest that: 'For pedagogical purposes, it might in fact be helpful to think about the various aspects of pronunciation along a teachability–learnability scale. Some things, say the distinction between fortis and lenis consonants, are fairly easy to describe and generalize—they are teachable. Other aspects, notably the attitudinal function of intonation, are extremely dependent on individual circumstances and therefore nearly impossible to isolate out for direct teaching ... In other words, some aspects might better be left for learning without teacher intervention' (1994a: 72–3).

It seems that a certain amount of English pronunciation cannot be learnt successfully in classrooms, no matter how much time and effort is expended on the task by teachers and their learners. However, as we noted in the previous chapter, as far as EIL is concerned, there seems to be a one-to-one correspondence between what is relevant (crucial to EIL phonological intelligibility) and what is realistic ('teachable' in the sense that learning follows teaching). We considered the possibility that motivation may have a critical role here. That is, where learners perceive relevance, they are highly motivated to learn a particular feature of the L2, whereas where they do not perceive relevance, they are unwilling to make the supreme effort needed to replace an L1 feature with an L2 feature. On the other hand, the argument could conceivably be expressed in reverse: where a feature of the L2 is widely unteachable, it becomes irrelevant to EIL.

As we work through the LFC in the following section, I will identify which phonological areas seem to fall into the unteachable category and which areas seem to have the potential to be learnt through pedagogy. If subsequent research should reveal cracks in the one-to-one correspondence between the teachable and the relevant, then it would still make sense for teachers to concentrate on the former and simply to draw attention to other aspects of the system that are necessary for EIL, but remain for later acquisition. In this way, learners could be primed for future learning by being made explicitly aware of features in the spoken output in receptive pronunciation work, without focusing on these features in productive work.

The identification of unteachable items is, to some extent, a matter of common sense and experience, and, to an even greater extent, predictable from a knowledge of transfer effects (see previous chapter). But as far as sounds are concerned, phonological universals are also able to inform the teachability–learnability debate, by providing concrete information about the level of difficulty in relation to the degree of markedness of an individual item or set of items. For example, most of the world's languages have approximately twice as many consonant as vowel phonemes. English, with 24 consonant and up to 20 vowel sounds, is marked in this respect, and we can therefore expect most learners to have problems with the English vowel system.

Another phonological universal relates to syllable structure. Most of the world's languages have syllables consisting of consonant + vowel, and rarely have consonants in word-final position. Again, English is marked in frequently having syllables and words which end in consonants, and in having many complex consonant clusters. Voiced consonant sounds are generally more marked than voiceless, especially in final position—one which they frequently inhabit in English words. Most of the English fricative and affricate sounds are marked, highly so when voiced, doubly so in final position. The voiceless fricative /θ/, however, is also highly marked, the voiced /ð/ doubly marked, and in final position triply so. We can thus predict particular difficulty with this sound for the majority of learners of English. (See pages 103–4 above, and Crystal 1987 Section 28, on phonological universals and markedness theory.)

Information of this sort thus enables us to identify sounds which are likely to prove especially difficult for learners and which, if intelligibility is not threatened, are probably not worth including in the LFC. This is the case with /θ/ and /ð/ (see next section). It also indicates which L2 areas we can expect learners already to have mastered within their L1s and on which we can build. However, while phonological universals provide useful support, they need to be treated with a degree of caution for two reasons. Firstly, it is by no means clear that *marked* equals *unteachable*. Indeed, it may turn out to be precisely the 'exotic' nature of certain sounds for L2 learners which sometimes makes them amenable to classroom teaching/learning (although success would depend to a great extent on the phonological skills of the individual teacher and on the intrinsic physical difficulty involved in producing the unfamiliar sound).

Secondly, the fact that a sound is marked, and therefore probably difficult for many learners to produce, does not automatically render it less important for intelligibility to the EIL receiver. In my data substitutions of /ɜː/, a doubly marked sound, caused intelligibility problems on several occasions. As we noted on the previous page, the mooted one-to-one correspondence between features which are teachable and those which are crucial to EIL phonological intelligibility may turn out to be less exact. If this were found to be so, we would be dealing with the LFC on two separate levels: as a specification of desirable NBES competence, and as a pedagogic construct. Teachers would then need to be informed about which features were not feasible for productive classroom teaching, and ways of introducing these features receptively, so that learners were primed to learn them for themselves should there be future opportunity for them to do so.

With the teachability–learnability distinction and the usefulness of knowledge of phonological universals (despite certain reservations) in mind, we move on to the LFC itself.

Features of the Lingua Franca Core

In Chapters 2 and 4, we examined data drawn from ILT interactions in which communication had broken down, and in which unintelligible pronunciation was wholly or partly the cause of the breakdown. The chief problematic areas were listed on page 132. We will now look at these in greater detail and consider why some phonological areas can be labelled 'core' and others 'non-core' or 'peripheral' in the context of EIL. While the LFC has something in common with Jenner's Common Core (see page 126), it diverges in important ways in order to accommodate the L2 speakers (and largely NBESs) who participate in EIL. In these areas, it is L1 speakers who will be obliged to make productive and receptive adjustments if they, too, wish to interact in English internationally.

The segmental–suprasegmental debate

One major phonological difference between EFL and EIL is the relative importance of segmental and suprasegmental features, something that was mentioned briefly in Chapter 2 (page 32). Indeed, some of these suprasegmental features—particularly those involving reduction—actually obstruct intelligibility for NBES receivers, whereas 'speech is intelligible—although it might sound slow, over-careful, etc.—without any reductions' (Adam Brown, personal communication). On the other hand, many segmentals are vital for the preservation of phonological intelligibility, as we noted in Chapter 2.

This represents an almost complete reversal of current phonological orthodoxy, since it has been widely argued for some years now that segmental errors have a rather less serious effect on intelligibility than do suprasegmental errors. Van Els and De Bot are unusual in stressing the importance of segmentals (though not beyond that of suprasegmentals). They argue that 'only an investigation of the relative contribution of both segmental and suprasegmental aspects to a "foreign" accent can ultimately reveal the relevance of the latter' (1987: 153); and almost a decade later, Anderson-Hsieh is able to report not only that very few studies have actually investigated the relative roles of the segmentals and suprasegmentals in intelligibility, but also that the few that have been conducted have been '*suggestive* rather than strongly conclusive of the greater influence of suprasegmentals' (1995: 17; emphasis in original).

Van Els and De Bot also warn against applying directly to the classroom the findings of research that does not itself actually take place in learning contexts. Thus, they contend, their own intonation experiment (1987) should not be used as evidence to suggest that learners will achieve better results if precedence is given to suprasegmentals in the early stages of L2 pronunciation teaching. More recently, Brazil has commented on the interdependence of the segmentals and suprasegmentals, arguing that 'the work students do in one area supports and reinforces the work they do in the other' (1994: 3). This seems to corroborate the view expressed in Chapter 2 that the most serious errors are those involving both levels. It also represents a significant shift in position from the more radical and commonly expressed view that 'the suprasegmentals are more basic and contribute more to intelligibility and accent. They should therefore appear first in textbooks and be mastered first by learners' (Brown 1991: 4; though note Brown's later shift to a more EIL perspective, as expressed on page 135).

The main point, however, is that those who give primacy to the suprasegmentals tend either to have 'NS–NNS' communication in mind (whether ESL in the USA or EFL around the world) or not to have considered fully the implications of EIL, nor carried out investigations to support or refute their claims. The LFC aims to establish a degree of segmental–suprasegmental balance appropriate to EIL. It neither advocates a return to the wholesale and indiscriminate teaching of the segmentals characteristic of virtually all pronunciation teaching in the UK and USA until the late 1970s, nor does it throw out the segmental baby with the bathwater and advocate the wholesale and indiscriminate teaching of the suprasegmentals. Rather, it takes into account the distinctive conditions that prevail in EIL as opposed to EFL and, consequently, the different needs of its interlocutors. In EIL classrooms, the prioritizing of the full range of suprasegmentals has lost validity for the majority of learners, and can only be defended where an individual learner's needs dictate such an approach, that is, in the following situations:

- the learner will in the future interact primarily with 'native' speakers of English;
- the learner has emigrated to an L1 English country or will be living in one for a prolonged period, and wishes to assimilate as fully as possible with 'native' English speakers;
- the learner, for personal or professional reasons, wishes to sound as close to 'native' speakers of English as is possible.

Even with these needs and the attendant motivations in place, many learners never acquire through classroom teaching all aspects of the English suprasegmental system because—as was mentioned earlier and will be discussed in greater detail below—some of them are simply not teachable, and can only be acquired over time (if at all) outside the classroom.

Core features

We turn now to the precise contents of the LFC—those items which, according to the ILT data, are crucial if pronunciation is to be intelligible. These fall into three main categories: sounds, nuclear stress, and articulatory setting. We will look at each of these areas in turn.

1 Segmentals

In this category I am including not only the consonant and vowel phonemes, but also certain phonetic realizations and methods of consonant cluster simplification.

Consonant sounds

RP and GA have 24 consonant sounds in common and the majority (including certain allophonic realizations) are essential in that conflations, substitutions, and elisions of these regularly cause a loss of intelligibility in the ILT data. Several of these phonemes, or very close equivalents, already exist in most other languages, at least in word-initial position. Others do not exist at all in most other languages or, if they do, are restricted to certain positions within a word. Inevitably there will be many differences across L1s in relation to both the segments they already share with English and the relative difficulty of producing and perceiving new segments. However, in contriving a phonological core for use by speakers from all L1s, we cannot be governed by individual L1 difficulties, and teachers will still have to refer to reference books, such as Swan and Smith (1987), in order to find out about the specific problems of particular L1 groups. But we can make some judgements about what to include in the EIL core or, more accurately, what to leave out by taking account of near-universal difficulties with certain sounds, in cases where the data indicate that intelligibility will not be compromised.

Consonant-wise, there are two candidates for omission from the core, i.e. the dental fricative pair /θ/ and /ð/. Substitutions of these phonemes did not cause phonological unintelligiblity on a single occasion in the data. Indeed, there is even an instance in the data of the opposite, i.e. where /t/ was interpreted as /θ/. This occurred when a Japanese learner was giving a presentation to a multilingual group on the subject of the Tarzan films. An Israeli learner asked him 'What do you mean, "thousand films"?' As Pennington points out, the dental variants [t̪] and [d̪] occur in many areas of Britain and in many indigenous varieties of English, such as African and Caribbean, as well as in many learner varieties. She argues that 'the recurrence of these variants in so many different areas may mean that the [t̪] and [d̪] pronunciations are in some sense simpler, or less marked, phonetically speaking, than are the interdental pronunciations of the phonemes /θ/ and /ð/' (1996: 65). This certainly seems to be the case when one takes degrees of markedness into account (see pages 103–4, 134). Thus, we have a situation where a high level of difficulty coincides with a low level of salience for EIL intelligibility.

Gillian Brown considers that 'when time is short, it is probably not worthwhile spending time on teaching /θ/ and /ð/ if the students find them difficult' (1974: 53). She recommends that learners be encouraged to substitute /f/ and /v/ rather than the other sounds commonly substituted (predominantly /t/ and /d/, but also frequently /s/ and /z/ and, by Japanese learners, /ʃ/ and /dʒ/). Brown's comment was made before the recent dramatic growth in the number of L2 speakers of English, and perhaps she herself would nowadays revise it in the light of this development. The LFC does not stipulate what should replace /θ/ and /ð/ but merely excludes them as not being necessary to safeguard EIL phonological intelligibility. My view, though, is that while /f/ and /v/ are relatively common among L1 speakers of English (for example, Londoners, and children generally), they are acoustically closer to the sounds they replace and bear a lower functional load than the other sound substitutions, most of these are also acceptable since they are widely used and recognized, and therefore do not threaten intelligibility. Use of the plosives /t/ and /d/, as we noted in the previous paragraph, is prevalent among L1 as well as L2 varieties of English, especially in the form of the dentals [t̪] and [d̪]. Meanwhile, the sound /s/ is acoustically so similar to /f/ that I have known L1 speakers of English, including myself, to mishear one as the other on a number of occasions, especially on the phone. The only possible exceptions, then, are currently (but not necessarily in the future) the Japanese substitutions, since they are by definition restricted in use and, thus, less familiar to all EIL receivers; and the use of /z/ which, although intelligible, elicited responses of irritation when used with high frequency (by a German speaker) in one of the studies. The last point touches on the issue of EIL acceptability, which we will examine in the final section of the chapter.

To summarize the LFC's position regarding substitutions of the fricatives /θ/ and /ð/:

- many L1 speakers of English use them (although at the time of writing, these sounds are still stigmatized in the L1 communities by speakers of RP, GA, and other more standard L1 varieties)
- the majority of L2 speakers of English find them far easier to produce[5]
- despite much classroom time expended on the RP/GA forms, few learners ultimately acquire them, including some BESs
- they are not necessary for intelligible EIL pronunciation.

Obviously, the decision as to whether it is worth making the effort to acquire the dental fricatives is one which can only be taken by individual learners according to their personal needs and wishes. It is thus crucial that teachers be aware of the factors involved in the L1 and L2 use of these sounds and in the L2 acquisition of them, so that they can help their learners to make informed decisions.

The other RP/GA omission from the LFC relates to a phonetic rather than phonemic feature. This is the use of dark (velarized) /l/, or [ɫ], syllabically (for example, in 'litt*le*') and before a consonant sound (for example, in 'mi*l*k'), or a pause. In some L1 varieties of English and, increasingly, in Estuary English (see Rosewarne 1996), this sound is becoming vocalic. According to Adam Brown:

Of greater importance than the distinction between clear and dark /l/ (which is regularly discussed in textbooks) is the option of using a

further alternative (which is seldom mentioned). This is found in certain native accents in contexts where RP has dark /l/, i.e. before a consonant and syllabically, as in *bill, middle* (RP [bɪɫ, mɪdɫ]). For some speakers, the tongue contact against the alveolar ridge is lost, such that the secondary tongue retraction towards the velum is left as the only articulatory gesture, often with some lip-rounding. As the articulation is now no longer consonantal but vocalic, a symbol such as [ʊ] is given to it in such pronunciations ([bɪʊ, mɪdʊ]).
(1991: 91)

The production of dark [ɫ] is problematic for most learners of English, and many never acquire it. On the other hand, its regular substitution with either clear /l/ or /ʊ/ is unproblematic for EIL intelligibility throughout the data. The majority of RP speakers already pronounce pre-consonantal dark [ɫ] as /ʊ/ in non-careful speech, although many would probably deny that they do so, and dark [ɫ] does not exist in Welsh English. It thus seems unreasonable to have 'higher' expectations of L2 speakers. As far as syllabic /l/ is concerned, although still stigmatized, the /ʊ/ substitution is found in British varieties and, along with schwa plus clear /l/, is typical of the speech of children.

Where syllabic /l/ follows the homorganic (i.e. produced in the same place) plosives /t/ or /d/, as in the words 'little', 'middle', 'settle', and so on, there is an added complication for learners because the plosives are now released laterally by means of lowering the sides of the tongue. This is a particularly difficult procedure for teachers to demonstrate and for learners to imitate and, as with /θ/ and /ð/, there is no pay-off for the immense effort involved in terms of ILT intelligibility. On the other hand, many learners already have the /ʊ/ sound, or something fairly close to it, while those who do not are able to acquire it with little difficulty. So despite Joanne Kenworthy's very reasonable concern that the /ʊ/ substitution is not at present intelligible to American L1 speakers of English and cannot therefore claim to be internationally intelligible (personal communication), its use is likely to spread in both L1 and L2 English: in L1 with the growing influence of Estuary English (see previous page), and in L2 with the growing influence of L2 varieties of English. For all these reasons, pre-consonantal and syllabic /l/ are not included in the LFC.

Further LFC consonant considerations relate to the choices to be made where RP and GA differ. As far as /r/ is concerned, I have opted for the GA rhotic variant, the retroflex approximant [ɻ], rather than the RP post-alveolar approximant [ɹ]. This is mainly because 'r' is indicated orthographically in situations (i.e. post-vocalic) where it does not feature in RP pronunciation when a word is spoken in isolation (for example, 'four') or is followed by another consonant (for example, 'four books') rather than a vowel (for example, 'four eggs'). Thus, the GA variant is simpler for both production as there is only one version to acquire, and for reception as it is always realized regardless of which sound follows. It also leads to simplification of the diphthong system (see below).

On the other hand, the LFC follows RP in its use of the consonant /t/. What this means in practice is that—leaving aside for a moment the aspiration involved in word-initial /t/ and the potential for elision when /t/ occurs word-finally (see below)—the sound is pronounced [t] in all environments. This contrasts with GA, where intervocalically /t/ becomes the voiced flap [ɾ]. Thus, the word 'matter' is pronounced ['mætə] in RP, but ['mærəɪ] in GA. Because this flap is phonetically closer to /d/ than to /t/, the modification has the potential to cause confusion—here, between the words 'matter' and 'madder'. Linguistic and extralinguistic context will normally be used by proficient speakers to clarify meaning where such ambiguity arises but, as we saw in Chapter 4, this is not the case for NBESs, who are more likely to base their interpretation on the acoustic information. For this reason, and also because the RP variant (like the GA variant of /r/) has a more reliable relationship with the orthography, and because one of the chief principles underpinning the LFC is to simplify the learning task as far as is realistically possible, the RP variant of /t/ is the one selected for the LFC.

The LFC also includes two phonetic features not generally included, let alone prioritized, in pronunciation courses. First, the aspiration [ʰ] following the fortis[6] plosives /p/, /t/, and /k/ when they occur in initial position in a stressed syllable. Without the help of this puff of air, a listener will find it more difficult to identify the sound as voiceless. Thus, an unaspirated /p/ may be mistaken for /b/, a /t/ for /d/, and a /k/ for /g/. This phonetic distinction is particularly important for NBESs, since they have a narrower band of tolerance than proficient L1 or L2 speakers, and are therefore more likely to interpret a phonetic variant categorically or, in other words, as a completely separate phoneme where such an alternative exists. This is also the reason why certain L2 phonetic approximations to L1 sounds are not acceptable in the LFC (see below).

The second phonetic feature to be included also relates to the fortis–lenis distinction, but this time is concerned with the differential effect of fortis and lenis consonants on the length of a preceding vowel sound. After discussing the sounds /ɪ/ and /iː/ as found in the words 'sit' and 'see' respectively, Dalton and Seidlhofer ask 'But what about the pair "seat"–"sieve"?'. Clearly, the vowel sound in the latter word occupies at least as much time as that in the former, despite the fact that /iː/ is commonly classified as 'long' and /ɪ/ as 'short'. The explanation is as follows:

> *Phonemically* speaking, in abstract categories, we also have a long /iː/ in 'seat' and a short /ɪ/ in 'sieve'. *Phonetically*, however, that is, in actual realization, the i-sound in 'sieve' may well be just as long as that in 'seat', due to the shortening effect of the final plosive. This is also the reason

why some linguists object to the long–short distinction and prefer the terms *tense* (for /iː/) and *lax* (for /ɪ/), according to the degree of muscle tension required to produce the respective sounds.
(1994a: 22; emphasis in original)

As Gillian Brown points out, the effect of a final consonant on the length of a preceding vowel 'is not usually stressed in manuals of English pronunciation and it is consequently often unknown to foreign teachers of English' (1990: 31),[7] to which I would add that it is just as likely to be 'unknown' to L1 teachers. The phonetic processes involved are complicated (though automatic for the speaker) and this is not the place to describe them in detail (but see G. Brown *ibid.*: 31–2 for a more detailed account). Nevertheless, the general principle, expressed with clarity in the extract from Dalton and Seidlhofer, is one which should inform pronunciation teaching more frequently than it currently does, for two reasons.

Firstly, intelligibility: learners do not automatically shorten a vowel before a fortis consonant. So, for example, the vowel sound in the word 'seat' may be identical with that in 'seed' and the vowel sound in 'pick' identical with that in 'pig'. To compound matters, it is difficult to produce a voiceless stop unless the preceding vowel is shortened, because the voicing of the vowel continues into the following consonant. The resulting ambiguity in words like 'seat' and 'pick' is likely to be more harmful in ILT, where receivers are less able to make use of contextual features in their interpretations, than in EFL.

Secondly, relative ease of articulation: it is nevertheless more comfortable to produce a shortened vowel sound before a fortis consonant than it is to retain full phonemic length, because both longer vowels and fortis consonants involve more muscular energy than do shorter vowels and lenis consonants. This is presumably why proficient speakers automatically make this length reduction. Learners, on the other hand, will not learn to do so automatically unless there is pedagogic intervention. Without this, they may, for the sake of articulatory comfort, be tempted to opt for the closest short (i.e. lax) vowel which, in the case of 'seat', would result in 'sit'.

Despite the underlying phonetic complexity of the operations involved, the basic pedagogic rule (shorten any vowel before a final fortis consonant and maintain the length before a final lenis consonant) is itself simple and thus learnable in the classroom. The time expended on teaching it will prove well worth the effort in terms of increased EIL intelligibility—unlike, for example, time spent on the sounds /θ/ and /ð/ or on certain aspects of connected speech and the intonation system, which we will come to shortly.

We will return to vowel length later, but before we move away from consonants, we need to consider the subject of consonant cluster simplification. The main issue here is that English syllable simplification is highly rule-bound, and that breaking the rules, particularly in the case of consonant deletion, is likely to be serious for intelligibility. We noted earlier that of the two methods commonly used by NBESs to simplify 'difficult' syllables, i.e. deletion and addition, the latter (comprising epenthesis and schwa paragoge) is less likely to compromise intelligibility since the underlying form is more easily recoverable. Indeed, epenthesis may even serve to clarify the consonants it follows and thus increase intelligibility for a less than fluent listener.

Occasionally addition can be problematic, though this is more likely to be the case if an epenthetic syllable is then stressed, as in the pronunciation of 'stroke' as ['sɪtrəʊk] (Peter Roach, personal communication), or where paragoge creates a homonym, for example where 'hard' is pronounced ['hɑːdə] (see Anderson-Hsieh 1995); and international students encountering the London underground for the first time regularly ask me what 'minder the gap' means. Otherwise, addition only seems to cause intelligibility problems in EIL when it serves to emphasize an error in a preceding consonant sound and thus compounds the error, as in the example of 'cartheft' pronounced ['kɑːˈtepətə] by a Korean speaker, cited in Chapter 2 (page 36).

On the other hand, consonant deletion is more of a threat to intelligibility. In L1 English, syllables are simplified by means of elision, which bears some similarity to the process of consonant deletion. However, the similarity is often superficial for, while elision is governed by the rules of English, consonant deletion operates in accordance with constraints on syllable structure within the learner's L1. Word-initially, English can have up to three consonant sounds (the first consonant in a cluster of three always being a /s/), and these can never be elided. The ILT data, however, contains several examples of learners simplifying initial consonant clusters by means of deletion, and of the consequent intelligibility problems for receivers. For example, a Japanese learner's rendering (in context) of the word 'product' as [pəˈrɒdʌkʊtə] was perfectly intelligible to her ILT receivers, whereas a Taiwanese learner's version ['pɒdʌk] was not. This was undoubtedly the result of the elision of /r/ rather than of word-final /t/, since the latter is a very common feature of English phonology and was not found to reduce intelligibility elsewhere in the ILT data.

The situation with word-medial and word-final English consonant clusters is very different. In some medial clusters, for example, 'listen' and 'castle', the orthographic 't' is no longer a feature of the spoken word, that is, elision of /t/ is obligatory. In other words, such as 'postpone' and 'Christmas' the 't' is not represented phonemically in the dictionary and would probably not be pronounced even if the word were being spoken carefully. In still others such as 'fact-sheet', 'friendship', and 'second class', while the 't' or 'd' may be represented phonemically in a dictionary transcript, it is regularly elided even in relatively careful speech (for example, the /t/ of 'fact-sheet' was not pronounced by an RP speaker as she carefully and slowly read out an address on BBC television).

In some words, a final cluster is so difficult to articulate smoothly that elision of one of the consonant sounds (often a /t/ or /d/) is permissible, and regularly occurs except in slow, careful speech. For example, the /t/ is generally elided in the words 'scripts', 'prompts', 'facts', and 'next week', and the /d/ in 'bands', 'finds', and so on. In cases like these (and see Brown 1991: 108–9, and page 101 above, for further examples and discussion), it does not make sense to insist—as do some pronunciation books such as Mortimer's *Elements of Pronunciation* (1985)—that learners should produce full clusters for fear of their simplifying in non-permissible ways. When faced with clusters that they find impossible to articulate, they will inevitably do so. Instead, pronunciation pedagogy should prioritize what is important for EIL intelligibility: that addition is preferable to deletion; that sounds in initial clusters should never be deleted; that where elision occurs in a final cluster, it is preferable to opt for a /t/ or /d/ where this is possible; and that although it is permissible to elide a final /t/ or /d/ where these occur in word-final clusters and the next word begins with a consonant sound (for example, 'stric_t rules'), this is not so if the next word begins with a vowel sound (for example, 'stric_t order')—which is not only stigmatized by L1 speakers but, far more importantly, risks unintelligibility in EIL.

Generally, the situation regarding consonant cluster simplification is the same in RP and GA. However, there is one cluster where they differ radically and for which the LFC follows RP rather than GA. This is the intervocalic '-nt-'. In words such as 'international', 'twenty', 'winter', and the like, i.e. where the '-nt-' occurs before an unstressed syllable, GA speakers regularly elide the /t/ (see Celce-Murcia et al. 1996: 65). Following its general principle of not introducing unnecessary complications and keeping sounds as close as possible to orthography, the LFC does not include this GA elision, and GA speakers would themselves be expected to produce an unelided '-nt-' cluster in EIL contexts.

Although, as a rule, the LFC requires learners to approximate rather than to imitate exactly the RP and GA consonant sounds we have been discussing, certain approximations were found in the ILT data to cause intelligibility problems. These approximations generally involved transfer from the L1 system. They resulted either in a sound which was unrecognizable or one which was perceived as being closer to another phoneme of English than to that intended. They are therefore excluded from the LFC:

- Spanish use of [β] for /b/ (especially between vowel sounds), which tends to be interpreted as /v/, for example, in the word 'habit', and for /v/, especially word-initially, for example, in the word 'very' which may then be interpreted as 'berry';
- Japanese substitution of [ɸ] for /h/ followed by /uː/ for example, in the word '_wh_o', and for /f/ for example, in the word '_f_ootball';
- Japanese approximation of the sound /w/ as [ɯ] in words such as '_w_ood';

- Japanese dropping of postvocalic /n/ and accompanying nasalization of the preceding vowel (or, to a lesser extent, and depending on phonetic environment, the substitution of /ŋ/ or /m/, the three sounds being allophones of /n/ in the L1). Thus, 'ban' becomes [bæ̃] and the '-ion' suffix is regularly realized as [ɔ̃];
- Greek and Spanish approximation of the sound /h/ as [x] for example, in the word 'house'.

This list is not exhaustive, but represents all the approximations which might be considered phonetically close enough to the target sound to be regarded as L2 regional variants, and yet which were problematic for intelligibility in the data upon which the LFC is based. Many other approximations, such as the frequently used dental [t̪] and [d̪] for the L1 alveolar plosives /t/ and /d/, were unproblematic in the data and therefore permissible LFC approximations (despite the fact that for many speakers [t̪] and [d̪] were used for both /t/ and /d/ and for the dental fricatives /θ/ and /ð/—a factor which reinforces the need to base decisions of this kind on solid evidence rather than on intuition, functional load, and frequency counts).

Vowel sounds

As regards vowel sounds, there are two considerations: quality and quantity. Vowel quality is concerned with tongue and lip position, and vowel quantity with relative length. While vowel quantity is reasonably stable across varieties of English, vowel quality is not. For example, RP speakers pronounce 'bus' as /bʌs/ while speakers of many northern British varieties say /bʊs/; RP speakers pronounce 'dog' as /dɒg/ while GA speakers are more likely to say /dɑg/.

This is the factor which led Jenner to prioritize quantity over quality in his Common Core (see page 125–6). But the view is controversial for at least two reasons. Firstly, the long–short situation is by no means as clear-cut as this suggests. All long vowels are not as long as each other or short vowels as short as each other (see above pages 140–1 and Brown 1990: 32, footnote). Nor is the same long or short vowel equally long or short in all phonetic contexts. As we saw earlier, its precise length depends critically on the nature of its phonetic environment and, in particular, on whether it is followed by a fortis or lenis consonant. Secondly, there are occasional situations where L1 varieties differ not only in quality but also in length. For example, speakers of RP and many other southern English accents refer to 'grass' as /grɑːs/, whereas in GA and many northern English varieties it is pronounced /græs/. However, as Adam Brown points out (1991: 20–1), the /ɑː/–/æ/ alternation applies only to a small group of words and thus does not seriously affect the vowel quantity proposition.

The vowel quality argument nevertheless holds good if we can assume that L2 speakers will, like speakers of non-standard L1 varieties, be consistent in the use of their preferred vowel qualities, and that they will also manage to incorporate length distinctions into them appropriately, particularly in relation to the fortis/lenis distinction and to nuclear stress (see page 153ff.). With sufficient guidance, this should be possible, and will in the process drastically reduce the pronunciation teaching load. It will at the same time remove one of the main problems facing the many teachers (L1 and L2) who do not themselves have standard English accents: that is, the implication that their accent is not appropriate as a pedagogic model. Learners, for their part, will no longer be puzzled by the fact that L1 speakers outside the classroom regularly pronounce their vowels differently from the way they themselves are being taught.

Two other factors concerning vowels are worth mentioning. The first relates more specifically to diphthongs. Because the LFC has opted for the rhotic variety of /r/, the diphthong inventory is already reduced from eight to five, as the three centring diphthongs /ɪə/, /eə/, and /ʊə/ (i.e. which end with a central vowel) are automatically excluded, and the schwa substituted with [ɹ]. Since devising his Common Core, Jenner has re-examined the status of the diphthongs and concluded that in fact only three, viz. the wide closing diphthongs /aʊ/, /aɪ/, and /ɔɪ/ are common to all NS varieties and therefore 'necessary for phonemic distinction and general intelligibility' (1995: 16). However, he concludes that diphthongs, like monophthongs, differ widely in quality among NSs and cannot therefore be accorded high priority in L2 teaching. As with the monophthongs, then, it is the length rather than the quality of diphthongs that is most salient for intelligibility. The LFC goes even further than Jenner's position and altogether eschews considerations of diphthong quality, with the proviso that whatever quality is used, the length must be that of a diphthong or long vowel, and the variant must be used consistently. This reflects the fact that diphthong substitutions did not normally cause problems in the data,[8] and also that L1 accents of English vary in their use even of the three wide closing diphthongs. For example, in South London, the word 'cake' is frequently pronounced /kaɪk/, whereas in RP it is /keɪk/, while in advanced RP, the /aɪ/ dipthong may be used in words such as 'house', that is, instead of /aʊ/.

One further point relates to the question of markedness. I hinted earlier at a possible tension between an L2 speaker's difficulty in producing marked sounds and an L2 listener's need for certain marked sounds to be pronounced correctly (see page 134). Where this is the case—as it seems to be for the vowel /ɜː/—it probably results from the fact that not only does the marked sound by definition not exist in the learner's L1, but also that it is infrequent in English (it is the least frequent monophthong in RP).[9] Thus it is unpredictable in the sense that it does not come easily to mind as a possible alternative to a pronunciation error.

In the ILT data there are several instances where the substitution of /ɜː/ with /ɑː/ causes an intelligibility problem, despite the fact that only quality and not quantity is involved. For example, in one case, a Japanese subject was discussing a picture with a Swiss-German subject (both were able to see the picture) and—referring to a bird in the picture—said 'I'd take the bird' but pronounced 'bird' as /bɑːd/. In this case, the error did not result in a word that was known to the listener, so the creation of a new word cannot be held responsible for the resulting incomprehension. In some of the other examples, however, the error did create another known word (for example, 'curtain' pronounced as 'carton', and 'birthplace' pronounced as 'bathplace')—although the substitution made little sense in the context. For this reason, I have made an exception in the LFC, and included vowel quality in relation to the sound /ɜː/. This is in accord with research by Schwartz (1980), whose data reveals a similar (non-comprehension) outcome as a result of the substitution of /ɜː/ with /ɑː/.

2 Suprasegmentals

In this section, we will be looking at the following: weak forms and other features of connected speech, rhythm, word stress, and intonation (in particular, pitch movement, nuclear stress, and word groups). Whereas the teaching of segmentals is straightforward, in the sense that we can for the most part provide learners with clear descriptions and generalizable rules, this is not the case with the suprasegmentals. Here, 'the rules' tend to be far more complex, and/or to operate largely at a subconscious level. Thus, the teachability–learnability distinction (see pages 132–3) becomes far more salient in decisions about what to include in the LFC.

Weak forms

Small structural items, such as the prepositions 'to' and 'from', the auxiliary verb 'have', the dummy operator 'do', the pronouns 'her', 'your', and so on (see Kenworthy 1987: 84 for a comprehensive list), possess both a strong form, in which full vowel quality is retained (i.e. the word is pronounced as in citation form), and a weak form, in which the vowel quality is modified and the length reduced, generally resulting in the sound schwa, itself the most frequent sound of RP and GA. In the latter varieties of English, strong forms are only used in certain situations, such as when a preposition occurs at the end of a clause ('What did you do that for?', where 'for' is /fɔː(r)/ rather than /fə/), or for emphasis ('It's her decision, not mine', where 'her' is /hɜː(r)/ rather than /hə/).

The theory is that through the speaker's weakening of these items, the listener's attention is able to focus on the more important (in terms of the speaker's message) content words. I will say at once that I am not at all convinced by the argument that it is necessary to weaken an unimportant item in order to highlight an important one, provided that the latter is adequately stressed (see below). British actors regularly fail to produce weak forms, as do speakers of certain L1 varieties of English (for example,

Scottish and South African English), without any consequent loss of intelligibility. Indeed, it is quite clearly the case in both RP and GA that speakers regularly and dramatically decrease their use of weak forms in situations where they are taking extra care to be understood, for example in television interviews and conference presentations. In fact, on at least two occasions during the past twelve months, I have attended conferences at which presenters delivered papers on the importance of suprasegmental features such as weak forms, in speech which was largely weak-form free.

Another argument in favour of weak forms is that learners should produce them because L1 speakers do so. Notwithstanding the previous point (i.e. that L1 speakers of varieties of English which contain weak forms in their inventories sometimes avoid them for the sake of clarity), this is not a valid argument for EIL. Here, what L1 speakers do in order to promote intelligibility when they communicate with each another—and even with L2 speakers—is irrelevant. In EIL, we are concerned above all with safeguarding intelligibility among speakers for whom English is nobody's L1. The interests of 'native speakers' are secondary to the enterprise.

Although weak forms are often taught in EFL classrooms in Britain—precisely because they are a feature of L1 use, and L1 teachers therefore find them easy to describe and model—learning rarely follows. The vast majority of learners, including many who become fluent bilinguals, use few weak forms other than 'a' and 'the'. In this sense, despite the fact that it is easy to formulate clear rules for weak form use, they are unteachable. Perhaps, through personal experience of learning English (an experience which, by definition, is not available to NS teachers), learners realize that weak forms hold potential problems of recoverability for their NBES interlocutors, who may find it difficult to retrieve the underlying full forms of reduced words (see pages 116–9 on the notion of recoverability). Thus, weak forms may actually hinder intelligibility in EIL. Another problem with weak forms is the contradiction, first pointed out by David Brazil (1994), of focusing in the classroom on a feature whose quality is precisely the result of speakers not focusing on it. This pedagogic focus may then, paradoxically, impede the later acquisition of weak forms in learning outside the classroom through exposure to L1 speech, and may explain why so few fluent bilinguals ever productively acquire weak forms other than the articles in their vernacular English.

The solution, as far as the LFC is concerned, entails strong and weak versions. In the strong version, weak forms are omitted altogether, since they are neither essential to EIL intelligibility nor unacceptable to L2 speakers of English in EIL contexts. It is then left to individual learners to perhaps acquire weak forms outside the classroom through prolonged exposure to the L1 (a process which, thus, will not be hampered by previous classroom focus), or to seek extra tuition (though, in my view, with a rather limited chance of success) if their needs are for EFL rather than

EIL. In the weak version, weak forms are not omitted altogether, but are adapted for EIL use, and this may be a more suitable approach for learners who themselves wish to teach English. It is based on the fact that, contrary to popular belief, all languages—and not only so-called 'stress-timed' languages—distinguish between stressed and unstressed syllables. But whereas English reduces both quantity and quality, many other languages, for example, Italian, retain a vowel's original quality and only reduce its length. This, then, is what I propose for English weak forms. Instead of teaching learners to produce schwa (and I am not here talking about schwa within words other than weak forms), which has so far proved to be a somewhat futile exercise, we could encourage them to shorten the vowel but retain its quality. Thus, we halve the task in hand, and remove at least the recoverability objection to the use of weak forms. On the other hand, many EIL learners will also need to understand L1 speakers of English in international contexts. These learners will still need to work on weak forms (in their traditional sense) *receptively* in the classroom, whatever approach is adopted for production, until the time comes when L1 speakers of English also take lessons in EIL and in accommodating their speech to that of their international interlocutors.

Other features of connected speech
These features occur in L1 and bilingual L2 English in fluent, non-careful speech which, as we noted in Chapter 4 (page 72), tends to have a speed of around 350 syllables a minute—and even faster for short stretches. They involve assimilatory processes, i.e. processes which aid the speaker's pronounceability by making articulation easier in such speech, chiefly elision, assimilation, catenation, linking of /r/, and intrusion of /j/, /w/, and, in RP, also /r/. The hearer's perceptibility, on the other hand, is aided by dissimilatory processes, in which a speaker subordinates his or her speech strategies to the hearer's needs by articulating more clearly (see Dressler 1984).

Two objections to the teaching of the features of connected speech productively thus arise. Firstly, dissimilatory processes rarely cause intelligibility problems for L1 and fluent L2 speakers of English. However, in EIL, where we are more concerned with intelligibility for NBES receivers, it makes better sense to prioritize the latter's ease of perception over the speaker's ease of production, since NBESs are less likely to make use of context to compensate for any deficiencies in the speech signal (see Chapter 4).

Secondly, most NBESs do not achieve speeds of anything like 350 syllables a minute in their speech. And at slower speeds, these features will be over-articulated, making speech more difficult for the speaker and attracting too much attention to themselves by the hearer, thus defeating the whole purpose. For example, as David Crystal has demonstrated (see the discussion on page 72), the sentence 'I wouldn't have been able to' in fluent speech may become /ə wʊbmpɪneɪblə/. Spoken more slowly by a learner who is being encouraged to use the various features of connected speech, it could come across like this: /ə wʊbəm pɪ neɪ blə/, with each 'syllable' being carefully articulated. In this case it would at best sound ridiculous and at worst be rendered completely incomprehensible. The point is that most—if not all—these assimilatory processes will be acquired naturally if learners' progress in their knowledge and control of the language is sufficient to enable them to speed up the rate of their speech. Too many pronunciation courses are based on the premise that learners will increase their speed through the acquisition of these processes rather than vice versa: teaching learners to say 'greem pen' instead of 'green pen', and the like, will not of itself quicken their speech. And even those learners who acquire the features of connected speech will still need to be able to articulate more carefully when they are communicating with NBESs.

As with weak forms, then, the features of connected speech are not included in the LFC, though, like weak forms, they will need to be taught for receptive purposes.

Rhythm

As we noted earlier (page 43), English is said to have a stress-timed as opposed to a syllable-timed rhythm. That is, stressed syllables are said to occur at roughly equal time intervals, with non-stressed syllables being 'stretched' or 'squashed together' in order to occupy the time between stresses. It is said to be the stress-timed rhythm of English which causes speakers to employ the features of connected speech which we considered in the previous section. On the other hand, in so-called 'syllable-timed' languages, syllables are said to occupy identical time intervals regardless of whether they are stressed, or of how many unstressed syllables occur between the stressed ones.

However, the concept of stress-timing appears to have little basis in reality. Ladefoged describes it as only a 'tendency' (1982: 224); Roach (1991) considers that if stress-timing operates at all, it only occurs in very regular, formal speech; and Cauldwell argues that the concept is a myth which persists partly because 'the data focused on consists of short stretches of speech (usually nursery rhymes)' (1996: 33). Any readers who doubt the truth of this should attempt to hold a stress-timed conversation. They will find it impossible to maintain such a rhythm for more than a few seconds while focusing on the content of what they are saying. The concept thus represents an idealized version of L1 English speech rhythm applying, where it does, only to very short snatches of authentic speech. Indeed, the work of Roach (1982, 1991), Brazil (1994), and Cauldwell (1996) points to 'stress-timed' languages having rather more in common with 'syllable-timed' ones than has generally been appreciated. And Marks suggests that there may be 'an atavistic element of perception at work', which results in our being 'predisposed, in order to make sense of our experience, to perceive regular rhythms where the evidence is actually fuzzy'. He therefore argues that the 'two kinds of timing may be of more interest in connection with the study of how people perceive and process elements of speech' than in terms of what they actually produce (1999: 196–7).

A more realistic approach to stress- and syllable-timing may be to regard language rhythms not as polar opposites but as occupying different points on a timing continuum. This approach could apply not only to different languages, but also to different contexts of use. For while it is possible that particular languages have a *tendency* towards particular points on the continuum, 'different types of timing will be exhibited by the same speaker on different occasions and in different contexts' (Roach 1982: 78). But oddly, while the 'corpus syndrome' (the automatic leap from research findings about what 'native speakers' do to their applications to ELT pedagogy) regularly occurs in relation to most other areas of the language (grammar, vocabulary, discourse patterns, many aspects of pronunciation), there seems to have been long and strong resistance to applying findings about rhythm. The consequence is that attempts are still being made to teach artificial, unnatural rhythm in ELT classrooms, mainly through rhymes and limericks.[10] This is not to suggest that in pedagogy artificiality is necessarily to be equated with inadequacy. Its value will depend on the precise use to which it is put. In the case of rhythm, stress-timed materials may have validity by providing a framework for the teaching of certain other features of the English pronunciation system which will be useful receptively and/or productively to learners, such as pausing between word groups and the lengthening of stressed syllables, provided that 'learners are not given the impression that this is how they should always speak English' (Marks 1999: 198).

Stress-timing, then, is not a feature of the LFC although, as I will discuss in the section on intonation below, the lengthening of stressed (nuclear) syllables seems to be crucial to intelligible English pronunciation.

Word stress

This is something of a grey area. Word stress seems to be reasonably important to L1 English receivers (though with provisos: see pages 39–40), but rarely causes intelligibility problems in the ILT data and, where it does so, always occurs in combination with another phonological error (see page 41–2). In addition, word stress rules are so complex as to be unteachable (see Roach 1991, especially pages 76–8, for examples to illustrate this point). On the other hand, misplaced word stress has a corresponding effect on the placement of nuclear stress and, as such, cannot be dismissed lightly. It also affects the aspiration following a word-initial fortis plosive, since this aspiration only occurs before a stressed syllable (see page 136). So while misplaced word stress may not, of itself, cause unintelligibility in ILT, the resulting failure to aspirate an initial /p/, /t/, or /k/ may do so, as these sounds may then be categorized as their voiced equivalents.

The full-scale teaching of word stress is not feasible and even if it were, it is not crucial to the intelligibility of individual words in ILT. But because of its implications for nuclear stress and sound identification, the LFC recommends providing learners with a number of general guidelines. For example, that the majority of two-syllable nouns receive stress on the first syllable and two-syllable verbs on the second; that certain suffixes, for example, -*ee* and -*ese* are stress-bearing unless the word modifies another ('He's ChinESE' as compared with 'He's a CHInese STUDent'); that some suffixes cause the stress to shift to the syllable preceding them, for example, '-ion', '-ic', and so on (and see Vaughan-Rees 1997: 9–10, 1999; and Levis 1999a for discussions of the most productive rules governing word stress patterns). But most importantly, learners need to be warned that there are many exceptions to all word stress rules and to be taught how to identify word stress in the dictionary.

Intonation

Here there are three principal areas of interest: pitch movement, nuclear stress, and division of the speech stream into word groups (tone units). As far as EIL pedagogy is concerned, the first is almost diametrically opposed to the second and third in its (lack of) relevance. We will look at these areas in detail to explain in the case of the first, why it is not included in the LFC and in the case of the second, why it is one of the most important features of the core.

Until very recently intonational materials tended to be particularly preoccupied with the attitudinal function of intonation, i.e. the possible attitudes that a 'native speaker' may be expressing when using one of the seven or so pitch movements (or 'tones') on the nuclear (or 'tonic') syllable within the word group (or 'tone unit'). For example, it was said that a rise-fall could mean that the speaker was impressed, being sarcastic or ironic, challenging, and so on. Nowadays, many intonation scholars accept that all this is very subjective, dependent on the individual speaker and on the specific context of the interaction, and thus impossible to generalize. Learners may well acquire these sorts of nuances through prolonged exposure to English, but we most probably cannot teach them in the classroom (see Taylor 1993).

There even appears to be a weakness in the claim for a grammatical function of intonation relating to pitch (i.e. pitch movement on the nucleus as being an indicator of grammatical structure, such that statements have a fall, *yes*/*no* questions a fall-rise, *wh*- questions a fall, and so on). According to Kreidler, 'Contrary to popular belief, all analysts of English intonation have insisted that there is no melody which is exclusively associated with one type of sentence: statements do not necessarily have a falling tune, questions do not necessarily rise. The tunes do not necessarily correlate with any specific kinds of grammatical structure' (1989: 182–3). McCarthy states the case even more strongly, arguing that there is 'much evidence to suggest that there is no one-to-one relationship between sentence-type and tone' and that 'the more we look at intonation and grammar, the more we are forced to conclude that they are separate systems which work independently, but in harmony, to contribute to discourse meaning' (1991: 106). Levis (1999b) produces important evidence to this effect in relation specifically to *yes/no* questions. He goes on to argue that

> because there is little clear meaning difference that can be attributed to intonation on yes/no questions for even native varieties, intonation on these questions is likely to play little or no role in intelligibility between inner, outer and expanding circle varieties of English and should thus be de-emphasized in pedagogy (ibid.: 378–9).

Some of the most recent work involving pitch movement is David Brazil's theory of 'discourse intonation' (Brazil et al. 1980; Brazil 1996, 1997). This is an elegant theory which has promoted much research into the workings of intonation within the 'native-speaker' framework. At the centre of the theory is the falling, or 'proclaiming', tone which speakers are said to use on the nuclear syllable to indicate that the information is in some way new, and the fall-rise, or 'referring', tone with which speakers indicate that the information is in some way shared or given (see pages 48–49 for fuller details). Many phonologists consider this to be a very satisfying account, and it may well turn out ultimately to be an accurate representation of what 'native speakers' do when they interact with each other.

However, there are two fundamental problems in attempting to apply Brazil's theory to L2 pedagogy. The first relates specifically to discourse intonation. Although the 'given' versus 'new' dichotomy seems very simple, certainly far simpler than links between tones and the expression of attitudes, in fact it is not at all clear. What counts as old or new information in any particular situation seems to involve many factors, and these are not necessarily present within the actual context of the interaction taking place. Thus, as with the use of tones to express attitude and even to indicate grammatical structure, this central feature of discourse intonation may be more easily acquired outside the classroom than generalized to the extent that it can be taught within it. In other words, it may provide important descriptive and explanatory information about 'native speaker' pronunciation, but it is not teachable.

The second problem relates to a difficulty inherent in any attempt to teach pitch movement, regardless of the theoretical underpinnings of the attempt. As we noted in the previous chapter, research conducted on unborn babies has strongly demonstrated that they can detect and react to pitch distinctions from around 26 weeks' gestation. It is not surprising that, having processed pitch from so early in their life cycle, people find it almost impossible later on to extract pitch movement for analysis. As I pointed out above (page 44), even experienced teachers regularly have problems in identifying pitch direction and often find that when they attempt to model a pitch pattern, it becomes unnatural or even wrong. And if teachers have problems when pitch is brought to the conscious level, there does not seem to be much hope for the success of their students in terms of the overt teaching of pitch.

Even if it were possible to teach pitch in the classroom, I do not believe that the use of 'native speaker' pitch movements matters very much for intelligibility in interactions among NBESs. This feature of the intonation system seldom leads to communication problems in the ILT data and, on the rare occasion that it does so, it is accompanied by another linguistic error— generally phonological, occasionally grammatical.

Nuclear stress, however, is a completely different story. Teachers and students alike have far fewer problems with what is often referred to as the accentual function of intonation. This is probably because nuclear placement operates at a more conscious level than the other aspects of the intonation system. Unlike pitch movement, it can be indicated easily in written form by means of italics, capital letters, underlining, and the like.

Nuclear stress, whether unmarked (on the last content word in the word group)[11] or contrastive (somewhere else), is the most important key to the speaker's intended meaning. It highlights the most salient part of the message, indicating where the listener should pay particular attention. And contrastive stress is especially important in English, as the language does not have the morphological or syntactic resources that many other languages have to highlight contrasts: English has few inflections, and its word order is relatively inflexible.

Nuclear stress is crucial for intelligibility in ILT. Although the majority of the phonological errors causing intelligibility problems that were described in Chapter 2 were segmental, a substantial minority involved intonational errors and, of these, almost all related to misplaced nuclear stress, particularly contrastive stress, either alone or in combination with a segmental error. The relatively high incidence in the data of communication problems caused by errors of this kind implied that while learners had come to rely on correct nuclear production and placement in order to interpret messages, i.e. they had acquired it receptively, they had not managed to acquire it for productive use.

To test out this hypothesis, I set up an experiment in which L1 and L2 speakers of English[12] were recorded reading sets of questions which began in an identical way but ended differently.[13] One set, for example, was as follows:

Did you buy a tennis racket at the sports centre this morning, or

- was it a squash racket?
- did you buy it yesterday?
- did you only borrow one?

– was it your girlfriend who bought it?
– at the tennis club?

Each subject was allocated one of four sets of questions and recorded reading them. In order to minimize the risk of their adopting an oblique orientation to the material (i.e. merely reading aloud without attempting to commununicate meaning), the contexts were personalized by means of using situations with which the subjects were very familiar, and by providing clear background information to the imaginary interaction taking place for each question. The subjects were asked to circle on their script any words they thought they had made a particular effort to stress.

After making the recordings, I removed the second halves of each question on the tape and played the first halves to the combined group of L1 and L2 speakers asking them, in each case, to predict the second half in each case. Success was, of course, dependent on each speaker's correct placement of contrastive stress and on each listener's ability to interpret the English nuclear placement system.

The L1 speakers, as one would anticipate, placed contrastive stress appropriately and correctly predicted all the second halves to the L1 questions. The L2 speakers correctly predicted around two-thirds of the L1 speakers' second halves. On the other hand, the L2 speakers misplaced contrastive stress in most of their first halves and, consequently, both they and the L1 subjects gained very low scores for predicting the L2 speakers' second halves (see Jenkins 1995, 1997 for more detailed accounts).

The experiment thus supported my hypothesis that learners acquire nuclear stress, and even contrastive stress, at the receptive level reasonably fast, but that they do not acquire it productively for far longer, and possibly not at all if they remain NBESs. And it is not just a question of placement: the method of production seems also to be implicated. One of the L2 subjects, an Italian speaker, correctly predicted three of his own second halves, despite the fact that he had not stressed the relevant syllable of the respective stem in such a way that any of the other subjects, L1 or L2, were able to identify it. Presumably he was signalling stress by some other means. Besides this, there were many examples of L2 subjects correctly circling words in their five stems, but not producing stress on these words in a way recognizable to themselves or the other subjects.

It seems likely, then, that nuclear—and especially contrastive—stress production and placement require overt classroom teaching of rules. Without such teaching, it is probable that NBESs will continue to expect nuclear stress to be correctly placed and produced by their peers, but will continue to misplace and misproduce it themselves. This will inevitably cause miscommunication in ILT. Even in those cases where learners' L1s do have contrastive stress (for example, Spanish[14]), the L1–L2 similarity will need to be made explicit through instruction, as learners do not necessarily notice similarities between their L1 and an L2 without their attention being drawn towards them. This is especially so in the case of marked items like contrastive stress. Learners seem to be reluctant to transfer marked items from their first to a second language, as is demonstrated by Kellerman's (1979) 'breken' study (in which advanced Dutch learners were asked to predict the transferability of different uses of the Dutch verb 'breken' to English, and opted for unmarked rather than marked uses).

Nuclear stress production and placement thus occupy an important place in the LFC. For EIL, and especially for NBESs, the greatest phonological obstacles to mutual intelligibility appear to be deviant core sounds in combination with misplaced and/or misproduced nuclear stress. And contrastive stress is particularly crucial in terms of the receptive–productive mismatch, as shown by both the experiment outlined above and the field data discussed in Chapter 2. Working on these aspects of intonation will therefore be hugely beneficial for international intelligibility.

There will be an equally large pay-off in terms of teaching and learning. We can teach learners how this nuclear syllable is produced, focusing, in particular, on its extra length—a feature that may be peculiar to English. But for learners to be able to maintain syllabic length comfortably, they will also need to work on articulatory setting and, again, this is something which can be taught and learnt in the classroom (see next section). The prominence thus accorded to the nuclear syllable will compensate for the lack of weak forms, just as it does in the speech of others who eschew the latter (see above, pages 146–8): learners will be understood through their foregrounding of the most important part of their message, without needing to reduce the less important part.

As far as nuclear placement is concerned, the rules, both unmarked and contrastive, are simple enough for learners to master in the classroom, 'carry around' with them, and automatize as procedural knowledge. Pedagogically, nuclear stress can be easily integrated receptively and productively into almost all classroom work: into the teaching of grammar and structure, lexical phrases, and the development of listening and speaking skills. Rules can be taught overtly, though with the caveat that it is not sufficient to tell students simply to stress the 'most important' word— they need help in working out how to identify this word. L1–L2 specific similarities and differences in signalling and placing nuclear stress can be discussed—and note the advantage held by the 'non-native' teacher in comparative discussion of this kind.

The final feature of the intonation system which we need to consider is that of word groups (tone units). This concerns the way in which English speakers divide their utterances into smaller meaningful units, or chunks, each containing one nuclear syllable (though complex word groups contain more than one nucleus). The division between one word group and the next is often achieved by pauses at the boundaries or, less commonly, by a change in key (overall pitch level) or rhythm.

We noted in Chapter 2 (page 45) that one of the factors regularly contributing to learners' problems with nuclear stress is their inability to segment the speech stream into word groups. Even if this were not so, it is difficult to see how teachers could explain the rules of nuclear stress placement coherently without reference to word grouping. So although the ILT data does not include examples of miscommunication caused specifically by the lack of (or inappropriate) word grouping, its potential to affect nuclear placement and its usefulness in pedagogic description necessitate its inclusion in the LFC.

A further advantage in prioritizing word groups, as we also noted earlier (see page 45), concerns planning time for non-bilingual speakers. As Brazil says: 'If, as I think is the case, the tone unit is the minimal stretch of speech for which assembly plans are made, this assigns an important purpose to the interval between them: it is the time the speakers can use for planning' (1996: 9). But in ILT, the listeners are also non-bilinguals. The interval between word groups thus not only helps speakers with planning, but also provides crucial support to listeners, by indicating which words they should process together for meaning, and providing them with the time to do so.

3 Articulatory settings

The third and final area of importance in the LFC is concerned not with individual features of the pronunciation system but with certain holistic factors involved in their production. Languages differ quite radically in their articulatory settings, with 'general differences in tension, in tongue shape, in pressure of the articulators, in lip and cheek and jaw posture and movement, which run through the whole articulatory process' (O'Connor 1973: 289).

Faulty articulatory settings make it far more difficult for learners to achieve (near-)target pronunciations in those areas which cause particular intelligibility problems in EIL, i.e. consonant and nuclear stress production. This is because articulatory settings act as a kind of link or pivot between the segmentals and suprasegmentals. On the other hand, mastery in this area both facilitates the production of core sounds and enables the speaker to manipulate these sounds to produce nuclear stress, i.e. to utter sounds with greater length, loudness, and (if the English tone system is ultimately acquired) pitch movement. If the articulators are not comfortably positioned, such manoeuvres will prove extremely difficult (see Jenkins 1998a), if not impossible, whereas 'concentrating on this holistic aspect of pronunciation ... makes it easier to allow suprasegmental and segmental aspects to work in unison' (Dalton and Seidlhofer 1994a: 142).[15]

As long ago as 1964, Honikman pointed out the difficulty of acquiring the pronunciation of a second language whilst maintaining the articulatory settings of the first—though in fact recent research by Jenner reveals that she was responsible 'not so much for an original idea ... but for restoring it to respectability' (1997b: 31) and traces the concept back to Sweet and others in the late 19th Century. Since Honikman's time, a small number of pronunciation writers (for example, O'Connor 1973; Bradford 1982; Jenner 1992; and Thornbury 1993) have likewise claimed the wisdom of starting holistically from setting and thence moving on to work on individual sounds. The implication underlying their claims is that learners of a second language approach its pronunciation with their articulators still geared to the production of their L1 sounds (and prosodic features—though these are rarely mentioned by name). Thus, they begin the process of trying to acquire the phonology of the L2 at a serious disadvantage, since many of its sounds are virtually impossible to produce unless the articulators adopt the same positions, types of movement, and degree of muscular activity as those employed by L1 speakers.

The difficulties that learners encounter in adapting to L2 articulatory settings generally relate to the types of movements that the articulators, particularly the tongue, lips, and velum (soft palate) engage in, the degree of muscularity and tension involved, and jaw, cheek, and lip posture. Bradford (1982: 17) suggests that the following aspects of articulation will cause problems for L2 learners of English:

- the fact that the main focus is the tongue-tip on the alveolar ridge, whereas in many L1s it is elsewhere;
- the relative laxness of all English consonants as compared with the excessive muscularity of some learners' L1s (for example, French and Italian);
- the tongue's centre of gravity in mid-to-forward position, leading to the centralization of vowels, whereas learners tend towards excessive vowel precision;
- the neutral character of lip movements with little rounding, spreading, or protrusion as compared with, for example, the vigorous lip-rounding and spreading movements of French speakers;
- the small degree of muscular effort involved in articulation; and the importance of the rest position for all articulators.

To this could be added the fact that L1 speakers of English tend to maintain their jaws in a loosely closed position and move them little (Honikman 1964). Problems in all these articulatory areas have the potential to lead to pronunciation errors at both segmental and suprasegmental[16] levels, and thus to affect intelligibility.

Voice quality, or phonation, may also affect intelligibility. Voice quality is the product of physiological activity in the larynx and tends to vary, sometimes quite drastically, from one L1 to another. Research has shown the voice quality of some L2 speakers of English to be less intelligible than that of others. For example, in one experiment designed to measure the intelligibility of L2 speakers of English, white noise was gradually reduced to the point where the raters could understand what was being said. It was concluded that understanding was far less a function of correct pronunciation than of voice quality: 'Voices which were less intelligible regardless of pronunciation were raspy, husky, hoarse, throaty, breathy, muffled, muted, falsetto, soft, and/or low. Clear, sharp voices were intelligible much sooner' (Leventhal 1980: 20).

Having made these points, there are, however, a couple of provisos. First, we are mainly concerned with intelligibility not for 'native speakers' but for other L2 speakers of English. All of the work cited above, on the other hand, has been carried out with L1 receivers chiefly in mind. Second, the goal of these writers is for learners of English to sound as 'native-like' as possible—a concept which has little relevance for EIL. Only Jenner sounds a note of caution: 'Many learners, on facing up to the realities of native-like voice quality and articulation ... may decide that although they wish to speak English fluently, they neither want nor need to sound like a native speaker. They may wish to preserve some vestige of a foreign accent as a mark of their identity or nationality, and as a signal to the listener to "make allowances"' (1992: 39). But note that even he seems to have L1 listeners (the people who will 'make allowances') in mind, and to entertain the idea of preservation of only a 'vestige' of the L2 accent. EIL has moved on a long way from this. Nevertheless, there is still a need for research to identify precisely which aspects of articulatory setting and voice quality are most crucial for the preservation of phonological intelligibility in EIL contexts. At present, all we can say with confidence is that some, but not all, aspects will probably turn out to be very important indeed.

Redefining phonological error and correctness for EIL

It is now time to redefine phonological error for EIL contexts of communication. The Lingua Franca Core is neither a pronunciation model nor a restricted, simplified core in the style of Quirk's Nuclear English (1982). Although contrived (in that it embraces features from GA, RP, and L2 varieties of English) and to some extent prescriptive, the LFC allows far greater individual freedom than the latter two approaches, by providing speakers with the scope both to express their own identities and to accommodate to their receivers (see the next chapter). In this sense it is, like a polymodel approach, 'based on pragmatism and functional realism' (Kachru 1992: 66).

The Lingua Franca Core
According to the LFC, phonological error in EIL involves an error in producing any of the following (not in any order of priority):

1 The consonantal inventory with the following provisos:
   - rhotic [ɻ] rather than other varieties of /r/
   - intervocalic /t/ rather than [ɾ]
   - most substitutions of /θ/, /ð/, and [ɫ] permissible
   - close approximations to core consonant sounds generally permissible
   - certain approximations not permissible (i.e. where there is a risk that they will be heard as a different consonant sound from that intended)

2 Phonetic requirements:
   - aspiration following the fortis plosives /p/, /t/, and /k/
   - fortis/lenis differential effect on preceding vowel length

3 Consonant clusters:
   - initial clusters not simplified
   - medial and final clusters simplified only according to L1 rules of elision

4 Vowel sounds:
   - maintenance of vowel length contrasts
   - L2 regional qualities permissible if consistent, but /ɜː/ to be preserved

5 Nuclear stress production and placement and division of speech stream into word groups.

Since the above areas are those in which pronunciation has the potential for EIL error, they are the ones which require pedagogic focus for production in EIL classrooms. Outside these areas, L2 variation should be regarded as regional accent variation akin to L1 regional variation, and pedagogy for EIL should be restricted to reception. Insistence on 'correctness' (i.e. 'nativelikeness') in the other areas can be described as insistence on conformity rather than on accuracy (Willis 1996; and see page 93 above). Indeed, accuracy in the sense of accuracy of meaning may be compromised if such conformity is insisted upon in non-core areas. This is because the use of some of the non-core features, like weak forms and other features of connected speech, may impede intelligibility in EIL whether spoken quickly by a BES or slowly by an NBES (see pages 146–9). And, in any case, the assumption that a 'native speaker' is the most intelligible, and therefore that conformity to 'native-speaker norms' will result in greatest intelligibility, is itself flawed. L1 speakers are only intelligible to L2 speakers if they provided the teaching model and, for the vast majority of the world's speakers of English, this is simply not so. Ultimately, it is probably true to say that L1 speakers of English are only more intelligible than L2 speakers of English to other L1 speakers (Barbara Seidlhofer, personal communication).

The LFC thus defines phonological error in relation to its effect on intelligibility in EIL contexts and by taking into account what is actually teachable and thus learnable in the classroom by most L2 speakers of English. There really is no justification for doggedly persisting in referring to an item as 'an error' if the vast majority of the world's L2 English speakers produce and understand it. Instead, it is for L1 speakers to move their own receptive goal posts and adjust their own expectations as far as *international* (but not *intranational*) uses of English are concerned. Intranationally, it remains the prerogative of ENL speakers in the inner circle and ESL speakers in the outer circle to define their own norms and thus what constitutes a pronunciation error (although the USA is to some extent an exception—see Chapter 8).

The LFC also drastically simplifies the pedagogic task by removing from the syllabus many time-consuming items which are either unteachable or irrelevant for EIL (compare the five main areas of the LFC with the ten of Jenner's Common Core on page 126). This will enable pronunciation teaching to take account of the ingrainedness and complexity of L1 phonological transfer discussed earlier, and thus become far more realistic in its goals in no longer aiming to 'reduce' all evidence of transfer in learners' accents. Instead, EIL teachers will be able to focus on the 'adding'[17] of a small number of essential core items, leaving precious time to work on these more thoroughly and therefore with far greater hope of success than erstwhile, and to develop their learners' accommodation skills (see next chapter).

Acceptability

One final point: I have as yet said little about the issue of EIL acceptability. In fact, as far as EIL is concerned, this is a less salient concern than it is in EFL. L2 speakers tend to be rather less judgemental over each other's pronunciation of English provided it is intelligible than do L1 speakers. James, reciting the views of Mey, says 'NSs are at their most authoritative on matters of phonology, less so on morphology, less still on syntax, and least on semantics. Moreover, this scale corresponds to a scale of the NSs' tolerance of linguistic deviance: they instinctively abhor phonological deviance, hate the morphological sort, merely dislike the syntactic, and can live with semantic deviance' (1998: 47). Such strength of feeling about the pronunciation of other L2 speakers of English was not once expressed during the course of my research. In fact, the only strongly expressed phonological attitude, voiced by a small number of respondents, was that they did not wish to sound like RP speakers. One (French) subject also admitted to feelings of embarrassment on hearing members of her own L1 group speaking English with a particularly strong French accent. In both these cases, the attitudes expressed relate to the issue of identity, an issue which we will examine in the final chapter.

As far as the LFC and phonological acceptability for EIL are concerned, there are two main factors. Firstly, is it acceptable to require L2 speakers of English to produce these core items? And secondly, is it acceptable to require L2 listeners to receive non-core items through the filter of speakers' L2 regional accents? As regards the first question, I can see little objection for those who do not wish to become more 'native-like' except that some may prefer to base their pronunciation on a particular L1 model, perhaps because they perceive it as having more prestige than others (see Saville-Troike 1996: 356). In fact, there is no reason why they should not do so if that is their preference.

In addition, there will always be learners of English who want or need to sound as 'native-like' as possible. But because of the international status of English, this group is not large. Discussing the learning of English for international uses as if it were no different from the learning of other foreign languages such as Spanish, McCarthy and Carter argue that they 'would feel cheated and patronized' if a teacher of Spanish did not inform them as to how its 'NSs' speak to one another (1997: 16). But as Prodromou points out in his response, 'Most people quite simply do not learn English to speak to native-speakers. On the other hand, people learn Spanish ... because they are interested in Hispanic culture for some reason (work or pleasure) and will therefore want a spoken and written model which will further this aim. There is a world of difference between English and, in fact, all other living languages at present' (1997: 19). *Pace* McCarthy and Carter (1997), I have no desire to patronize those learners who wish to sound 'native-like' by telling them that they should/need not go to such lengths: it is their decision, not mine. My only proviso, in both these cases, would be that they should also learn the LFC in order to equip themselves for international communication. But doing this would actually involve very little additional work: merely the learning of the GA or RP version of a small number of items and the developing of accommodation skills (see Chapter 7). Otherwise, the only group who will initially have major objections to producing the LFC is likely to be the 'native speaker' group, but we will leave discussion of this problem to the final chapter.

As regards the second factor, the issue of reception of L2-influenced non-core items, because speakers will have a shared phonological core, and because they will also have learnt how to adjust their speech to accommodate to their different interlocutors, I do not envisage any serious problems. They speak the language with each other because they have the desire to communicate, and it is in the interests of all parties to try to understand each other and to be understood. None has a vested interest in the language *per se* or the feeling that it belongs more to them than to their interlocutors. It would be foolish to dismiss language attitudes as having no role in EIL, and this is a question to which we will return in the final chapter. However, for the time being I will simply suggest that assuming learners receive sufficient exposure to other L2 accents of English as part of the pedagogic process of developing their accommodation skills, the acceptability problem—if one arises at all—should be minimal.

I have said that the LFC allows speakers plenty of scope to adjust their pronunciation in order to accommodate to their receivers, and it is precisely to the developing of this skill that we turn in the next chapter.

Notes

1 Note Bhatia's (1997) use of the term 'added'—an important concept in the context of EIL, and one which we will take up in the final chapter in the discussion of accent addition.

2 'Dense fog now covers the whole of southern England, with visibility at a maximum of eighty metres. The airports of Heathrow, and Gatwick are unlikely to receive incoming flights until approximately eleven hundred hours. Aircraft are being diverted to Manchester, Prestwick or Paris.'

3 *ELT Links*, joint British Council–IATEFL SIG Symposium, University of Vienna, September 26–28 1996.

4 In a one-way ANOVA (Analysis of Variance) test. The variation between groups was significant at the 0.01 level.

5 The majority who do not have problems in producing /θ/ and /ð/ are speakers of English from Greece, Iceland, Spain and those Arabic speakers familiar with literary/classical Arabic.

6 This refers to the force of articulation, i.e. the amount of muscular tension used in the production of the consonant. The fortis consonants are those which are often referred to as 'voiceless' and the lenis as 'voiced'. However, this is strictly true only in the phonemic sense, and not necessarily in terms of phonetic realization, which will depend to some extent on the phonetic environment. Hence the terms 'fortis' and 'lenis', though less frequently used, are more accurate than 'voiceless' and 'voiced'.

7 There are some notable exceptions to this, such as Judy Gilbert's *Clear Speech* (1993), but most of the small number of pronunciation manuals which cover this important distinction are reference works for teachers, for example, Celce-Murcia et al's *Teaching Pronunciation* (1996), rather than coursebooks for use by students.

8 The one exception was the word 'toys' in which the diphthong /ɔɪ/ was pronounced as /aɪ/, thus giving the word 'ties'. The intelligibility problem may have resulted simply from the fact that the pronunciation of the diphthong produced a recognizable word (although it was not a word appropriate to the context being discussed). The other possibility is that Jenner's assessment of the need to retain the quality of these three diphthongs is correct, but as this was an isolated example of unintelligibility, I remain unconvinced.

9 This is an example of the way in which evidence drawn from frequency counts can be used to explain phenomena in the naturally occurring ILT data and to influence decisions as to the LFC's content, rather than to dictate them.

10 The people who advocate the teaching of weak forms are often those who also encourage the reciting of limericks. However, limericks nearly always begin with the two words 'There was', in which the 'was'—in order to preserve a stress-timed rhythm—is pronounced in its strong form /wɑz/ rather than its weak form /wəz/, which defeats the purpose of stress-timing altogether.

11 A group of words which forms a meaningful unit within the stream of speech, contains one nuclear syllable, and is separated from the previous and/or following word group(s) by a pause.

12 The L2 speakers were of an upper-intermediate level of proficiency and had been in Britain for two months at the time of the recording.

13 Each question consisted of two word groups.

14 Though while in English the contrastive item can remain implicit, for example, 'My son's bought a NEW computer', in Spanish the contrast must actually be stated, for example, (the Spanish equivalent of) 'My son's bought a NEW computer, not a second-HAND one'.

15 See Jenner (1992); Thornbury (1993); and Jones and Evans (1995) for a range of teaching strategies for working on articulatory settings and voice quality in the classroom.

16 The diaphragm and vocal cords play the greater part at suprasegmental level, with the former controlling the breath flow and thus the loudness aspect of stress, and the latter—along with the diaphragm—controlling pitch.

17 See the final chapter for a discussion of accent reduction and accent addition.

7 Pedagogic priorities 2: Negotiating intelligibility in the ELT classroom

Certainly, it is important for learners ... above all to have understood the implications of the well-established sociolinguistic maxim that linguistic consistency is not normal and indeed would be dysfunctional in a language used in a real speech community.

Milroy 1994: 168

In Chapter 4, I argued that listeners engaging in interlanguage talk are generally reluctant or even unable to compensate for one another's phonological shortcomings by utilizing contextual and cotextual cues to interpret meaning and, consequently, that phonological intelligibility is essential to successful ILT communication. In Chapter 5 we examined the influences exerted by the L1 on L2 pronunciation and, by extension, on the design of any phonological core. Then, in Chapter 6, I presented my core phonology for EIL, the Lingua Franca Core (LFC). This prioritizes for teaching those features which were identified in a corpus of ILT data as being crucial to the preservation of phonological intelligibility and which, because they also take into account the complex workings of L1 transfer, are pedagogically feasible.

However, while the teaching of the Lingua Franca Core is necessary, it is not sufficient. Although the LFC comprises only features which are considered to be teachable, in the sense that learning is likely to follow teaching, we cannot guarantee that all learners will make the effort to learn the core or, subsequent to learning, will actually use it at all times in all appropriate interactions. Inevitably there will be occasions when factors such as processing overload, nerves, strong emotion, and the like intrude. These, in turn, may cause a speaker to revert automatically to earlier and more firmly established pronunciation habits and so, very probably, to pronunciation containing L1 transfer in the core areas.

In Chapter 5 we noted that, generally speaking, there seems to be a one-to-one correspondence between the *relevant* (items essential for EIL intelligibility) and the *realistic* (items which are teachable), and between the *irrelevant* and the *unrealistic*. I argued, though, that if a particular feature was potentially unteachable because of strong transfer effects, but was also crucial to EIL intelligibility, then learners' motivation to be intelligible may override unteachability. This, I suggested, is so in the case of word-initial consonant clusters. Owing to the interaction of transfer with universal processes, consonant clusters in any position in a word are very difficult for most adult learners of English, but in word-initial position, the deletion of sounds threatens EIL intelligibility.

It may be, then, that what is crucial to intelligibility sometimes becomes teachable when learners discover its contribution to effective communication. But this is unlikely always to be the case. And if, as a result of future research, some features which I have designated 'non-core' turn out, after all, to be core, then the outcome may depend on their *degree* of unteachability, or difficulty. If, because of the interaction of transfer with universal or developmental processes, they are at the extreme limit of unteachability, then the best we can do is to prime learners for future learning by drawing their attention to these features. Learners will then be better placed to acquire them for habitual use through any future lengthy exposure outside the classroom. If features are unteachable for automatic use, but are produceable by means of great conscious effort, learners will need pedagogic input to enable them to appreciate both why it is sometimes necessary for them to make this effort, and precisely what is involved.

In essence, there are two issues at stake here, though they are, in fact, two sides of the same coin. On the one hand, speakers need to develop the ability to adjust their pronunciation according to the communicative situation in which they find themselves. This means that they need to be able to assess the relative necessity of pronunciation intelligibility for their interlocutor of the moment and, where this is high, to make the crucial adjustments that will guarantee it for that particular interlocutor. In other words, they need to be able to 'accommodate' (or more specifically, 'converge') towards their listeners. On the other hand, listeners also have a role to play. At the end of the first chapter, I spoke of the need for receivers of English, both L1 and L2, to develop greater tolerance of accent difference in general, and the ability to adjust their expectations to accommodate the specific interlocutor in the specific communication event. Listeners engaged in ILT have to accept that they cannot expect target pronunciation, even in the core areas, one hundred per cent of the time, and that they must learn to cope with a certain amount of L1 transfer.

In this chapter, we will consider what these productive and receptive accommodation skills involve, and how pedagogic means can be contrived to enable learners to develop them. But because the concept of accommodation is crucial to the discussion of phonological intelligibility that follows (just as the concept of L1 transfer was crucial to the discussion of the LFC), and because the term 'accommodation' is used somewhat loosely to cover a range of (often very general) meanings, we will first establish what accommodation entails according to accommodation theory.

Throughout the chapter, I will for the most part be using the term 'ILT' (interlanguage talk) in place of the broader 'EIL' (English as an International Language). This is to make clear that our interest in accommodation is grounded in interactions among non-bilingual English speakers (NBESs), that is, interactions in which the need for phonological intelligibility is similar for all interlocutors. Bilingual speakers of English, like L1 speakers, have far greater contextual and cotextual resources at their disposal, so that where accommodation occurs, it is less likely to be motivated by a desire for interlocutor intelligibility which, I will argue, is the prime motivation for accommodation in ILT.

Accommodation theory and intra-speaker variation in ILT

Our concern with accommodation skills relates specifically to their potential to enhance phonological intelligibility in ILT. In essence, we are dealing here with the question of *intra-speaker interlanguage variation* (see Chapter 3), in our case specifically the variation between correct and incorrect core phonological forms. In accounting for this variation, accommodation theory offers important pointers for the devising of classroom procedures that will encourage variation in the direction of correctness, when the intelligibility of core phonological items is crucial to the success of an interaction. So before we move on to the pedagogical implications, we will consider precisely why and how accommodation theory is able to account for phonological variation in ILT and, in so doing, will identify these pointers.

Accommodation theory (more correctly, Communication Accommodation Theory, or CAT)[1] is not the only theory which has been proposed to account for the variation between correct and incorrect forms in interlanguage. Nor has it been proposed that accommodation theory provides a unitary model to account for all levels of interlanguage variation. But several accounts of IL variation concur on the importance of social context and, in particular, the role of audience factors. Bell (1984), for instance, argues that variation is the result of adjustments, or accommodations made by speakers according to their interlocutors' personal characteristics, general speech style, and specific linguistic usage. He thus identifies social factors which are responsible for triggering both psychological and cognitive processes.

A description of the many other theories and models attempting to account for IL variation lies well beyond the scope of this book. Anyone wishing to pursue these should refer to Tarone (1988) for the most comprehensive survey of IL variation to date, as well as to the shorter surveys of Wolfram (1991), Ellis (1994), and Jenkins (1995). However, the main surveys of IL variation conclude, like Bell, that despite certain shortcomings, accommodation theory offers the most satisfactory explanation for IL variation to date. And, for reasons which we will consider, it is particularly relevant to phonological variation in ILT.

The accommodation framework

The theory originated in its earlier form of Speech Accommodation Theory (SAT) to account for the motivations underlying adjustments in people's speech, in particular the cognitive and affective processes underlying the speech strategies of convergence and divergence (making one's speech respectively more and less like that of one's interlocutor). The goals of such speech adjustments were claimed as one or more of the following: evoking the addressee's social approval, promoting communicative efficiency between interlocutors, and maintaining a positive social identity (Beebe and Giles 1984). The many studies conducted within the accommodation framework have tended to place greatest emphasis on the first and third of these goals, and the majority of them to investigate L1 interaction. However, studies of IL variation tend to focus on the motivation of communicative efficiency as being better able to account for adjustments made by L2 speakers in certain speech situations.

Accommodation theory draws on four social-psychological theories in order to explain style shifts. Firstly, the theory of similarity attraction, which claims that people are more attracted to those who share similar beliefs and attitudes than to others. Secondly, social exchange theory, according to which people weigh up the rewards and costs of alternatives before they act, usually selecting the alternative which will result in the greatest reward and smallest cost. Thirdly, the theory of causal attribution, which suggests that people evaluate one another's behaviour according to their interpretation of the motives underlying that behaviour. And fourthly, intergroup distinctiveness, according to which people attempt to maintain their group identity by retaining their distinctiveness from other groups. Beebe and Zuengler (1983) point out that it is possible for two or more of these facets to be operating at the same time to cause variation in a speaker's language and to offer an explanation for the strategies of convergence and divergence, which form the basis of accommodation theory.

The first work on accommodation was published in the early 1970s, when Giles (1973) demonstrated the phenomenon of interpersonal accent convergence in an interview situation, and introduced his 'accent mobility' model. He argued that instead of explaining situational variation by means of Labov's 'attention to speech' paradigm and the formality or informality of the context, the focus should shift to processes of interpersonal accommodation and, in particular, to receiver characteristics. These processes were subsequently incorporated into SAT and led to a plethora of further research by Giles and others, in which a wide range of speech variables were manipulated in a number of different settings. In its original form, SAT 'aimed to clarify the motivations underlying speech and intermeshed in it, as well as the constraints operating upon it and their social consequences' (Giles, Coupland, and Coupland 1991b: 6), by means of focusing on speech convergence and divergence, and attempting to explain the cognitive and affective motivations underlying them. Later, the theory was broadened to include other strategies, such as complementarity (which occurs in situations such as interviews, where role discrepancies are to be expected) and over-/under-accommodation. In more recent years, its scope has been further extended to incorporate a whole range of non-verbal and discursive dimensions of social interaction, which are reflected in its change of name to Communication Accommodation Theory (Giles and Coupland 1991: 63).

In essence, convergence is a strategy by which individuals adapt to one another's speech (SAT) and other communicative behaviours (CAT) in terms of a wide range of linguistic and prosodic features, such as speech rate, pauses, utterance length, pronunciation and, in the case of CAT, non-vocal features such as smiling and gaze. Divergence, on the other hand, refers to the way in which speakers emphasize speech and non-verbal differences between themselves and their interlocutors. Divergent strategies range from a few pronunciation and content differences to abuse and the switch to another language. Convergence is a strategy of identification with the communication patterns of an individual and thus internal to the interaction. Divergence, by contrast, is more often a strategy of identification with the communicative norms of a reference group and thus external to the interaction, and therefore predicted to occur more frequently in interactions where speakers have very different social identities. Maintenance, a third accommodation strategy, is in effect a type of divergence in that interactants preserve their speech patterns and other communicative behaviours across situations, in order to maintain their group identity.

Within these broad categories are a number of distinctions. Both convergence and divergence may be upward, by means of a shift towards a prestige variety, or downward by means of a shift away from it. They may also be uni- or multi-modal (respectively at one, and two or more levels), partial or total (where total would indicate a one hundred per cent matching of the interlocutor's speech on the dimension under consideration), symmetrical (reciprocal) or asymmetrical (non-reciprocal), large or moderate, and objective or subjective (convergence/divergence respectively to what is actually heard or to a belief about the interlocutor's speech, in other words, to a stereotype). There have also been found to be optimal rates of convergence (Giles and Smith 1979), with the phenomenon of 'overaccommodation' occurring when a speaker is considered by the recipient to be making more adjustments than necessary, and thus often leading to miscommunication despite the speaker's precise intention to produce the opposite effect (see Coupland et al. 1988, Zuengler 1989).

Of the three main motivations found to underlie convergence and divergence, the first two (to gain the interlocutor's approval and to communicate efficiently) relate primarily to convergence, and the third (to maintain a positive social identity) to divergence. In its unmarked form, convergence relates to the theory of similarity attraction, reflecting a speaker's often unconscious desire for identification with another, and the consequent adjustments made to his speech in order to sound more similar to the other. Various studies have shown that through convergence speakers may increase their attractiveness, predictability, intelligibility, and interpersonal involvement in the eyes of their interlocutor (Giles et al. 1987). Thakerar et al. point out, though, that 'the magnitude of speech convergence will be a function of the extent of the speakers' repertoires' (1982: 218), and this is something we will need to bear very much in mind in relation to ILT.

The second and third motivations for convergence, i.e. communicative efficiency (also referred to as 'communicational efficiency', 'communication efficiency', and 'communicative effectiveness') and identity maintenance, are psychological rather than affective in essence. A desire for communicative efficiency which, as stated above, may be the principal motivation for convergence, can lead to the cognitive organization of a speaker's output. This involves the speaker's organizing of his or her speech to take the recipient's requirements into account which, in turn, leads to increased intelligibility. Thakerar et al's (1982) seminal study of psychological convergence and divergence has demonstrated how a complementary relationship, such as that of interviewer and interviewee, can increase mutual predictability, which is also likely to facilitate understanding. More recently, research into discourse attuning has shown how a speaker takes into consideration the recipient's ability to understand, i.e. his or her 'interpretive competence', and has postulated a range of 'interpretability' strategies (see Coupland et al. 1988).

The communicative efficiency motivation is of particular relevance to ILT research. Speakers who find themselves together in an attempt to accomplish a particular task, the successful accomplishment of which is to their mutual advantage, will be instrumentally motivated to facilitate communication in order to achieve a successful outcome. If these speakers come from different linguistic and cultural backgrounds, then accommodative processes will have a far greater role in enhancing mutual comprehension than they would in communication between speakers from similar backgrounds. In particular, when widely differing accents come into contact in such speech situations, their users will probably feel strong internal pressure to converge phonologically in some way, in order to promote their own intelligibility.

The communicative efficiency motivation will be discussed in this chapter as the primary motivation for attempts at phonological convergence, and thus for IL phonological variation in ILT contexts. In other words, variation in these contexts can largely be viewed not as the negative lapsing into error of intermittently correct items, but as the positive making of effort (whether consciously or subconsciously) to rectify intermittently incorrect items, even though the speaker's repertoire and level of competence may conspire against this intention.

In proposing the updated 'reformulated SAT', Giles et al. argued that 'SAT presents a broad and robust basis from which to examine mutual influences in communication, taking account of social and cognitive factors, and having the scope to cover the social consequences of speech shifts as well as their determinants and the motivations underlying them' and has 'the flexibility of relevance at both interpersonal and intergroup levels' (1987: 34). For the future, they suggested that, among other things, 'an SAT perspective might have applied relevance for situations rife in potential miscommunication and misattribution' (ibid.: 41). With this in mind, we will move on to consider the accommodation framework in relation to ILT, a context which—as we have already seen—is 'rife in potential miscommunication'.

Accommodation theory: an explanation for phonological variation in ILT

Since L1 pronunciation is to a considerable extent the product of habit, its features are likely to be transferred automatically in the production of a second language. The transfer process commonly results in an abundance of L1-specific pronunciation 'errors' of the kind we observed in Chapter 2, which by definition vary from speakers of one L1 to another. Such phonological deviations from the target pronunciation are most likely to occur when there is a lack of monitoring of pronunciation performance, as contrasted with syntactic and morphological errors, which often occur despite monitoring, as a result of learners' processing difficulties relating to degree of knowledge and control of the L2.

Turning to hearer factors, we noted at length in Chapter 4 that NBES receivers have a tendency to process language with minimal reference to contextual cues and instead to focus primarily on the acoustic signal. Error-free pronunciation in terms of the subset of error types (i.e. the LFC) that was proposed in Chapter 6 is therefore crucial as a first stage in facilitating the NBES hearer's ability to interpret spoken interlanguage. However, interlanguage pronunciation is rarely free even of this subset until a relatively late stage in the SLA process. And to compound the problem, because of their L1-specific nature, phonological transfer errors potentially pose a far greater threat to ILT listeners than do errors from other linguistic areas, where there is more common ground among NBESs (see Ioup's 1984 study comparing written and spoken ILs). The subjects who took part in my ILT studies, when interviewed, invariably cited their interlocutor's pronunciation as the cause of mis- or non-understanding.

So, because the problem operates at both speaker and hearer level in ILT, phonological transfer errors are far more likely to lead to problematic communication here than they are in 'native/non-native' interaction. However, the principal motivation for most adult learners of English is their wish to be able to communicate intelligibly with other speakers of English, and in the 21st Century, these are most likely to be NBESs from *different* L1 backgrounds. Thus, we can predict that in those ILT situations where the conveying of information is highly salient to speakers, they will monitor their pronunciation and attempt to adjust it by means of some sort of convergence towards that of their NBES addressees. Where they are successful, the result will be a decrease in the phonological differences between themselves and their addressees, so rendering their speech more intelligible to the latter. In this respect, it seems that the motivation underlying convergence in ILT, that of communicative efficiency, is the same as the motivation which underlies recoverability. For, as we saw in Chapter 5, it is the desire to promote addressee comprehension which determines the selection of certain phonological simplification strategies over others—in particular, epenthesis over consonant deletion.

On the other hand, the socio-psychological concepts of intergroup distinctiveness and identity assertion in which accommodation theory was originally rooted are rather less relevant to ILT. For while the notion of group dynamics is central to accommodation in ILT, these dynamics are bound to operate very differently when membership moves from that of an L1 group to that of a global community. Tarone asks 'what is the speech community of the second-language learner? Where all learners speak the same native language and share the same culture, this may be clear. But what about the case of the ESL classroom where nearly every learner may come from a different native-language background? With what speech community(ies) does a learner in this situation identify?' (1988: 118).

The EIL speech community is a complicated one. On the one hand, speakers are claiming membership at a global level; they are speaking English as a lingua franca in order to make themselves intelligible to other members of the EIL community and would not wish to diverge phonologically, since to do so would be to jeopardize intelligibility and thus defeat their very purpose in using English. On the other hand, the majority will not want to lose their L1 identity when they speak their L2 English and this will mean preserving something of their L1 accent. The Lingua Franca

Core solves the dilemma by providing scope for both convergence and maintenance: NBESs are encouraged to converge on those L2 features which are essential to intelligibility in ILT, but are at liberty to maintain those features of their L1 where intelligibility is not at stake.

The promotion of interlocutor comprehension was first mooted as a *primary* motivation for speech convergence by Thakerar et al. (*1982*) and has subsequently been researched by others such as Shockey (*1984*) and Takahashi (*1989*). Giles and Coupland, the originators of accommodation theory in the 1970s, have more recently claimed for it 'cognitive organization versus identity-maintenance functions', arguing that 'increased intelligibility is a valuable byproduct of convergent acts and may on occasion be the *principal* motivation for accommodating' (*1991*: 85; emphasis added). The latter is undoubtedly true of ILT, whose unique set of speaker and hearer factors mean that pronunciation errors (i.e. in core areas) at best necessitate much negotiation of meaning and consequent interruption to the flow of conversation, and at worst cause a total breakdown in communication. Perhaps most importantly for our present purposes, accommodation theory not only explains why and how NBESs attempt to adjust their pronunciation in order to decrease the differences between themselves and their NBES interlocutors but, in so doing, also provides clues as to how pedagogic intervention may increase the success rate of these attempts.

A number of problems have, nevertheless, been raised in relation to the application of accommodation theory to IL variation. For example, Tarone has argued that since most of the work has been done with dialect speakers or fluent bilinguals rather than with L2 learners, we have not accumulated sufficient second language data to examine IL variation within this framework. Again, she considers that some style shifts in IL may not be caused by interlocutor effects but by situational norms and 'the communicative demands of different genres' and, therefore, that 'group membership and the individual identity assertion associated with it may be only one of several possible causes of interlanguage variation' (*1988*: 50–1). The latter point, though, can be countered with the argument that the current accommodation (CAT) framework by no means limits the causes of IL variation to 'group membership and the individual identity assertion'. The communicative efficiency motivation is also considered important, particularly in 'native/non-native' (as opposed to same-L1 'non-native') communication, and is thought by some, including myself, to be by far the most salient factor in ILT. To this can be added that 'the communicative demands of different genres' are likely to be inextricably bound up with interlocutor effects.

Despite her objections, Tarone summarizes her account of the empirical evidence for interlocutor effects on IL variation by making two points:

> ... first, there does seem to be clear evidence that second-language learners produce different variants in response to different interlocutors; but, second, there are surprisingly few studies documenting this effect. There are a number of interesting hypotheses which could be explored by further research, but clearly more data are needed.
> (ibid.: 92)

Referring specifically to SAT, Tarone reiterates Beebe's claims (in a 1982 plenary address) that the approach provided by SAT has a number of advantages over the 'attention to speech' model:

> ... it focuses upon determinable social and social-psychological factors like multiple group membership and more directly inferrable factors like identity assertion as causes of IL variation rather than postulating an unobservable intermediary process of 'attention' ... it allows the researcher to determine the origin of the variants which make up the different styles of interlanguage ... to analyse interlanguage as well as foreigner talk and code-switching within the same framework ... to study shifts in amount of talk, speech rate, duration, pause and utterance length, stress, pitch, intonation, and even in the content expressed—none of which are factors easily analysed in terms of grammatical correctness.
> (1988: 49)

Zuengler, in similar vein, concludes that 'CAT appears promising as a theory of L2 sociolinguistic variation' and that 'it is essential that further research be conducted within a CAT paradigm to determine the extent to which the theory can help us explain the complexities of nonnative speech' (1991: 233–4).

The accommodation framework in previous interlanguage variation research

A problem which we have already identified for research into accommodation in IL and ILT settings is that most of the work has been conducted in either L1 dialect or L2 fluent (bilingual) contexts. There has nevertheless been a small but steady growth in the study of second language learners within the accommodation framework, although almost entirely in 'NS–NNS' rather than ILT contexts. And disappointingly, accommodation theory applied to interlanguage variation—like other sociolinguistic theories of IL variation—has often been discussed with little by way of empirical support from L2 data, with researchers tending to rely on L1 data and anecdotal evidence. So although accommodation theory has been recognized as having the scope to account for synchronic variation in interlanguage, as Zuengler (1991) points out, there is as yet no large body of L2 data to give substance to the view.

The majority of studies of IL variation conducted within the accommodation framework focus on phonological variation.[2] Although these studies all find evidence of accommodative processes at work in IL variation, their results are not all significant. Zuengler (1989) accounts for this in terms of linguistic proficiency: some forms may simply not be in the NBES's repertoire. This means that however strong a speaker's desires to converge, they will be unable to do so where these items are concerned.

We will consider in more detail two areas of research into IL accommodation which have particular relevance for ILT itself: research into the communicative efficiency motivation, and that into the role of speakers' L2 repertoires.

Communicative efficiency and interlanguage

Several sources attest to the growing importance that researchers have begun to attach to communicative efficiency since the early 1980s. At the level of content, Giles and Smith (1979) had already focused on the issue in the early days of SAT. They had drawn attention to the fact that speakers take into consideration the listener's knowledge and converge by, for example, using less jargon with an interlocutor who does not share their expertise, in order to increase mutual intelligibility. The first study to suggest specifically that increased intelligibility rather than social approval may be, in many cases, the central motivation for accommodative behaviour was that of Thakerar et al. (1982). Others have subsequently taken up their claim. For example, Bell argues that 'in concentrating on approval seeking as a reason for style shift, accommodation has often overlooked a more transparent motivation: a speaker's desire to be understood' (1984: 199). Coupland (1984), reporting a personal communication from Thakerar, suggests that communicative efficiency is more relevant than social approval in his own study of accommodation in a travel agent setting.

Where interlocutors have different accents, particularly in bilingual situations, mutual intelligibility becomes an increasing problem and, as Bell points out, 'the sharper the linguistic differences between codes, the larger the issue of intelligibility looms, the stronger are the pressures to accommodate to the audience' (1984: 176). Describing the doctoral research of Shehadeh (1991), a Syrian researcher then at Durham University, Lynch reports that in his investigation of conversation between L2 learners of English, Shehadeh demonstrates that 'certain types of pair and group work create conditions for interaction in which learners push each other to speak more comprehensibly and more accurately' (1996: 77). In the second half of the chapter, we will return to the topic of pair and group work and the ways in which they can be manipulated in the classroom to induce accommodation.

A study carried out by Takahashi (1989) to investigate accommodation within an ILT setting lends particularly strong support to the claim that speakers are likely to converge towards the speech of their interlocutors in ILT contexts chiefly in order to promote intelligibility. Takahashi examined the speech adjustments of six female Japanese learners of English, three of intermediate level and three of advanced level. All were interviewed by a high and low proficiency Japanese and a high and low proficiency Spanish speaker of English. Their conversations were analysed with respect to four quantitative variables: the length of speech and fluency; the amount of talk; the number of questions; and the use of meaning negotiation. Although Takahashi did not consider them in her own study, she recommends that similar future research would do well to investigate qualitative changes to L2 speakers' pronunciation and syntactic complexity.

In analysing her data, Takahashi found the interlocutor to be an important factor in influencing the subjects' speech at both linguistic and psychological levels. Of particular interest to us is her discovery that the advanced speakers converged at a statistically significant level towards the proficiency level of their interviewers: they increased the amount of speech with their high proficiency interviewers and decreased it with their low proficiency interviewers. By contrast, the intermediate speakers spoke more than their low proficiency interlocutors, but less than their high proficiency interlocutors. Thus it appears that convergence occurred on this variable where it was within the competence of the L2 speaker to adjust her speech in the direction of that of the interviewer. Where this was not so, however, convergence did not occur.

Accommodation and IL repertoire

This leads straight into our second central issue: that of the speaker's repertoire. In the case of Takahashi's lower and intermediate level subjects, they did not increase their amount of speech to converge on that of their higher-level interlocutors because it was not within their repertoires to do so. L2 speakers engaged in ILT are very likely to have the motivation to adjust their speech in the direction of their receiver, but not to have the ability to do so. And in this respect, pronunciation provides a particularly strong barrier to successful convergence, chiefly because 'in addition to the social and psychological factors that affect all language performance, L2 speech is always subject to L1 interference' (Beebe and Giles 1984: 18). And as was discussed earlier at some length, such 'interference' (preferably 'transfer', or better still, 'crosslinguistic influence') is reflected most extensively at the phonological level, and in ILT tends to involve movement away from a target form in different directions.

It appears, then, that speakers engaged in ILT have not only competence limitations regarding the target language, but also repertoire problems in relation to their different-L1 interlocutors. In particular, they are unlikely to be able to match their partners' pronunciations, on account of the L1-specific nature of many of them. At the same time, however, their motivation to adjust their speech in order to promote greater intelligibility for their NBES interlocutors is in all probability very high. Thus, as Beebe and Giles warn, when we extend accommodation theory to SLA data, it is important that we consider repertoire limitations: 'for it is the tension between limitations in *ability* to converge ... and *motivation* to converge that makes second-language data unique ... With native speakers and fluent bilinguals, we assume that the ability to converge is there. With second-language learners, the capability may not be there' (1984: 23; emphasis in original). In effect, the spirit is willing but the flesh is sometimes weak.

Having considered the relatively small amount of research into the use of accommodation by IL speakers that is most relevant to our interest in ILT, we will take a brief look at the phenomenon of *foreigner talk*. Although this concerns adjustments made in the speech of an L2 speaker's 'native speaker' interlocutor, foreigner talk is of interest because it provides useful insights into both the features of L2 speech which elicit such adjustments, and the role of the communicative efficiency motivation in determining the type and degree of adjustments.

Foreigner talk

The phenomenon of foreigner talk (henceforth FT) was first documented in the early 1970s, the term being introduced by Ferguson (1971). It refers to the simplified register which 'native speakers' use to address 'non-native speakers' and is, Ferguson suggests, like baby talk, a reflection of the formers' belief about the way the latter speak. Arthur et al. describe FT as arising from language users' 'unconscious ability to make a number of coordinated adjustments in their language that have the net result of simplifying and facilitating communication' (1980: 113), thus making a case for FT as accommodation motivated by communicative efficiency. Such simplification, they argue, can be elicited by an interlocutor's 'non-native' accent.

Much information on the linguistic features of FT has been gathered. The most salient characteristics are generally agreed to be the following: less syntactical complexity, fewer pronouns, the use of higher frequency vocabulary, more clearly articulated pronunciation (to the extent of unnaturalness, for example, by the avoidance of contractions and weak forms), slower speech rate, more questions (often for the purpose of checking understanding), as well as the tendency to speak more loudly, and to repeat. However, there is still no general agreement as to exactly what triggers FT, or why it varies across 'native speakers' or across combinations used by the same speaker on different occasions.

Two studies, Varonis and Gass (1982) and Gass and Varonis (1985a), investigate what features of 'non-native' speech elicit FT. Varonis and Gass (1982) reveals that when 'native speakers' are asked for information both by other 'native speakers' and by 'non-native speakers', they differentiate between the two groups in terms of the forms of response used, even when the latter group have spoken in grammatically correct language: when replying to the 'non-natives' the 'native speakers' repeated the most important part of the message, usually with rising intonation such as would normally be associated with a question. The study goes on to investigate why this should be so, and finds that when 'native speakers' evaluate and react to the speech of 'non-natives', the most salient factor is 'the comprehensibility of the total linguistic input from the non-native to the native', and that such comprehensibility 'may be achieved in a number of different ways through the interaction of various linguistic and social factors'. The authors consider these to be pronunciation (a major factor), grammar, familiarity with topic, familiarity with person, familiarity with speaker's native language, fluency, and social factors (ibid.: 132).

Gass and Varonis (1985a) builds on this, as does other work by the same authors. For example, Gass and Varonis (1984) found that a 'native speaker's' familiarity with 'non-native' speech in general affected positively the 'native speaker's' ability to understand a particular 'non-native speaker'. This in turn is likely to reduce the amount of FT used (a point not actually made in the study). Gass and Varonis (1985a) demonstrate that 'non-native speaker' proficiency is determined mainly by pronunciation, fluency, and comprehension. During the course of an interaction, the 'native-speaker' subjects appear to reassess their interlocutors on the basis of their own ability to understand them (this ability at least partly determined by pronunciation), and to adjust their speech accordingly. FT modifications are apparently greatest for those 'non-native speakers' who are involved in a large number of negotiations of meaning during the middle section of the interaction.

The authors account for their findings by suggesting that the 'native speakers' determined that their interlocutors were more difficult to understand than they had originally predicted them to be. This leads the authors to claim that 'comprehensibility is one variable that triggers NS speech modification' or, in other words, FT. They also suggest that 'it is intuitive that NS modifications to NNSs are made for the purpose of increasing the possibility that the NNS will comprehend' (1985a: 54), though they point out that this may involve perceived rather than actual comprehension, since evidence of lack of comprehension is not a precondition for FT. Indeed, such talk was used before the 'non-native' interlocutor had demonstrated either comprehension or the lack of it.

We therefore have some possible explanations for the use of FT: as a response to the incomprehensibility of 'non-native' speech; as a response to apparent 'non-native speaker' lack of comprehension; and as a function of 'native speaker' stereotyping of their interlocutors. However, none of this explains the variation found in FT. Zuengler suggests that placing FT within the framework of accommodation theory 'will clarify much of the variation ... and bring a coherence to the literature' (1991: 235). Zuengler starts by examining 'native speaker' goals in communicating with 'non-native speakers'. She argues that many of these coincide with the speaker goals conceptualized in CAT, particularly the desire for communicative efficiency and mutual comprehension. Likewise, it may be a particularly strong goal in certain types of 'native/non-native' interaction. For, as Zuengler points out, observers have noted a greater use of FT when 'native speakers' and 'non-native speakers' are involved in a two-way exchange of information than in one-way communication from the 'native speaker', as a result of greater concern for (mutual) comprehensibility.

Zuengler claims that for many 'native speakers' interacting with 'non-native speakers', two dimensions are salient: perceived ethnic and cultural difference, and the linguistic/communicative competence of the 'non-native speaker'. She argues that the 'native speaker' partner, having one of the goals of CAT (concern for mutual comprehensibility, a desire to gain the interlocutor's social approval, or a desire to maintain distinctiveness), will encode the strategies of convergence, divergence, or maintenance. Thus, FT adjustments to speech rate, pronunciation, and so on can be explained as the manifestation of convergence,[3] and a lack of FT features as the manifestation of maintenance or divergence reflecting an interlocutor's desire to maintain distinctiveness from the 'non-native' interlocutor.

ILT and accommodation: some conclusions

Beebe and Giles argued long ago that accommodation theory has the potential for 'breaking away from its essentially social-psychological mold and emerging more centrally and ... into the interdisciplinary arena' (1984: 9). This is precisely the situation as regards ILT, whose variation between correct and incorrect core phonological forms is fully explicable within an accommodation framework but largely outside the theory's original social-psychological parameters. As we saw in the data presented in Chapter 3, convergence in ILT manifests itself in non-traditional ways—that is, in a closer approximation to core target forms rather than in adjustments in the direction of an interlocutor's (incorrect) core forms—in situations where interlocutor comprehension is particularly salient. This is, perhaps, to be expected, bearing in mind speakers' repertoire limitations described above and the other phenomena peculiar to ILT discussed in Chapter 3.

But having established that accommodative processes occur in this manner in ILT, we need to incorporate the research finding into pedagogy for it to be meaningful. As Widdowson argues, unless the findings of IL research can be exploited 'to enable language teachers to contrive the most effective conditions possible in classrooms' for the language learning process to take place, by 'providing particular kinds of warrant for teacher intervention, then they are of little pedagogic value' (1984: 324). As far as accommodation is concerned, instead of leaving it to chance as we have done hitherto (albeit through ignorance rather than design), we can begin to plan ways of developing further in our learners the accommodation skills which the vast majority already possess in their L1 and are clearly motivated—but not always able—to utilize in their L2 English, particularly in ILT contexts.

As far as the pedagogic enterprise is concerned, the first step has already been taken. In order to reduce phonological errors, we must first understand their variable nature. This we are able to do by recourse to accommodation theory, according to which the greatest influence on the accuracy or otherwise of pronunciation in ILT is the salience of interlocutor comprehension. Where L2 phonological items are not fully acquired, speakers are likely to make the effort to adjust in the direction of correctness, rather than transferring the easier alternative from their L1, where they perceive a strong need for interlocutor comprehension, but to produce incorrect forms where they do not. We move now from theory to practice: to a consideration of how our knowledge of accommodation theory and its relevance to IL in general, and to ILT contexts in particular, can be put to good use in teaching.

Accommodating classrooms

So what are the implications for a pedagogy which aims above all to maximize learners' success in international contexts? To summarize what we have established so far:

1 understanding in ILT contexts is heavily dependent on phonological intelligibility;
2 phonological intelligibility resides in the correct (target-like) production of a group of core items;
3 NBESs desire and may be able, under certain conditions, to accommodate towards each other by converging on these core items.

However, the accommodative ability is embryonic in IL. In the vast majority of cases, pedagogic intervention is necessary if NBESs are to accommodate to their ILT interlocutors successfully, both productively and receptively, and in larger groups—quite possibly containing members of their own L1 group—as well as in different-L1 pairs (see below on the issue of conflicting group membership). We need, as teachers, to have the knowledge of precisely what these 'certain conditions' involve and of the extent to which it is possible for learners to rise above them, as it were, and accommodate to their interlocutors even where the particular linguistic and/or extra-linguistic circumstances render this more difficult.

Even when the conditions are ideal, accommodation in the traditional sense (i.e. speakers converging on their interlocutors' pronunciations) rarely occurs. In so far as NBESs share a common purpose, it is to get closer to each other in terms of the L2. They do not want to acquire one another's pronunciation errors and as long as their motivation for accommodating to their interlocutor remains purely that of communicative efficiency, they seem to have some sort of inbuilt mechanism (conscious or subconscious) which safeguards against this outcome. Even if, over a prolonged period of time, the motivation subsequently broadens to include that of social approval, realizations of traditional convergence only very occasionally occur. Among the half dozen examples in my data are the following: a Japanese learner converged on the speed and stress patterns of a Swiss-French peer; another Japanese learner occasionally used terminal devoicing (for example, she pronounced 'sad' as /sæt/) during the information exchange phase of some of her interactions with her Swiss-German partner; another Swiss-German learner occasionally echoed the American pronunciations of his Japanese interlocutor. These cases of traditional convergence involved friendships which had became very close, though only the longest one (that between the Japanese and Swiss-French learners, who were together daily for six months) resulted in acquisition in the sense that the Japanese learner's speech continued to manifest the Swiss-French characteristics when not in the company of her Swiss-French friend.

As a rule, though, interlocutors do not converge on one another's L2 accents even during the interaction, let alone afterwards. And even where speakers from different L1s actually *share* common transferred features in their English pronunciation, the same appears to be true, at least for those speakers who have not had much previous exposure to one another's accents. For example, in one interaction in my data, a Japanese speaker was recorded in extended communication with a Portuguese speaker (from Portugal) for the first time. Prior to this, the Japanese speaker had never communicated with a Portuguese L1 speaker, and the Portuguese speaker had had very limited exposure to Japanese accents. Both subjects had a tendency to drop final /n/ and nasalize the previous vowel sound. For example, the Japanese subject pronounced 'Japan' as [dʒæpæ̃] and 'considered' as [kɔ̃sidəd]; the Portuguese subject pronounced 'inland' as [-[ĩlænd]. Each makes this transfer error several times during the social exchange task, but when they move on to the information exchange task (where intelligibility is far more salient: see Chapter 3), the Portuguese subject does so only twice and the Japanese not at all. This is very different from the outcome in the same-L1 pairs, where the number of (shared) transferred features actually increased from the social exchange phase to the information exchange.

This suggests that in interaction between those from non-familiar L1 backgrounds, convergence takes the form of an attempt at the blanket replacement of 'high risk' L1 features rather than an attempt to match the interlocutor's similar pronunciations. It is very likely that both specific pedagogic intervention and repeated exposure to the other accent are necessary before interlocutors even become aware of such similarities across L1 accents. The latter point supports Bell's claim that people naturally converge more to each other in their speech on subsequent occasions (1984: 62), although more research is needed to support the claim for ILT.

The above all runs counter to the fear, frequently expressed by teachers and learners alike in multilingual classrooms, that learners will somehow acquire one another's pronunciation errors. Research in this area suggests that the fear is unfounded (see, for example, Porter 1986; Lightbown and Spada 1999). My own findings lead to the same conclusions. Even over time, subjects did not reveal more than a small sprinkling of one another's phonological transfer errors and, apart from the single example described above, it is inconceivable that they actually 'acquired' these errors in the sense of retaining them outside the accommodative situation. Both lack of repertoire and psychological resistance would militate against such acquisition.

Optimum conditions for accommodation in ILT

Having dismissed the phenomenon of traditional convergence as being largely irrelevant to ILT contexts, we move now to a consideration of the ideal conditions to elicit productive and receptive accommodation of the type we have identified in ILT: that is, productively the replacement of transferred items in the core with more target-like forms, and receptively the mental adjustments that render a listener more able to cope where such transfer replacement fails. I have argued above, in line with accommodation theory, that where certain conditions prevail, ILT interlocutors have a strong desire to make these adjustments for the sake of mutual intelligibility. However, successful realization of this desire is often another matter. While NBESs clearly do meet with a modicum of success when they make sufficient effort—as demonstrated by the data presented in Chapter 3—pedagogic intervention is needed to enable them to take maximum advantage of the conditions which elicited the wish to accommodate in the first place.

Below is a list of the conditions most likely to induce speaker and listener attempts to accommodate phonologically towards one another:

Conditions for productive convergence:
- interlocutor intelligibility is the most salient aspect of the interaction to the speaker
- the speaker appreciates the listener's difficulties in making use of extralinguistic context

– the target item is within the speaker's repertoire and can be produced effortlessly
– there is no processing overload to prevent a focus on pronunciation.

Conditions for receptive convergence:
– the receiver is motivated to understand
– the receiver has had prior exposure to the speaker's accent
– the receiver has had prior exposure to a range of L2 accents and has developed a tolerance of difference
– the receiver does not have a fear of acquiring the speaker's transfer errors
– the receiver is linguistically and affectively able to signal non-comprehension.

These conditions divide into two further categories: interlocutor factors and situational factors. The former comprises the speaker's phonological repertoire and awareness of listener difficulty with context, and the receiver's familiarity with other L2 accents, attitude towards L2 errors, and ability to signal non-comprehension. The latter comprises those features of the situation which increase the speaker's motivation to be intelligible and the listener's to understand, and the processing load on the speaker. In all these cases, it is a relatively straightforward matter for teachers to devise appropriate classroom activities that will help their learners build on whatever pre-existing motivation to accommodate they already possess, and develop whatever skills they have already acquired in this direction.

Before turning to specific ideas for contriving and enhancing these conditions in order to develop learners' accommodation skills in the EIL classroom, I will discuss these conditions in greater detail, focusing on how they can be maximized through classroom teaching, to increase the likelihood that learners will in the future be able to translate their accommodative desire into linguistic action. Because there is often a considerable degree of overlap between productive and receptive conditions, I have regrouped the items, for the purposes of the discussion which follows, into the interlocutor and situational factors outlined in the previous paragraph.

Interlocutor factors

Phonological repertoire
In this category, we are concerned above all with speaker and hearer phonological repertoires. Because interlocutors, by definition, are both speakers and receivers, in practice both sets of repertoires (productive and receptive) are necessary for all participants engaged in ILT. On the one hand, speakers need within their productive repertoires the features identified as crucial to intelligibility in the Lingua Franca Core and, moreover, need to be able to produce these items with relative ease. This means

184 The Phonology of English as an International Language

that most, if not all, NBESs will need to acquire some new pronunciation habits in the core areas. Without these additions to their pronunciation repertoires, speakers will lack the essential resources to enable them to adjust their pronunciation in the direction of more target-like production, no matter how strong their desire to do so.

On the other hand, receivers need to range far beyond the limits of the LFC in their receptive repertoires in order to be able to cope with the inevitable failures of their interlocutors to make core adjustments when other factors intrude and make it difficult for them to do so. This involves two factors. Firstly, the addition to learners' receptive repertoires of a range of L2 and L1 accents of English. Initially these should be the accent varieties of those speakers with whom they are most likely to interact, but over time they will be able to add to this repertoire. The best way for this familiarity to be achieved is through repeated pedagogic exposure to other accents, with attention in the early stages of exposure being drawn to areas of difference, especially where these areas are core items and thus 'high risk'. Secondly, learners need to develop a greater awareness of the fact of L2 variation in general (particularly in core areas) and a readiness to attempt to cope with it, especially when faced with a completely 'new' accent. In fact, the second development should eventually occur automatically as a consequence of the first—although both can undoubtedly be speeded up by appropriate classroom teaching. L2 speakers of English thus become 'inter-accental' speakers of English (see Chapter 8).

Context

A second interlocutor factor relates to a speaker/receiver difference in the use of extralinguistic context, something that I touched on earlier (page 90). In the ILT data, there are occasions when interlocutor comprehension was highly salient to the speaker, and yet the latter did not make the effort to adjust non-target-like core pronunciations. My interpretation of these instances is that when deciding how much effort to invest in replacing phonological transfer, speakers weigh up (whether consciously or subconsciously) the risks involved for their interlocutors. If clear extralinguistic cues are available—such as the elicitation pictures used in my studies—speakers may decide that it is safe to relax their controls on pronunciation. In this case, transfer will only be replaced if the item is fully within the speaker's repertoire, i.e. is part of procedural as well as declarative knowledge. And this will be particularly so in cases where a phonological item is especially problematic for a speaker. For example, Japanese speakers of English famously have problems in producing /r/ which they regularly conflate with /l/ (far more so than vice versa) and the problem is inevitably far greater in the production of clusters such as /gr/ than in that of the single sound (see pages 90–1). This may well account for exchanges such as that reproduced on page 82, where the Japanese speaker, aware that her partner had a picture of a grey house before him, did not make the effort to produce the /gr/ of 'grey'.

It seems, then, that contextual cues are far more salient to L2 speakers than to listeners. Speakers, whether L1 or L2, tend to opt for the route of greatest ease where they do not predict negative effects for their listeners. In the case of ILT, speakers seem to lose sight very temporarily of the context-interpretation difficulties that they themselves have as listeners, and relax their control in relation to a difficult pronunciation if such context is available. Some sort of awareness raising is required here to enable NBESs while in the act of speaking to keep in mind their listener's orientation to context.

The ability to deal with non-comprehension

Again, this is something that I mentioned briefly in an earlier chapter (page 77), where I pointed out that many NBESs appear to be reluctant to signal their non-comprehension, particularly in ILT interactions. This reluctance may be the result of a listener's desire not to lose face by admitting non-understanding. Or, more plausibly in ILT, it may be the result of their desire not to cause an interlocutor's loss of face by pointing out that their speech is incomprehensible. This seems to be particularly so where pronunciation is concerned. As I described earlier, many of my subjects found one another's pronunciation difficult to understand, but a number were not prepared to mention the fact in their interlocutor's presence, and either wrote about it on their questionnaire or told me in private. In this case, their concerns probably relate to the issue of identity, and the fact that—as these subjects were aware from personal experience—one's identity is very closely bound up with one's L1 accent in L2.

A third possibility for the reluctance, however, is a purely linguistic one: a lack of appropriate language with which to signal the non-comprehension politely. As regards both the second and third possibilities, specific teaching can both demonstrate the helpfulness (to speaker as well as listener) of the listener's signalling their non-understanding, and provide linguistic models of ways to do so. As far as accommodation is concerned, in the absence of such signals, speakers will lack one of the main incentives to adjust their pronunciation, that is, evidence of their lack of intelligibility for their receivers.

Fear of phonological error acquisition

We considered this issue earlier (pages 181–2). The main point to emphasize here is that learners generally do not acquire the phonological errors of their peer groups. This only ever seems to happen in the case of the formation of very strong friendships, where the motivation for accommodation shifts along the *convergence continuum* away from communicative efficiency and in the direction of solidarity (the more common motivation for convergence in L1–L1 interaction)—see Figure 7.1. As I have already pointed out, in converging with an interlocutor, a speaker may indeed produce an occasional phonological error typical of the latter.

But the key word here is 'occasional'. The phenomenon is rare and the retention of these errors as acquired items (i.e. used in the absence of the specific interlocutor) is rarer still.

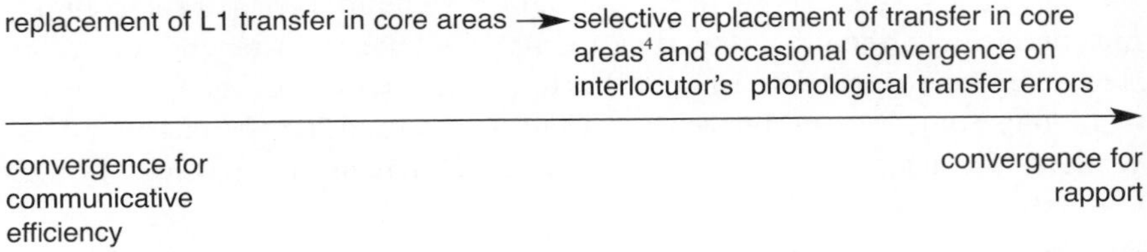

replacement of L1 transfer in core areas ——➤ selective replacement of transfer in core
                                            areas[4] and occasional convergence on
                                            interlocutor's phonological transfer errors

———➤

convergence for   convergence for
communicative   rapport
efficiency

Figure 7.1: Convergence continuum: changing motivations for convergence over time

And, in fact, the opposite is far more likely to happen, much to the surprise of learners when the evidence is presented to them. When I recorded learners in same-L1 pairs at the end of a ten-week period, during which I had recorded the same learners in different-L1 pairs, the results, as we saw earlier (pages 58–63) were extremely telling. When learners interacted with a partner from a different L1, they made many fewer pronunciation errors than they did in interactions with a partner from the same L1. Far from acquiring their different-L1 partner's errors, the chief influence of this partner was to cause them to make fewer of their own typical transfer errors. The subjects involved in this particular study were shocked when they listened to the recordings of their same-L1 dyad interactions, although they pointed out that they had understood one another rather more comfortably than they had understood their different-L1 partners. Nevertheless, they decided to take their CAE Speaking examination with the latter because they felt their performance would be rated more highly by the examiners if they made fewer phonological transfer errors.

Situational factors

Motivation to be understood / motivation to understand
These productive and receptive convergence factors are two aspects of the same phenomenon: the salience of intelligiblity to both speaker and listener. For whatever reason, in certain exchanges, interlocutors are particularly concerned that the speaker's words will be interpreted correctly, and are both aware of the potential for the latter's pronunciation to impede such intelligibility. One of my studies focused on the amount of convergence when interlocutors were engaged in an exchange of information in order to complete a task as compared with that in undirected social interaction. The findings were clear: when interlocutor intelligibility is highly salient, speakers make a much greater effort (and are successful) in replacing L1 transfer in core areas with closer approximations to the target. This pattern was replicated in various types of different-L1 dyads: all male, all female,

male-female, and across a range of L1s, age groups, and educational backgrounds. The findings were also confirmed by the subjects themselves in questionnaires. Most subjects nominated pronunciation as the main—or even the only—cause of miscommunication in ILT and, in several cases, claimed to alter their speech, particularly their sounds, as a function of the L1 of their interlocutor, and/or to try to speak English in a more 'standard' way than they did with 'native speakers'.

Clearly, the salience-of-intelligibility motivation is one that can be exploited in classroom communication activities in order to give learners useful practice in accommodating to their interlocutors in this way. In the final section of this chapter, we will consider some of the possibilities.

Processing overload

We have already considered this speaker-oriented factor to some extent in the discussion of context. The crucial point is that when speakers are simultaneously having to process language at a number of different levels— lexical, grammatical, and discoursal, if they encounter processing difficulties, they tend to reserve their conscious efforts for the latter levels and, in areas where their pronunciation is still variable, to 'allow' it through lack of focus to return to more established (i.e. L1) habits. Thus, even when interlocutor intelligibility is salient, there may not be sufficient attention available for phonological convergence.

Again, pedagogy can help learners to cope better with such situations. Initially, in order to provide learners with as much opportunity as possible to practise accommodating to one another, teachers can ensure that their tasks do not cause any such overload. But this, of course, will not prepare learners for interaction outside their classroom. Gradually, therefore, the linguistic load can be increased but, at the same time, another factor should be introduced. That is, through the task design learners need to be made aware from first-hand experience that when they have to make linguistic choices, compromising on pronunciation is likely to be the most damaging one in terms of their intelligibility: they should not treat it as though it were the last in the queue for conscious attention.

Teaching accommodation skills

Hassall distinguishes between 'explicit EIL' 'where informed discussion proceeds in an open conscious manner with individuals who have the capacity to contribute', and 'implicit EIL' 'where models and materials have to be chosen for the students and presented to them' (1996a: 422). The former is the stuff of discussion and debate among academics, and it is the latter that is more relevant to the language teaching we are here concerned with. Elsewhere, Hassell talks thus of implicit EIL:

> … its goals are realistic being concerned with communication between non-native speakers and closely related to the importance of English

in different cultures and communities. The adjustment in perspective necessary to promote EIL rather than EFL/ESL in the classroom increases the legitimacy of student speaking to student in the classroom not just as a preliminary to non-native/native speaker interaction but as English speaker to English speaker.
(1996b: 70)

It is precisely this concept of 'student speaking to student' that is so crucial to the classroom acquisition and development of phonological accommodation skills to prepare learners for ILT communication outside the classroom. In fact, it is *only* such interaction that is able to promote these particular skills. More controlled, teacher-led activities undoubtedly have their purposes, but without student–student interaction we remain with EFL or ESL, that is, with students whom we have prepared for communication with 'native speakers'.

Table 7.1 summarizes the differences between the two basic types of classroom activity.

	Teacher-led input/interaction	ILT peer group interaction
IL phonology	• controlled practice of core items	• opportunity to practise accommodation skills
	• exposure to non-core NS pronunciation features	• exposure to other IL varieties
SLA	• grammatical accuracy • L2 pragmatic competence	• comprehensible input → intake • more opportunities for output

Table 7.1: Summary of the effects of teacher-led and ILT interaction on IL phonology and SLA

I have included the section on Second Language Acquisition (SLA) in general, in order to reinforce the point that teacher-led activities cannot by themselves promote EIL acquisition. They provide learners with good L2 grammatical and pragmatic models and opportunities to practise them in a more controlled way. However, EIL learners do not necessarily require the full and unmodified 'native-speaker' grammatical inventory, and they certainly do not need to acquire English 'native-speaker' pragmatic behaviour, particularly at the sociopragmatic level, to function appropriately in the English language in international contexts.

As regards IL phonology, controlled teacher-led work is of direct benefit to learners in providing them with models and practice opportunities of the features in the Lingua Franca Core. This is an essential prerequisite to classroom work on accommodation skills, as learners will not be able to converge with one another on more target-like pronunciations if it is not within their capacity to produce them—and this is particularly the case with nuclear stress. An extensive focus on the LFC sounds, including drilling and tailor-made minimal pair work (see A. Brown 1995), will enable learners to develop new automatic motor plans. Clear demonstrations of the rules of nuclear and contrastive stress and practice activities, again involving minimal pairs, will help learners move from receptive to productive competence in this problematic area.

But it is in ILT activities that learners have the opportunity to develop the appropriate use of these items and, in particular, their accommodation skills. At the same time, they receive valuable exposure to other IL varieties, which helps them develop their receptive competence for EIL. Less controlled pair and small group work, particularly involving information exchange, will provide an ideal climate. As Gass and Varonis (1991) point out, activities involving a two-way exchange of information are better than those which are only uni-directional, because they involve more negotiation of meaning and thus more opportunities for learners to adjust their pronunciation, modify their receptive expectations, signal non-understanding, and the like.

Examples for lower proficiency levels are activities involving directions and diagrams: both learners have the same map or basic diagram and have to describe to one another what they need to do in order to complete them. At higher levels, the same basic strategy can be used, but greater sophistication can be introduced. For example, following the reading of a text on the psychology involved in supermarket layouts, learners could design their own layouts, do a standard describe-and-draw activity and then, still without seeing one another's plans, compare and discuss them, and arrive at an optimum solution. Although this type of activity is concerned above all with the quality of the interaction which takes place between the learners, it should not be forgotten that the teacher is still in ultimate control and has crucial roles both as classroom manager (selecting and setting up the activity appropriately for the particular learners) and as provider of feedback on performance. While learners often discover for themselves where their faulty pronunciation or faulty reception has caused a breakdown in communication, it is generally the teacher who is able to pinpoint precisely what has gone awry, and to comment also on the suitability of strategies used, such as the asking for repetition or clarification.

Possibly the most useful ILT activity of all to promote phonological accommodation in multilingual classrooms[5] is student–student dictation. Brodkey demonstrated the usefulness of dictation in measuring mutual intelligibility almost three decades ago (1972). Rimmer has more recently argued that 'dictation has a special relationship with pronunciation because of the importance of listening skills' (1997: 36). This is only half the story as far as ILT is concerned, because ILT dictations involve learners in dictating to one another, which maximizes the possibilities for exposure to different L1s in ILT classrooms. For example, learners could take turns in dictating a number of statements about themselves, all except one of which were false, and the task of the listener(s) would be to take down only the statement they thought to be true.

Activities like this involve optimum exposure to one another's accent varieties, as students will continue to ask for repetition until they think they have understood what was said. Above all, such activities provide useful insights for both speaker and listener as to which areas of their respective ILs provide the greatest obstacles to intelligibility in ILT. Feedback should include a discussion between speaker and listener(s) of who was responsible for anything that was taken down wrongly, i.e. was it an error of production or reception? (See Gilbert 1993 and Rimmer 1997 for other suggestions for dictation activities.)

Receptive competence in ILT is gained through exposure to a wide range of varieties of accent so that learners develop the ability to interpret other pronunciations than those of their teachers and co-L1 speakers. Where teaching takes place in multilingual environments, the competence-through-exposure process will, to some extent, occur naturally if slowly. But it is unlikely to go far enough in typical short courses. Published materials are not essential—and as yet, there are, in any case, few recordings of ILT available. However, learners can, themselves, be recorded speaking together, whether in naturalistic conversations, interview-type situations, or task-based interactions such as those in the CAE Speaking examination. The recordings can then be exploited as material for listening texts in the same way that 'NS–NS' interactions are used for listening skills work in ELT coursebooks.

In addition to such 'covert' exposure to one another's accents, learners can usefully engage in contrastive work to make their pronunciation differences explicit. By this, I mean that specific classroom work can focus on different IL accents by making pronunciation a topic of classroom discussion. Such discussion could highlight learners' pronunciation differences, and thus make explicit the more subconscious exposure to different IL accents that occurs naturally in multilingual classrooms and, to some extent, through listening materials in monolingual ones.

Allwright argues for a more profound pedagogic value of discussions of language itself within a communicative model of language teaching, pointing out that teachers have not fully exploited their potential. He considers that such discussions can provide an opportunity for enhanced learning, since 'better understanding is likely to result if learners discuss their learning and share various understandings … They may learn directly from each other, or, more likely, they will learn from the very act of attempting to articulate their own understanding' (1984b: 158). Thus, discussions of this nature would be of benefit not only to learners' receptive phonological competence, but also to their overall second language acquisition. Specific activities could be of the 'How do you pronounce x?' type, where 'x' is anything from a single sound to a lexical phrase. The process requires handling with tact, however, so that learners are not made to feel that value judgements are involved and are aware that in many cases (the non-core areas), their pronunciation differences do not involve errors, but are perfectly acceptable L2 variants on a par with L1 regional differences.

In the previous paragraph I referred to a classroom activity that was beneficial not only for phonological accommodation, but also for SLA in general. In Table 7.1, the 'Summary of the effects of teacher-led and ILT interaction on IL phonology and SLA' (see page 188), I suggested that ILT is beneficial to SLA by providing learners with more comprehensible input, which then becomes intake. This relates to a body of research produced in the 1980s showing that the speech adjustments resulting from negotiation in pair work and small group work indirectly benefit the receiver's language acquisition by virtue of a link between the adjustments made in such work and the comprehensible input necessary for acquisition. See, for example, Larsen-Freeman (1985); Long (1985); Long and Porter (1985); and Pica and Doughty (1985). Larsen-Freeman (1985) argues that peer input is often more accessible to learners than 'native-speaker' input. In classrooms, apparently 'inaccessible' teacher input may reflect a reluctance on the part of the learner to negotiate with the teacher because of the power differential, particularly in whole-class situations, where there is the added fear of appearing foolish in front of the peer group (see Pica and Doughty 1985; Rulon and McCreary 1986).

Doughty and Pica (1986) claim that the significance lies not in group work itself but in the nature of the tasks that are carried out within the group framework. Information gap tasks, particularly two-way tasks, they contend (as do Gass and Varonis 1985b; and see page 189 above), promote far more negotiation arising from comprehensibility problems than do other task types. The manipulation of output in order to restore comprehensibility is thought to result in optimally adjusted input for the receiver. Such negotiation of meaning is held to occur most extensively in groups of mixed-L1 backgrounds, and it is thus ILT that potentially offers the greatest benefits to SLA for both speakers and receivers: while speakers are motivated to adjust their speech and, in particular, to replace their L1 phonological transfer in core areas, hearers (as a direct consequence of such adjustments) are provided with comprehensible input.

One major problem in all that I have said above is that it depends to a large extent on the availability of ILT classroom interaction and this, by definition, is impossible to organize in monolingual classrooms. However, more English teaching is carried out around the world in monolingual than in multilingual classes, and here, as my same-L1 pairs data demonstrates, L1 transfer does not reduce phonological intelligibility but actually increases it. Thus, in monolingual classrooms where students are being prepared for EIL, it is necessary for teachers to spend some time initially on helping students to adjust their perceptions so that they are aware of the extent of the problem. Although not ideal, this can be achieved to some extent by playing tapes of L2 English speakers from a variety of L1s.

The fact that in ILT there is a need for speakers to make phonological adjustments in core items in the direction of more target-like pronunciation, and that the opposite is true of same-L1 interaction in English, may explain why the accents of learners in monolingual classrooms tend to fossilize earlier in their development than those of learners in multilingual classrooms. Apart from the fact that they are exposed only to same-L1 accents (and, perhaps, those of 'native speaker' teachers), learners are not motivated to replace their pronunciation transfers in order to be understood. Allwright refers to the dangers of 'classroom pidgins' developing in homogeneous groups of learners (1979: 178), while Long and Porter (1985) argue that learners in groups composed of mixed-L1 backgrounds avoid the monolingual group problem of the development of classroom dialects intelligible only to speakers from the same first language. Bygate maintains that monolingual groupwork 'at least allows and at worst encourages fossilization and the use of deviant L2 forms' (1988: 76–7). Similarly, Aston (1986) refers to the negotiation of meaning by learners from a monolingual background as leading to the negotiated acceptance of non-standard forms. The situation is summed up in Figure 7.2.

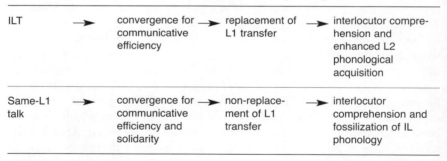

Figure 7.2:   Model of predicted phonological outcomes in ILT and same-L1 talk

One final point with regard to accommodation in EIL classrooms relates to the optimum group size. Pica and Doughty argue that because two-way tasks are likely to be most effective when only two participants are involved, 'pair rather than group work on two-way tasks may ultimately be most conducive to second language acquisition' (1985: 132). Our interest is not so much with SLA—however beneficial a 'side effect' this constitutes— but with developing learners' productive and receptive accommodation skills for the purposes of international communication in English.

Nevertheless, for different reasons, I have come to the same conclusion as to pair work being preferable to group work. One reason is that it is obviously a more complex matter to converge (albeit on a more target-like pronunciation) with more than one interlocutor. In my larger group data, I consistently found that speakers seemed to be unable to adjust their pronunciation. Quite possibly it seemed too difficult a task to approach and they did not even make the attempt. In a larger group it is, of course, quite possible to abdicate all responsibility and leave others to do the speaking, and this was always the case with one or two learners in any group.

However, there is a much more problematic issue at stake here, and this relates to groups where there is more than one representative of an L1 present. Here, the presence of a same-L1 interlocutor seems to mutually reinforce their L1 identities. This, in turn, leads to phonological convergence which, as we noted earlier, at first takes the form of subjective convergence, but gradually becomes objective convergence as the interaction progresses. And identity is not the only factor involved: embarrassment also plays a part. Many of my subjects admitted to feelings of embarrassment in situations where they had to speak English with members of their own L1 group. They found it unnatural to use a lingua franca when there was no authentic need for them to do so and therefore increased L1 phonological transfer not only for the sake of mutual comprehension and the expression of group identity, but also as a response to their embarrassment.

Obviously much thought will have to be given to the problem of accommodation in groups containing members of the same L1. This is a reasonably frequent situation internationally, and the EIL enterprise will to some degree be threatened if research is unable to identify and pedagogy to implement a solution. Somehow the feelings of group identity that remain grounded in the same-L1 cohort within a larger EIL group need to be encouraged to shift outwards, to identify with the EIL group as a whole. Phonological accommodation should then follow automatically, since the primary motivation will become EIL intelligibility rather than L1 identity. For the time being, however, it seems that different-L1 pairs provide the best context for the classroom development of EIL accommodation skills.

At this point, we have come full circle in that ILT is both problematic discourse and the solution to the problem, to the extent that the difficulties encountered by speakers engaged in ILT can be solved by appropriate pedagogy in multilingual classrooms. There are still a number of unanswered questions, some of which will be dealt with in the final chapter. Others, such as the problems in relation to monolingual classrooms and larger groups will remain for another day. But whatever developments take place in the next few years, one thing is almost guaranteed: accommodation will play a major role in international uses of English. As Nelson says, 'the community of speakers will by sheer numbers and geographical distribution require active accommodation from all participants to retain a high degree of intelligibility across varieties' (1992: 337). The need to eschew the 'dysfunctional' linguistic consistency to which Milroy (1994) refers (page 165) is as critical in the EIL speech community as in any other, and probably more so as far as pronunciation is concerned. NBESs must be prepared both to cope with major pronunciation differences in the speech of their different-L1 partners and to adjust their own pronunciation radically for the benefit of their different-L1 hearers. And this sort of preparation can only be achieved through pedagogy.

Notes

1   Originally Speech Accommodation Theory, or SAT.
2   These are: Beebe (1977, 1981); Beebe and Zuengler (1983); Berkovitz (1986); Flege (1987); Takahashi (1989); Zuengler (1982, 1987, 1989).
3   Though Kasper points out that 'convergence strategies used by NS to achieve mutual comprehension and to facilitate NNS' conversational participation can in fact result in *divergence*, by creating or exacerbating the very problems they were designed to forestall or solve. Frequent foreigner talk adjustments such as completing, rephrasing and restating the NNS' utterances can produce an asymmetrical distribution of "interactional authority"' such that 'the practice of expert-novice-convergence ... appears more ambiguous in social messages than is usually assumed: instead of facilitating novice participation, it may accentuate asymmetry and produce psychological divergence' (1997: 354; emphasis in original).
4   'Selective replacement of transfer in core areas' refers to the following phenomenon: with increasing familiarity with a particular interlocutor's IL accent, speakers appear gradually to switch from the blanket replacement of *all* core items (where this is within their competence) to a selectivity based on the particular interlocutor's receptive needs—which themselves simultaneously decrease. The same process is probably true of increasing familiarity with an accent *per se*, i.e. not only that of an *individual* speaker, though future research is required to clarify the extent to which this is the case.
5   See page 192 for suggestions for monolingual classrooms.

8 Proposals for pronunciation teaching for EIL

The past is a foreign country: they do things differently there.

L.P. Hartley, *The Go-Between* (Hamish Hamilton 1953), Prologue

The time has come to draw together the threads of the preceding chapters and consider the wider implications for pronunciation teaching. In Chapter 6, I advocated the use of a phonological core, the Lingua Franca Core, in pronunciation teaching. Then, in Chapter 7, I described how phonological accommodation (convergence) functions in interlanguage talk, and suggested ways in which it can be contrived in ELT classrooms. My approach to pronunciation derives essentially from a concern for the sociolinguistic factors involved in the use of English as an international lingua franca—now the most frequent use of spoken English around the world. My argument is that unless pronunciation teachers (and materials writers) are conversant with these factors, they are in danger of remaining confined within a narrow pronunciation methodology of the type that has dominated the field for so many years, instead of being able to adapt their approach to the international needs of many of their students.

What is called for, then, is a major reconsideration of the way in which pronunciation is currently dealt with, not only in L2 English classrooms but also in phonology teacher education and in research, since the latter two have considerable influence on the former. For example, it is not valid to promote the findings of research conducted into intelligibility for 'NS' listeners as having relevance for EIL, where the majority of listeners are themselves L2 speakers. Neither is it helpful on teacher education courses to describe English phonology primarily in terms of 'NS' models, when 'NSs' are a worldwide minority of English speakers. Yet both these approaches are still the rule and both feed directly into classroom teaching and published pronunciation materials.

In pronunciation, probably more than in any other area of ELT, there is an urgent need for a completely new paradigm. Braj Kachru describes the broader situation in words that have particular resonance for pronunciation teaching:

What is needed is a shift of two types: a paradigm shift in research and teaching, and an understanding of the sociolinguistic reality of the uses and users of English. We must also cease to view English within the framework appropriate for monolingual societies. ... The traditional presuppositions and ethnocentric approaches need reevaluation. In the international contexts, English represents a repertoire of cultures, not a monolithic culture. The changed sociolinguistic profile of English is difficult to recognize, for good reason. The traditional paradigm ... however undesirable, continues to have a grip on the profession. What makes matters more complex is the fact that active interest groups want to maintain the status quo.
(1992: 362)

The following is an extract from a very recent British Council publication, but one could be forgiven for assuming that it was written during a much earlier era:

The incredible success of the English language is Britain's greatest asset. It enhances Britain's image as a modern, dynamic country and brings *widespread political, economic and cultural advantages*, both to Britain and to our partners.

The British Council plays a vital role in further extending the use of English around the world and exposing people to the *richness of British culture* ...
(The British Council, *Conference prospectus*, ELT conference 1998; emphasis added)

My purpose in quoting this extract is not to attack or ridicule the British Council, but rather to provide a typical example of the 'grip on the profession' of the 'traditional paradigm' to which Kachru refers, and of the 'colonial discourses that have come to adhere to the language' (Pennycook 1998: 191). The 'richness of British culture' is something that, in the light of international developments in the English language, would now be more appropriately covered within British Cultural Studies than as part of mainstream English language programmes. But such a move would lead in turn to a reduction in the 'widespread political, economic and cultural advantages' to which the prospectus refers, once fewer learners of English saw the need to study British culture, let alone to travel to Britain to carry out their studies.

Views like those of the British Council, and comparable interest groups in the USA, such as the English Only movement, remain immensely influential among both the general public and the ELT profession, in their promotion of the notions that English is somehow a 'better' language than others, and that standard British or standard American English (despite difficulties in defining these) are in some intrinsic way superior to other, especially L2, varieties of the language. The latter notion is nowhere so influential as in the field of pronunciation teaching, where close links between accent and attitude are ever present, whether overtly stated or simmering just below the surface. The success of such interest groups in tuning in to and 'justifying' an already existing prejudice towards certain accents of English, thus bears much responsibility for the fact that pronunciation teaching at the start of the 21st Century is still predicated on outmoded assumptions, dating back to the middle of the 20th Century and beyond. I shall take up this issue a little later in the chapter.

When I first began researching EIL phonology, I was careful to exclude the ENL settings, particularly the USA, from my comments and to condone their continued promotion of the 'NS–NNS' interaction paradigm. More recently, however, I have come to a rather different conclusion. Those who speak English as a second language in the USA are thought to number around 12 per cent of the total population, and their number is increasing year on year with continuing immigration into the USA. If this percentage is correct, they account currently for around 30 million people (Crystal 1995: 108–9),[1] in other words, the equivalent of more than half the total population of the UK. And Hispanics alone are predicted to number over 80 million by the year 2050 (Crystal 1997: 122). American society is becoming ever more multilingual/multicultural, such that in New York, for example, there are now speakers of around 150 different first languages.[2] In addition, there are demographic differences across the US with, in some areas, very high concentrations of particular L2 groups, such as Hispanics.

While one might assume that the purpose of immigrants to the US in learning English is to enable them to communicate with its 'native speakers', many of whose forebears, it should be remembered, were nothing of the kind if we go back a mere generation or two, and to integrate into 'native-speaker' society, this view is naive. A more likely scenario, according to many Americans with whom I have discussed the issue, is one in which immigrants from different L1 countries are excluded from many areas of 'native-speaker' society and end up communicating as much, if not more, with each other. This is particularly so in the workplace where, as Lippi-Green (1997) reports, those with non-standard English accents tend to be excluded even to the extent of being denied employment. The continued promotion of intelligibility for 'NSs' as the overarching goal of pronunciation teaching is thus irrelevant to many needs of many learners.

Adult ESL classes in the USA, like EFL classes in the UK, tend to be multilingual in composition. Yet because of the concern with intelligibility for 'NSs', there seems to be little inclination to exploit the pedagogic reality in the sorts of ways described in the previous chapter. Valuable learning opportunities are thus being lost to students in the USA in the same way as they are to trainee teachers in the UK (see page 200). Nor is there any suggestion that in this highly multilingual/multicultural society, L1 speakers of English should be making some of the concessions (both receptive and productive) to facilitate mutually intelligible pronunciation when 'NS–NNS' interaction does take place.

The desire to make L2 speakers conform phonologically to the 'NS' standard should perhaps be considered in the context of massive and ever-increasing immigration into the USA. Widespread negative attitudes to bilingualism are thought to be, at least in part, the result of fear of a threat to the primacy of the English language in the face of this immigration (see Pennycook 1998; L. Milroy 1999). Comparably negative attitudes exist towards L2 accents of English among members of both the general public and the ELT (TESOL) profession. As L. Milroy says, 'A major instantiation of American language ideology … presents itself overwhelmingly as a negative and sometimes demonstrably irrational attitude to languages other than English, and by association to English spoken with a "foreign" accent' (1999: 179). In the ELT profession, negative attitudes to foreign accents are not uncommon among pronunciation experts. These people inevitably have an interest in preserving the phonological status quo for, should L2 accent varieties gain some sort of legitimacy, this would in turn render obsolete the current pronunciation-teaching paradigm whose main purpose is to enable L2 speakers to understand and be understood by L1 speakers with GA accents.

The main point to bear in mind, then, is that in spite of claims to the contrary, in multilingual/multicultural ENL countries, of which North America is the example *par excellence*, the pronunciation needs of learners are to a large extent similar to those of learners in EIL communication contexts. I will return to this issue later in the chapter, when discussing the need to educate NSs in EIL pronunciation.

So what is the solution for English pronunciation teaching in the 21st Century? Kachru (1992) calls for two types of paradigm shift in ELT: one in 'research and teaching', and the other in our 'understanding of the sociolinguistic reality of the uses and users of English'. In terms of pronunciation, the two are inseparable: as I implied at the beginning of this chapter, a shift in sociolinguistic understanding will facilitate and inform a shift in approaches to pronunciation research and teaching. In practical pronunciation terms, if EIL is genuinely to be—at least accent-wise—the language for all English speakers that its name implies, I see these shifts leading to radical change in four main areas: firstly, in pronunciation in teacher education; secondly, in the testing of pronunciation; thirdly, in the status of 'NNS' pronunciation teachers; and fourthly, in the need for (EIL) pronunciation learning for 'NSs'. I will consider each of these areas in turn and then, in the Afterword, look to the future of the phonology of EIL.

An overhaul of pronunciation teaching in English language teacher education

The major obstacle to the modernizing of English pronunciation teaching in recent years has been the failure to *educate* teachers. That is, to provide teachers with the facts which will enable them to make informed decisions in their selection of pronunciation models, as opposed to *training* them to reproduce unquestioningly a restricted range of techniques in order to promote all aspects of a single model, in whatever teaching context they should find themselves. And yet, if my proposals are taken up, it should be possible to educate teachers phonologically even, to some extent, on short initial courses, since the time saved by focusing on a smaller range of core features can be put to good use in discussion of the sociolinguistic rationale which underpins the core (see Sutter 1999).

However, on many programmes—I have in mind certain short (for example, four-week) initial training courses, such as the Trinity College and UCLES (University of Cambridge Local Examinations Syndicate) Certificates—the selection of a model is not dealt with at all. Rather, it is assumed that teachers need to be equipped with a cursory knowledge of one of the two main 'native speaker' prestige models, that is, RP or GA, regardless of where in the world they intend to teach subsequently. In British-based courses the assumption is that teachers will teach RP, and in American-based courses that they will teach GA. Amusingly, some phonologists of these two inner circle countries regard their own national prestige model as the international standard pronunciation of English and the other group's model as non-standard.

On longer courses, whether British-based inservice courses such as the UCLES Diploma in English Language Teaching to Adults (DELTA), American pre-service master's degrees, or European (non-British) pre-service undergraduate degrees, the assumptions are no different. The approach is still oriented towards educating teachers in either RP or GA or, occasionally, providing a choice of either; the knowledge base is simply less cursory. The implications of sociolinguistics and social psychology for the teaching and learning of L2 English pronunciation are rarely even mentioned. Yet once teachers have gained some classroom experience and have, themselves, returned to the (teacher education) classroom, these are precisely the areas in which they need to be better informed. Only a study of these subjects will ensure that teachers are well equipped, phonology-wise, to move on in their careers rather than—as so many do—stay in the same place teaching in exactly the same way for the rest of their working lives. In the next two sections I will discuss in detail the aspects of sociolinguistics and social psychology that are most crucial for pronunciation teaching. For the moment, though, we will look more closely at the status quo.

The chief distinction between teacher training and teacher education is essentially that whereas training provides teachers with a number of techniques, or 'recipes', for reproduction in whatever teaching context they find themselves, education should enable them to adapt their teaching to that context: to mediate between the language and the specific group of language learners. To this extent, pronunciation education is failing. Teachers cannot mediate if they are not in possession of the facts which would enable them to do so. They may be aware of the existence of a phenomenon known as 'English as an International Language', 'Global English', 'World English', or the like, but they are unlikely to have been asked to consider the implications of this phenomenon for the teaching of pronunciation (or, for that matter, of grammar, lexis, or discourse). And yet it is at the phonological level that the EIL varieties differ most from each other and, thus, where teachers need to be best informed if they are to prepare their students to communicate effectively in EIL contexts.

Recently, there has been some progress in the direction of inter-nationalization on, for example, the UCLES CELTA and DELTA, in 'the coming together of the schemes for native and non-native speakers under the new framework'.[3] In theory this means that 'NNS' teachers are eligible for places on CELTA and DELTA courses. In practice, though, many such teachers continue to be refused places at many centres,[4] just as they were on the old CTEFLA and DTEFLA, on the grounds of their L2 accents and grammar 'errors'. Where it occurs, this practice not only represents indefensible discrimination against particular groups of English speakers, but it also disadvantages 'NS' trainee teachers. For thus, the latter are denied access to the very representatives of the 'changed sociolinguistic profile of English' whose pronunciation varieties they need to study; and so the vicious circle closes.

At certificate level there is rarely time available for a detailed study of phonology. At diploma level, where teachers are thought to be educated rather than trained, phonology is often studied in greater depth. To date, there have nevertheless been few concessions in terms of internationalization, in the sense that there is still no principled discussion (if any discussion at all) of the selection of internationally appropriate pronunciation models. The same assumptions operate on most DELTA phonology courses at the start of the 21st Century as did when I began teaching on them in the 1980s. A typical syllabus covers the sounds, features of connected speech, word stress patterns, rhythm, and intonation of RP. The goal of teaching is assumed, without further discussion, to be the reasonably close approximation of this accent, though with the increasing acknowledgement that comfortable intelligibility for a 'NS' *listener* is often sufficient and that a totally native-like accent is generally unrealistic as a goal. And to this extent, the current situation is less satisfactory than it used to be. For whereas we used to consider that, with sufficient teaching and learning, it was possible for L2 speakers to achieve a native-like accent, nowadays we still think the latter accent is best, but no longer that learners will be able to achieve it. Their accents are doomed to be second best.

It was this phonological status quo—apparently so resistent to change—that prompted me to offer a presentation at the 1998 International House London Teacher Training Conference, *Transigence and Transaction*, entitled 'Phonology for international uses of English: time to tell the truth to trainees'. The blurb in the conference programme read as follows:

> Over the past decade, the use of English in international contexts has increased dramatically, such that interaction is now more likely to take place between two non-native speakers of English than between a native and a non-native speaker. The phonological implications of this interaction pattern shift are immense: many of the pronunciation features that we doggedly describe to trainees are of minor importance or even obsolete in terms of international intelligibility and acceptability. In this talk we will consider how to make phonological descriptions more realistic for trainees and what else they need to know besides, so that they can help their learners acquire pronunciation that will facilitate intelligibility in international communication.
>
> *Transigence and Transaction*, Conference Programme page 8[5]

In the presentation itself, I argued that those who embark on teacher training/education programmes are no longer being told the truth about English pronunciation because the phonological descriptions with which they are being provided are based on an outdated premise, that of 'NS–NNS' as the prevailing English interaction pattern.

In Chapter 6 above, I dealt at length with my remedy for this 'untruth': a core approach based on 'NNS–NNS' interaction. An approach of this sort seems to me to be the only possible way forward for an international language spoken by millions of people from a wide range of first languages. It makes good international sense for the phonological needs of the majority (the L2 speakers) to be prioritized and those of the minority (the L1 speakers) to be relegated to a back seat. In the light of future empirical[6] research, the Lingua Franca Core (LFC) may be found to require modifying in certain ways. But this does not invalidate the principle itself.

The first stage in the overhaul of pronunciation in ELT education for EIL, then, is to present teachers with the LFC and its rationale. First of all, teachers need to be made aware of the role of pronunciation in intelligibility in EIL interactions, and of the phonological features central to such intelligibility. This includes an understanding of how the LFC features are produced and, therefore, a certain amount of phonetic training—something which has been noticeably lacking in the majority of 'NS' teacher training/education courses for many years. There is also a need for discussion of the non-LFC items and the reasons underlying their non-core status (such as non-teachability and non-relevance, both of which were discussed in Chapters 5 and 6). For EIL pronunciation classrooms, this much should be mandatory, even on very short teacher training certificate courses such as CELTA.

However, for the immediate future, ELT students will also need to acquire the non-core areas receptively in order to be able to understand 'NSs' face-to-face (for example, in British, American, or Australian universities) or, more likely, in the media. In effect, this means that pronunciation teacher education should cover the full range of phonological features of at least one of the main 'NS' varieties of English—even though teachers will not thence be expected to pass this on to their students for productive use. In addition, and more importantly in the longer term, their students will need help in understanding a range of L2 accents of English. Pronunciation teacher education therefore requires major adjustments in this direction. At the theoretical level, a component on L2 accents of English should examine, in particular, the workings of L1 phonological transfer (see Chapter 5) and the distinctions between a model and a norm (see Chapter 1). At the practical level, teachers need guidance in ways of using contrastive work in monolingual and multilingual classrooms, in order to provide their students with exposure to these different accents and to encourage accommodation in core areas (see Chapter 7). This much should be mandatory on more advanced teacher training/education diplomas such as DELTA.

But, as I went on to argue at the International House presentation, the Lingua Franca Core (and non-core), while necessary for EIL teacher education, is not sufficient: the truth, but not the whole truth. Teachers will be unable to form a deeper understanding of its rationale, and thus make informed use of it for their own pedagogic ends, unless they also study certain aspects of sociolinguistics and social psychology. We will consider now the important contributions that these two overlapping disciplines have to make to teacher education[7] for EIL pronunciation teaching.[8]

The sociolinguistics of EIL phonology

Any phonology course which is designed for teachers of EIL as opposed to EFL or ESL, and which intends to educate at the conceptual level rather than train at the technical level, is morally obliged to consider L2 accent within a framework of sociolinguistic variation rather than within one of 'NNS' error. In the foreign country of the past, to rephrase Hartley, English was learnt to enable those who spoke other first languages to communicate with native speakers of English and, possibly, to identify with and gain membership of a particular L1 English (usually British or American) community.[9] English was a 'foreign language' in the sense that any other language learnt today for the purposes of 'NS–NNS' communication is 'foreign', for example, French as learnt by Japanese L1 speakers, Italian as learnt by German L1 speakers, and so on. This being so, learners were expected to conform to the pronunciation (usually RP or GA) which constituted membership qualifications. Noticeable differences in pronunciation between L1 and L2 speakers could, then, legitimately be described as phonological errors on the part of the latter, and attempts be made to eradicate them.

On the other hand, EIL membership is by definition membership of an international rather than of an L1 English community. Admittedly, even in this context, it is still possible to consider English a 'foreign' language to its L2 speakers up to a point. But here we need to distinguish between the *process* of learning English and the *product* which learners acquire. The language is undoubtedly foreign (in the sense of being unfamiliar or even strange) to learners in the earlier stages of the learning process, when they have not yet been able to master it sufficiently to enable them to appropriate it for their own purposes. But after learners have achieved a certain level of proficiency such that they are able to communicate successfully (and this level is lower than many would suggest—certainly no more than upper intermediate as defined by examination systems such as those of UCLES),[10] English has by definition become part of their personal linguistic repertoire, one of the choices available to them in their daily communications. And since these communications are most likely to operate on an international basis, i.e. with other L2 speakers, at this stage it no longer makes sense to talk of a 'foreign' language. Instead, English is an international language with all the sociolinguistic implications for its pronunciation that such a shift involves.

The study of EIL pronunciation within a variationist framework entails a consideration of the notion of standard accent and of the facts of accent variation. The following is an outline of the aspects of these two areas that I consider to be crucial in a sociolinguistics course for EIL pronunciation teacher education. Where relevant, I have referred the reader to other sources for a more comprehensive coverage of the issues.

The notion of standard accent

The first area that teachers need to consider is the notion of standardness of accent. In fact, the term 'standard' is particularly difficult to define in relation to accent. As Trudgill points out, 'There is one thing about Standard English on which most linguists, or at least British linguists, do appear to be agreed, and that is that Standard English has nothing to do with pronunciation' (1999: 118). Standard English (or, more accurately, Englishes[11]) can be spoken with any regional accent. In other words, despite the popular misconception, standard accents have nothing to do with Standard English, something of which it is essential for pronunciation teachers to be aware before they begin making decisions about appropriate pronunciation models. While Standard English is a social dialect (Trudgill 1999), and a 'minority variety' at that (Crystal 1995: 110), it is also the favoured educational model, particularly in its written form, throughout whole countries, and non-users are discriminated against in many written and certain formal spoken contexts. It therefore makes good sense to teach Standard English grammar and vocabulary to L2 speakers so that they are able to use them (or not) as appropriate—but see Widdowson's corollary: that we should 'at the same time respect the propriety of other forms of English as proper to different needs and purposes' (1993: 326).

The same situation does not obtain for English pronunciation. As Standard English is a social dialect, so RP and GA (or 'network American') are social accents. There are major differences between them in that RP is marked for class, while GA is 'what is left behind when all the non-standard varieties spoken by disparaged persons such as Valley Girls, Hillbillies, Southerners, New Yorkers, African Americans, Asians, Mexican Americans, Cubans, and Puerto Ricans are set aside' (L. Milroy 1999: 174). Nevertheless, each is commonly described as a 'standard' accent or even 'no accent', and is promoted in pronunciation courses for L2 learners as being both the standard and the prestige accent with intrinsically superior qualities.

However, less than 3 per cent of the British population now speaks RP in a pure form (Crystal 1995: 365). In other words, over 97 per cent of the population is said to speak with a non-standard accent which, in the case of educated speakers, is often a regionally-modified RP (ibid.). In America, the situation is less extreme, but the trend still runs in the same direction. Around 33 per cent of the combined population of the USA and Canada speaks with a GA accent or, to put it the other way, around two-thirds of the population do not. Thus, the so-called 'standard' accent is not by any stretch of the imagination used by a majority in either geographical context.

Turning to the prestige factor, this relates to the social origins of the two accents rather than to any particular intrinsic qualities. RP has links with classism (see Chapter 1), while GA is linked to racism, as the above quote from Milroy makes abundantly clear. The case of RP demonstrates the point that no intrinsic merit underlies the selection of prestige accents, rather that it is a social process involving attitudes towards particular groups of people and thence by association towards their accent. The novelist Beryl Bainbridge recently used the occasion of a dinner in honour of her success in the W.H. Smith literary award to rail against regional accents, especially those of her home city, Liverpool, as 'nasal' and 'stupid' (*The Observer*, 7 March 1999). She recommended that children with regional accents take compulsory elocution lessons, as she herself had done.

However, before the expansion of the English public schools in the later 19th Century, neither RP nor any other standard accent was associated with upper class privilege, and regional accents were the norm among all classes. Prime Minister Gladstone, who had attended Eton earlier in the century, apparently spoke throughout his life with a Liverpool accent (cf. Honey 1989). Not surprisingly, as soon as listeners are unaware of the social connotations, aesthetic judgements do not seem to favour prestige accents. In other words, we are concerned with 'imposed norm' rather than 'inherent value': 'the norms are "imposed" by those in the know, the stereotypes which link beauty, or harshness, or comedy to a set of sounds are unavailable to others' (Edwards 1994: 96).

Although speakers with broad non-standard accents are undoubtedly discriminated against in both the UK and the USA, this time it does not make good sense to promote the so-called standard accents among L2 speakers as a safeguard against such discrimination. This is not only because of their minority use by L1 speakers and their lack of intrinsic qualities, but also because of the facts of accent variation (see next section) and because of the inextricable link between accent and identity, which I will discuss in a later section. A better policy would be to educate L1 schoolchildren in the facts of L2 accent difference, much as Wolfram is currently advocating in the USA in relation to different L1 dialects (see page 227).

These, then, are the main factors in relation to standard accent that need to be presented for the consideration of EIL pronunciation teachers. Useful background reading can be found in Wilkinson 1995; Lippi-Green 1997; Bex and Watts 1999; and Milroy and Milroy 1999.

The facts of accent variation

We looked at inter-speaker language variation in Chapter 2, where I discussed the widespread and inevitable extent of this phenomenon, and the role of language attitudes in the general preference for linguistic conformity to some perceived standard and the corresponding antipathy towards linguistic variation. In the previous section I discussed the two main accent varieties commonly regarded as standard, RP and GA, pointing out that neither can consider itself 'standard' in terms of its spread of use among L1 speakers and that neither can lay claim to being 'a standard' in the sense of possessing some sort of intrinsic superiority over other accents.

But the difficulty goes still further: neither RP nor GA represents a monochrome accent. Especially in the case of RP there is no single version, but a range of versions depending on the speaker's age, social class, and even region. In particular, 'among younger speakers this variety is apparently becoming much more blurred round the edges than it was once assumed to be' (Milroy 1994: 168). For example, in an area of the southeast of England around London and Essex, Estuary English, which has a number of distinctive features (see Rosewarne 1996), is influencing the development of RP among the young. Teachers need to be aware, then, that if for some reason, they decide to teach RP rather than adopt the core approach, they are not teaching a universally identical accent; and that they may even be in danger of passing on to their students an accent which is inappropriate to their age group.

Thus, accent is subject to variation even within a single ·L1 variety considered to be standard. But for EIL, it is not sufficient to limit the discussion to L1 varieties. And as soon as we come to consider L2 accents of English, there are a number of other issues involved. For anyone teaching pronunciation for EIL, education in the following facts of phonological variation is critical. Because accent variation is discussed on a number of other occasions, the relevant chapters are indicated in parentheses, in order to avoid unnecessary duplication:

1 Accent variation is the rule and conformity the exception (Chapters 2 and 3).
2 In view of the nature of phonological transfer, the influence of L1 pronunciation on L2 English accents is inevitable (Chapter 5).
3 It follows points (1) and (2) that there is nothing intrinsically wrong with L2 pronunciation which does not conform to a 'NS' accent but varies in the direction of the speaker's own L1 (Chapter 2).
4 Such variation does not equal incorrectness provided that the variation is in areas designated non-core, i.e. not crucial to intelligibility (Chapter 6).
5 In these cases, L2 variation = L2 regional accent. 'NNS' accents are thus entitled to parity with NS regional accents (Chapters 2 and 6).
6 And since EIL speakers have L2 regional accents, the most relevant models are provided by fluent bilingual speakers who share the learner's L1 (this chapter, below).
7 On the other hand, the assumption that a 'standard' 'NS' accent is internationally intelligible is a myth: 'NNS' accents are often more intelligible than 'NS' accents in EIL contexts, and so there is less to be gained from teaching the latter for production (Chapter 4).
8 Exposure to a wide range of 'NNS' regional accents is also an essential part of learning EIL. This applies even more to teachers than to their students and, as Taylor (1991: 433) points out, 'in view of the great variety of pronunciations that teachers and learners will be expected to deal with, teachers will have to be even more phonetically aware than they are now ...' (Chapters 6 and 7).

One final point about accent variation. Accents change over time and EIL accents are in this respect no different. Once teachers have accepted the broad principle that L2 accents are not merely 'errors' where they differ from L1 accents, they need to be prepared for the possibility that changes to the EIL core/non-core categories may be introduced by L2 speakers themselves—and, in fact, that this is ultimately the more likely scenario. I have already discussed (in Chapter 6) the influence of L2 speakers on the sounds /θ/ and /ð/. In the coming years, like David Crystal (see page 15), I predict that other influences will emerge and necessitate changes to the LFC, and that these influences will be 'NNS'-led. 'NS' teachers must therefore guard against their instinctive reaction, that is, to interpret any 'NNS' innovation as error.

The social psychology of EIL phonology

Crystal points out that 'The need for intelligibility and the need for identity often pull people—and countries—in opposing directions. The former motivates the learning of an international language, with English the first choice in most cases; the latter motivates the promotion of ethnic language and culture. Conflict is the commonsense consequence when either position is promoted insensitively' (1997: 116).

For teachers of EIL pronunciation, one of the most crucial elements in their education should surely now be the role of L1 identity in L2 accents. With English being spoken around the globe in an ever-expanding range of communicative contexts, one of the only means available to preserve L1 identity is, increasingly, L1 accent. However, the use of an L1 accent in L2 may—as we have seen in previous chapters—threaten mutual international intelligibility and, thus, the whole purpose of an international language of communication is defeated. The issue of accent therefore requires extremely sensitive handling by English teachers. Quite remarkably, however, it is rarely, if ever, even mentioned in pronunciation teacher training/education, and is brought up as a consideration only in a very small minority of pronunciation books for teachers, such as Dalton and Seidlhofer (1994a) (which, not insignificantly, is the work of two 'non-native speakers').

One of the main motivations underlying my approach to phonology for EIL is to avoid the kind of insensitivity towards the L1 identities of L2 learners of English that Crystal refers to. Indeed, as we noted in Chapter 6, such insensitivity is all the worse for having no basis in phonological necessity. A 'native-like' accent is not necessary for intelligibility in EIL. There is no need for learners to eradicate as far as possible the phonological features that mark them as coming from a particular L1 group. In fact the whole concept of 'accent reduction' (the term is used more widely in the USA than in the UK, but the concept itself is alive and well in the UK) is flawed in the context of EIL accents. Here again, a radical change of approach is called for, and the one I propose centres on the concept of 'accent addition'. Because the subject has not yet, to my knowledge, been discussed in the literature, I will explain in some detail what I mean by accent addition, and how I believe it should be incorporated into pronunciation in teacher education.

Accent addition

The starting point is the phenomenon of the inability of the vast majority of adults to master an L2 accent as contrasted with their mastery of other features of the L2. This is traditionally explained by psycholinguists as the result of an age-related diminution of phonological ability—the 'Critical Period Hypothesis'—involving, for example, loss of the ability to perceive L2 sounds and loss of articulatory motor skills. The general consensus sets the critical period at close to puberty (for example, Scovel (1998) sets it at around twelve years of age, although Long (1990) produces evidence suggesting it may be even earlier, perhaps as young as six).

Social psychologists, however, tend to regard adult learner retention of L1 accent in L2 not as a function of age *per se*, but as a response to conscious and subconscious feelings of L1 group identity which, predictably, develop and strengthen with age. Daniels refers to L1 accent as the 'umbilical cord which ties us to our mother'. He argues that 'whenever we speak an L2 we cut that cord, perhaps unconsciously afraid of not being able to find it and tie it up again when we revert to L1' (1995: 6). The implication is that the more closely speakers approximate the L2 accent, the greater the risk they subconsciously fear of losing their L1 accent (however unlikely this is in reality)[12] and with it, their L1 roots. Anne Pakir, the Singaporean scholar, made the accent-identity link explicit in her plenary at the 1998 TESOL Convention in Seattle: 'meddle with my accent', she warned, 'and you meddle with my identity'. And the fear is not likely to be dispelled by the use of the term 'accent reduction' and approaches to pronunciation teaching that imply to learners that the goal is precisely to rid them of an undesirable and deviant L1 accent in L2 and—by extension—an undesirable and deviant identity.

In fact, the whole concept of accent reduction is predicated on a basic contradiction. Second Language Acquisition (SLA) is concerned with gain rather than loss. According to the *Oxford English Dictionary*, 'to acquire' is 'to gain a skill, habit etc. by one's own ability, efforts, or behaviour'. SLA thus by definition involves the gaining of a second language, the provision of an additional resource. By this token, an L2 accent is not an accent reduced but an accent gained: a facility which increases learners' choices by expanding their phonological repertoires. And accent reduction makes still less sense in relation to *receptive* pronunciation skills: not by any stretch of the imagination could one argue that learners are reducing their receptive phonology in order to understand a new pronunciation system. The concept of reduction is no more viable in relation to pronunciation than it is in relation to other aspects of language. Interestingly, we never hear references to 'grammar reduction' or 'vocabulary reduction'. No writer of L2 pedagogic grammars or vocabulary courses would entertain the notion that learners need to reduce their L1 grammar or vocabulary in order to acquire the L2.

What I suggest instead for EIL pronunciation teaching is the opposite approach. That is, to think not in terms of reducing the L1 accent but of *adding* the L2 as far as is necessary for mutual phonological intelligibility: in other words, the concept of 'accent addition'. The term itself first came to my notice via an e-mail list in the words of Swedish phonetician Olle Kjellin,[13] although his interpretation of the concept represented by the term is rather different from my own. This is what Kjellin actually said:

> We are not dealing with '(foreign) accent reduction', but rather 'accent addition'. It may be the same thing, but I sense an important difference in attitude towards it. And towards 'accents'. We cannot remove an accent that somebody has, be it native or foreign. But we can give those who want it the key to how to best pretend to be a speaker of another accent. With that aspect, there cannot be any talk about 'losing one's identity', or the like.

Although the idea of pretending to be a speaker of another accent is not one which sits at all easily with an EIL approach to pronunciation, the change of attitude Kjellin advocates is a vital one. Judy Gilbert, the American phonologist, responded (by e-mail) to Kjellin's claim, quoting David Mendelsohn[14] as follows: 'accent reduction ... has always suggested something negative to me, like the need for removing a stain or blemish. The idea of adding an accent (or giving access to the practical use of a useful new code) seems better from a human feelings standpoint, as well as more accurate'.

The important decision for EIL—assuming that, unlike Kjellin, we are not aiming for 'native-like' pronunciation as the outcome of accent addition—is what we should add to what. And here, it is essential to bear in mind the fact that in EIL, the primary need of L2 speakers is to be able to understand each other rather than L1 speakers. To guarantee international phonological intelligibility, there must be unifying features among the different L2 accents. But if the concept of addition is to be meaningful, we must also find ways of taking more account of speakers' L1 accents and building on them in pronunciation teaching.

My suggestion would be a five-phase accent addition programme, where only the first phase is mandatory (as goal rather than guaranteed outcome) for EIL. The other four are optional, with their take-up depending on the sociolinguistic profile of the individual learner. They are not optional, however, for the teacher: even minimally trained teachers need to be competent in dealing with at least 1–4 in their classrooms. The five phases, in (for the majority of EIL learners) descending order of importance, are as follows:

1 *Addition of core items to the learner's productive and receptive*
repertoire
This phase involves the acquisition of the EIL core features (the LFC) but not

the non-core features. Thus, learners endeavour to add to their repertoire a number of core items that they can then use when they engage in EIL interactions, while in the non-core areas, the retention of L1 forms indicates (L2) regional accent rather than incorrectness. In neither core nor non-core areas, then, is there any suggestion of accent reduction. Full details of the core and non-core features are set out in Chapter 6 above.

2 Addition of a range of L2 English accents to the learner's receptive repertoire

Inevitably some learners will not acquire complete productive competence in the 'mandatory' core, but will continue to use certain L1 features instead of adding the relevant L2 core features. For this reason it will be useful for learners to be exposed to a range of regional L2 accents of English and to familiarize themselves with their salient features. This process will be even more effective if target interlocutors can be identified and exposure be focused on their English accents.

3 Addition of accommodation skills

This refers both to learners' acquisition of the ability to adjust their pronunciation in response to a specific interlocutor's receptive needs by selecting appropriately from their productive pronunciation repertoires and to the ability to adjust their (receptive) expectations in relation to the interlocutor's own pronunciation (see Chapter 7).

4 Addition of non-core items to the learner's receptive repertoire

These are, in effect, the omissions from the mandatory core. They are irrelevant to intelligibility in 'NNS–NNS' interaction and, in some cases, are unteachable for productive use because of learning constraints such as complexity and lack of generalizability. Nevertheless, it will be useful for learners to acquire these items receptively if they intend to communicate with L1 speakers of English.

5 Addition of a range of L1 English accents to the learner's receptive repertoire

Although the few published materials which include accents of English other than RP and GA tend to focus on other L1 accents, exposure to them is far less important for the majority of learners. Nevertheless, some learners are likely to need to communicate with L1 speakers of English who have regional accents, and in these cases, it will be helpful to provide them with exposure to these accents so that they can add them to their receptive repertoires.

This programme is very far removed from notions of accent reduction. Learners who achieve all five phases will be phonologically greatly enriched. They will have expanded their productive and, to an even greater extent, their receptive repertoires, without losing anything of their L1 accent in the process. Their English accents will still include many features of L1 pronunciation transfer (in non-core areas), and by this means, L2 speakers will preserve their own L1 identities even as they identify with other L2 speakers in international settings through the use of core features and accommodation. The difference is that now the transfer is evidence of a legitimate regional accent rather than of error.

To return to the comments I made at the beginning of this section, it is crucial to the future of EIL that L2 accents are handled in a sensitive manner. Intelligibility is central to EIL, but this does not any longer mean intelligibility for 'NSs'. Anachronistic attempts to promote the latter and, thus, to compromise learners' L1 identities unnecessarily, are doomed to failure. It is no longer acceptable to expect learners to do what one speaker at the TESOL 1999 Convention recommended, that is, to 'put on their American face' (or, for that matter, their British one) in order to produce and receive pronunciation for the benefit of 'native speakers'. Now that we have empirical evidence demonstrating that many L1 phonological features are irrelevant to EIL intelligibility, there is no good reason to expect learners to acquire these features and, by implication, in the process to obliterate as much as possible of their L1 accents and, along with these, their L1 identities. A programme of accent addition such as I have outlined above seems to make much better sense in both ethical and practical terms.

One other major obstacle that must be overcome in this respect, however, is the attitude of L2 speakers of English themselves, including teachers of English, to their own accents. This is the *linguistic insecurity* that Labov, who coined the term, used to explain the findings in his 1966 study of social variation in New York City. Edwards describes 'the general tendency for non-standard dialect speakers to accept the often negative stereotypes of their own variants' as revealed by the way in which members of low-status groups regularly adopt the unfavourable reactions of high-status groups to their speech in matched guise tests'. He considers that 'this "minority-group reaction" is a revealing comment on the power and breadth of social stereotypes in general, and on the way in which these may be assumed by those who are themselves the object of unfavourable evaluation' (1994: 99). As Lippi-Green puts it, these minority-group speakers 'become *complicit* in the process' (1997: 242; emphasis added).

The problem for EIL is that 'NNS' accents (and their owners) have been subject to prejudice in and from the British and American centre for decades, such that even in these multicultural days it is difficult for speakers of English with L2 accents to gain places on teacher training courses and just about impossible for them to secure jobs teaching English in either country. Unsurprisingly, then, they have developed an inferiority complex about their English. They have come to regard the real experts of English as an *international* language as being 'NSs' of English as a *national* language, and themselves as second best, and continue to do so even though they are now the majority-group speakers.

This is demonstrated, for example, by Dalton-Puffer et al. (1997), whose empirical research among Austrian university students of English 'confirms the low status the non-native accents have amongst their users and that overall preference for the three native accents' (the latter being RP, near-RP, and GA). Similar findings are reported by McKay (1995, cited in Bamgboşe 1998) for a group of international students of ESL at the University of Illinois. It is crucial for the future of EIL that teacher educators whether 'NS' or 'NNS' take on the task of counteracting this 'minority-group reaction', not least because the group concerned is, in fact, the *majority*. (For further discussion, see pages 215–27 on the need for radical changes in the status of 'NNS' pronunciation teachers.) A programme of accent addition should go some way towards resolving the 'love–hate relationship' that many L2 speakers have with 'NS' English accents (Bamgboşe 1998: 7), such that at one and the same time, they both consciously value 'NS' over 'NNS' accents but fear acquiring them.

An overhaul of pronunciation testing

In Chapter 6, I presented the case for redefining phonological error for EIL. This, in turn, has major implications for the testing of learners' pronunciation. Correctness can no longer be assessed in relation to 'NS' (for example, RP or GA) phonological norms and intelligibility for 'NS' judges. Instead, we should be thinking about EIL norms and intelligibility for BES judges, preferably 'NNSs', from L1s other than those of the learner. This is all the more important now that many speaking examinations are conducted in communicative settings, with candidates interacting with one another rather than with the assessor(s). In such examinations, it is essential to assess pronunciation, not in a vacuum, but within the context of the interaction taking place. That is, are speakers able to adjust their pronunciation appropriately to accommodate their interlocutors? However, to date little progress appears to have been made in this direction. As Lowenberg argues, it is still the case that 'most researchers in testing appear to assume implicitly that the benchmark for proficiency in English around the world should be the norms accepted and used by "native speakers" of English' (1992: 108). By this token, any departure from 'NS' norms should automatically be considered evidence of deficiency, of interlanguage error rather than international variety.

Some of the data on which I based my Lingua Franca Core were collected during practice for one particular speaking examination, Paper 5 of the Certificate in Advanced English (CAE), a University of Cambridge Local Examinations Syndicate (UCLES) examination considered to represent a low-advanced level of competence. Because all UCLES speaking examinations now adhere to a communicative model with similar format and descriptors, my comments on the CAE speaking examination can be taken to refer to all five examinations from elementary through to high-advanced.

Two of the CAE descriptors[15] refer respectively to accent and to intelligibility. As far as accent is concerned, the requirement is not adherence to 'NS' norms, but that there should be 'little accent' or that any L1 influence should not be 'obtrusive'. This is problematic. Firstly, the reference to 'little accent' is ambiguous. Presumably a speaker would not be penalized for having an RP accent. The 'little' must therefore be intended to have the force 'little that departs from RP (or other "NS" prestige accent)'. Secondly, how does one define 'obtrusive'? The obtrusiveness of an accent is largely dependent on the perspective of the receiver: in the case of CAE, the 'NS' assessors and the 'NNS' co-candidate (who may or may not share the speaker's L1). L2 speakers, as we noted above, appear to have a strong and overtly expressed preference for 'native-like' accents (see above, page 211 on the 'minority-group reaction'). On the other hand, according to Porter and Garvin (1989), 'NSs' do not appear to consciously favour 'NS' accents and disfavour 'NNS' accents to the same extent that 'NNSs' themselves do. However, the social-psychological literature reveals considerable 'NS' bias against 'NNS' accents (see pages 207–12), even though this may well operate below the level of consciousness. The danger is, then, that while 'NS' assessors may not give low marks for pronunciation to candidates who have a particular type or degree of L1 phonological influence in their accent, subconscious bias may lead them to reduce marks in other more flexible global categories such as 'Task Achievement' or 'Interactive Communication'.

Moving on to intelligibility, CAE (and subsequent models of other UCLES speaking examinations) shows signs of progress by establishing closer links than hitherto between pronunciation and communciation of the message or, in other words, intelligibility. What has not been properly thought through, however, is the issue of 'intelligible for whom?'. The descriptors refer to 'the listener', but does this refer to the assessors or the co-candidate? People inevitably judge the intelligibility of speech according to their own level of understanding and in this respect, CAE assessors—in my experience over several years—are no different. Typical comments made to me by co-assessors when unable to understand candidates' pronunciation include words to the effect that one candidate only understood the other because they were both, for example, Spanish, or because they had prepared for the exam together. Lowenberg points to the paradox of a situation in which the norms expected to be followed in an interaction are those of 'NSs', 'even when no native speakers are involved' (1993: 104). Clearly, in testing pronunciation, greater account than this must be taken of the 'candidate interface': the ways in which they adapt their pronunciation to facilitate one another's understanding, and the extent to which they successfully achieve mutually intelligible pronunciation. The level of understanding achieved by the assessors is irrelevant in this regard.

Nevertheless, the solution is not to be found in the opposite extreme, that of regarding any successful communication between candidates as indicative of acceptable pronunciation, and any deviation from 'NS' English pronunciation as evidence of a regional variety. As regards the latter point, Simo-Bobda argues that unless we define (describe and codify) new local norms clearly, 'many students and teachers ... [will] understand this idea to mean that whatever is incorrect can be defended as a feature of local English' (1999: 29). If we adopt a core approach, however, the problem for EIL is not as extensive as it is for the New Englishes (i.e. the intranational ESL varieties) which Simo-Bobda has in mind. The latter are each individually faced with a mammoth task of codification, whereas for EIL, we are dealing with one international set of pronunciation requirements, and accepting as regional variation all that lies outside its limits. Paradoxically, EIL pronunciation testing should then become more rather than less rigorous—less subject to the personal perceptions and biases of examiners, and more closely related to abilities in specific phonological areas.

The other important consideration for EIL testing is the need to test speakers' ability to accommodate towards one another. As we noted in Chapter 3, no speaker's production is invariant and in interlanguage talk (ILT) the most likely cause of intra-speaker phonological variation is communicative efficiency: the desire to be intelligible to an interlocutor. This, as I demonstrated, leads to phonological convergence. However, in ILT, convergence is manifest, not as it is in communication between speakers of the same language, but in ways that more resemble the adjustments made in Foreigner Talk. In same-L1 interaction, speakers motivated to converge do so by shifting their accent in the direction of their more/less standard interlocutor's pronunciation. In Foreigner Talk, on the other hand, NSs signal convergence by articulating more clearly and slowly as part of the overall strategy of simplifying their speech in order to render it more comprehensible to an apparently non-proficient L2 speaker.

In ILT the situation is more complex. Speakers are not likely to converge on an interlocutor's L1-influenced pronunciations for two main reasons: firstly, the pronunciations are not within their productive repertoire; and secondly, in the context of an examination, they would not wish to jeopardize their own performance by voluntarily producing items which might be regarded by the examiners as errors. The convergent strategy employed in ILT is therefore one of convergence on a more target-like pronunciation of relevant core phonological items, i.e. not in cases where interlocutors share a particular non-target feature (for example, German and Turkish NBESs both tend to substitute /v/ for /w/). As we saw in Chapter 3, this convergence occurred at statistically significant levels both in different-L1 as compared with same-L1 pairs, and in information exchange as compared with social interaction tasks.

On the other hand, same-L1 pairs were found to converge on their mutual L1 accents—since there was no communicative need to converge on the target—and thus to increase the amount of L1 phonological transfer in their speech. Indeed, the subjects involved claimed that they found one another easier to understand when transfer was increased in this way. In other words, when interlocutors share the same L1, a stronger L1 accent is communicatively more effective than a less 'obtrusive' one, and is therefore likely to be produced even in testing situations where it may lead to the candidates being awarded low marks for pronunciation.

In order for pronunciation testing to be relevant to EIL, two major changes urgently need to be effected. Firstly, whether or not an examination is conducted communicatively, descriptors need altering radically so that the candidates' pronunciation is only being tested in relation to the core areas, rather than in relation to all the features of a native-like accent. This will involve the retraining of assessors, and include their familiarizing with a wide range of L2 English accents, so that they are able to discern when a candidate is making adjustments to accommodate an interlocutor. Secondly, in communicative testing, methods need to be devised for assessing candidates' pronunciation performance according to the success or otherwise of the communication between them, independently of assessors' personal ratings of the quality and intelligibility of the pronunciation. The principal criterion in EIL pronunciation testing should be that candidates understand one another's pronunciation and find it acceptable. However, identifying a way to measure this and make the approach feasible is likely to prove extremely difficult.

Radical improvement in the status of 'NNS' EIL pronunciation teachers

The proposition that 'NNSs' are better placed than 'NSs' to teach English to second language learners is not one that is likely to meet with widespread approval among teachers of either group at present. Nevertheless, there are compelling reasons why we should give the proposition our serious attention and consider its implications for the future of EIL in general and of pronunciation teaching in particular.

The background to the 'NS–NNS' teacher debate

As Nayar argues, 'the concept of the native speaker, particularly for a language with such a trans-national and trans-ethnic profile as English, creates some insidious pragmatic problems'. One of these problems relates specifically to the 'NS–NNS' teacher debate. This is the way in which the concept 'confuses language identity with academic and pedagogic excellence'. Nayar continues as follows:

The discourse of Applied Linguistics as well as the vast amount of supporting material brought out by the ESL/EFL enterprise have created and perpetuated the image of the native speaker as the unquestionable authority of not just language ability but also of expertise in its teaching. Native speaker status is often seen as the *sine qua non*, automatically bestowing authenticity and credibility on a teacher, as an English Language expert or even a teacher trainer. As an initial gate-keeping shibboleth, nativeness can assume primacy over pedagogic expertise or actual language competence in the ELT enterprise.
(1998: 287)

In order to set the scene for the discussion which follows of 'NNS' and 'NS' teachers in relation to EIL pronunciation teaching, I will first present the main questions that have been raised as to the legitimacy of this higher status accorded 'NS' teachers of English, beginning with a quotation from Henry Widdowson, which is reproduced here at length because it neatly encapsulates the central issues:

... teachers of English are required to teach not English as a general linguistic phenomenon but English as a subject—a subject which keeps company with others on the curriculum—history, physics, geography and so on. Now nobody, I think, would suppose that somebody who lived through a particular period of history was especially well qualified to teach it as a subject—that the best teachers of the history of the Second World War, for example, are a diminishing group of octogenarian old soldiers who have actually lived the experience. Similarly, it would surely be odd to argue that the best teachers of the geography of, say, the Austrian Alps are Tyrolean shepherds because they have a unique intimacy with the landscape ... Of course these people have a wealth of intimate experience which can be drawn upon as data, and so they can serve as expert **informants** on certain aspects of the subjects concerned. But this does not make them expert **instructors**.

The same kind of argument applies to the subject English. And in our case the subject is English **as a foreign language** (EFL). It has generally been the case, I think, that teachers of EFL have been considered (or consider themselves) as teachers of English which happens incidentally to be a foreign language. In this definition of the subject, English is paramount and its speakers privileged. But we can also conceive of EFL as the teaching of a foreign language which happens to be English. Now the focus of attention is on the foreignness and not the nativeness of the language, on what makes it foreign, and how, as a foreign language, it might be most effectively taught.

Now when it comes to expertise in the teaching of foreign languages, those in the English speaking world have little to offer. In this respect, the fact that their own language is so dominant does them a disservice. The British[16] are not noted for their ready acquisition of any language other than their own. The record of foreign language instruction in their schools has, generally speaking, been one of dismal failure. And yet there is this pervasive assumption that they are naturally expert in the teaching of a foreign language to other people ... But why should the British claim any authority to advise on foreign language teaching, in which they have no credible credentials at all? It seems perverse. And yet such authority is claimed. And furthermore, it is conceded. Why?

Because there is this persistent confusion, I suggest, between the phenomenon English as a native language, and the subject English as a foreign language, and the invalid assumption that arises from it that experience in the one readily transfers to an expertise in the other. In other words, that pedagogic competence in EFL follows easily on from a linguistic competence in E—the FL can be added on without too much effort or trouble. Start with native speaker ability, add on a little common sense, or perhaps a brief rudimentary training in technique, get hold of a resource book, and hey presto, you are an EFL teacher, eligible for employment, a genuine article with customer appeal.
(1994b: 1.10–1.13; emphasis in original)

Although Widdowson refers specifically to EFL, I believe his argument to be even more pertinent in the context of EIL, and particularly EIL pronunciation teaching. But before I move on to discuss my reasons, it is important that we consider the implications of the above passage. We are concerned, on the one hand, with knowledge of the subject English and, on the other, with the ability to teach this subject. Widdowson's gist is that 'NS' teachers are, by and large, equipped with knowledge only in a 'privileged' intuitive sense, and with pedagogic competence only to a 'rudimentary' degree. By contrast, he goes on to argue, 'NNS' teachers know the 'subject' English, in an explicit rather than intuitive sense, by virtue of having themselves learnt it as a 'foreign' (i.e. second rather than first) language and as a result of this, their pedagogic 'credentials' are more 'credible'.

Some 'NS' teachers, on learning of this line of argument, take great exception to it. For example, Martin Parrott writes of his anger at the 'assumption that (native-speaking) language teachers are ignorant about the systems of English 'as a foreign language' and dismissive of theoretical issues'. He continues: 'Native speakers can't make themselves into non-native speakers but, in my experience, native speaking teachers are avid language learners and analysts and researchers of their learners' languages and linguistic strengths and difficulties in learning English' (1998: 20).

Similarly, in response to an article written by George Kershaw (1996), in which the advantages of 'NNS' over 'NS' teachers are enumerated, Steve Saxton raises a number of objections. He counters Kershaw's claim that 'NS' teachers have limited knowledge of the English language by enumerating his own credentials: '... I did English O-level in the days when grammar was still part of the syllabus, then A-level, then a BA in English, then Certificate, Diploma and Masters in TESOL', adding that 'there is a frightening number of people with similar qualifications' (1997: 48–9). Moving on to Kershaw's characterization of 'NS' teachers of English as uninformed monolinguals, Saxton asks 'But who are these people? I can't recall any native-speaker colleagues who didn't have at least one other language. For myself, I have fluent Swedish and German, passable French ..., basic Turkish and a smattering of a few other languages', again adding 'This is nothing special among TEFL professionals: my impression is that many are far better linguists than I am' (ibid.: 49). Saxton concludes that the case for NNS teachers is being spoilt by the setting up of 'a target of an uncompetent and/or unqualified native speaker'. On the contrary, he points out, 'Like many others, I have sunk thousands of pounds of savings and valuable months and years in postgraduate qualifications. We are not trading on the fact of being native speakers alone' (ibid.).

Saxton and Parrott are right: but only up to a point. Of course there are institutions which provide excellent English language teacher education for native speakers, just as there are others which provide minimal training in English teaching for non-native speakers. There are 'NS' teachers who have undergone a process of teacher development similar to that which Saxton describes, just as there are 'NNS' teachers who have not approached their professional development with anything like this degree of rigour. It cannot possibly be said that all 'NNS' teachers 'know' English and are skilled pedagogues, while the opposite obtains for all 'NS' teachers, and one is bound to sympathize with (the minority of) 'NS' teachers who, like Saxton and Parrott, have invested much in their own education and are justifiably aggrieved by claims to the contrary.

However, two factors are inescapable. Firstly, while the education of many 'NNS' teachers of English, particularly in Europe, extends over several years, the vast majority of British, as well as a number of American and Australasian, 'NS' teachers of English are trained only to certificate level.[17] That is, they have attended a four- (or very occasionally five-) week teacher training course or its part-time equivalent, such as the UCLES CELTA course and the Trinity College TESOL Certificate. This is the kind of 'rudimentary training in technique' to which Widdowson refers. In the space of four weeks trainees have to acquire both teaching skills and knowledge about the English language and, inevitably, they do not proceed very far with either. If they are eventually to be competent teachers, it is therefore essential that they continue learning 'on the job'. Their development as teachers will thus depend largely on the teaching environment in which they subsequently find themselves. And given that better language schools are often prepared to employ only those teachers certificate with grade 'B' or above, many of the novice teachers who have merely 'passed' their certificate (grade 'C'), i.e. the vast majority, could well find themselves in less supportive, less teacher-development-friendly institutions, where they have little opportunity to continue learning about the language and developing their teaching skills. Such institutions are also far less likely to encourage their teachers to progress to higher level qualifications such as diplomas and master's degrees, let alone to finance these.

Secondly, and rather more crucial in the context of EIL, is 'NS' teachers' previous language learning experience. And here there are two considerations. The first is that, *pace* Saxton, a great many 'NS' teachers do *not* speak other languages. Again, there will always be exceptions, but in both Britain and America, monolingualism is the norm and this applies as much to teachers of English as it does to the rest of the 'NS' population. The second relates to their lack of experience of learning English as a second rather than a first language. Even if 'NS' teachers do have experience of learning other languages, they cannot replicate the experience of learning English in this way. As Seidlhofer argues:

> Most importantly perhaps, the non-native teacher has been through the process of learning the same language, often through the same L1 'filter', and she knows what it is like to have made the foreign language, in some sense, her own, to have appropriated it for particular purposes. This is an experience which is shared only between non-native teachers and their students. One could say that native speakers know the destination, but not the terrain that has to be crossed to get there: they themselves have not travelled the same route. Non-native teachers, on the other hand, know the target language as a foreign language. Paradoxically, it is precisely this which is often perceived as a weakness, although it can be understood, and drawn upon, as an important resource. This shared language learning experience should thus constitute the basis for non-native teachers' confidence, not for their insecurity.
> (1999: 238)

Seidlhofer's point is that 'NNS' English teachers' personal knowledge of the 'route' that their learners are travelling can only ever be a strength, never a weakness. In other words, 'NNS' teachers have privileged knowledge which informs their teaching, particularly if they share their learners' L1 and have thus learnt English through 'the same L1 "filter"'. But even if they do not share the same L1 as their learners, the very fact of their bilingualism by definition provides these 'NNS' teachers with insights into the learning of English which are unavailable to 'NS' teachers, especially to the monolingual majority.

There is, of course, a sense in which 'NS' teachers also have privileged knowledge. However, theirs relates to the English language rather than to its teaching. This is the intuitive knowledge which Widdowson describes as 'intimate experience which can be drawn upon as data' (see page 216). It includes (I assume) a knowledge of idiomatic usage, slang, phrasal verbs, puns, proverbs, cultural allusions and the like, all of which can present difficulties to 'NNS' teachers if they occur unexpectedly in their classrooms. But the essential point is that as far as EIL is concerned, this sort of knowledge of the English language is irrelevant. If EIL is to succeed as a worldwide lingua franca, its speakers will have to avoid this sort of cultural baggage.

EFL is a different matter.[18] Those who still choose to learn EFL have made a decision to learn the English of its native speakers of one variety or another, rather than the more 'NNS'-oriented EIL. This is their prerogative and it would be patronizing indeed to deny them the option. And in this case, 'NS' teachers have the cultural and linguistic, if not the pedagogic, advantage. As Medgyes argues on behalf of 'NNS' teachers, 'To us, English is full of mystery both from a linguistic and from a cultural point of view ... by definition we have a less reliable knowledge of the English language than NESTs [native-speaking teachers of English]. In addition, we are likely to have relatively scanty information about the culture, or rather cultures, of English-speaking countries. Yet in the classroom we have to appear to be well-informed sources in both respects' (1994: 38). Elsewhere, Medgyes states: 'With respect to language competence, I regard it as axiomatic that all non-NESTs are deficient users of English' (1992: 345).

Although Medgyes accepts that English is now 'the primary language of international communication' (1994: 1), he regularly discusses its L2 teaching—as in the previous paragraph—within the original EFL, or 'NS–NNS', paradigm. In this regard, he considers—and appears to accept as inevitable—that 'NNS' teachers have an 'inferiority complex' (ibid.: 38). This is because they cannot, as Seidlhofer puts it, 'get into the skin of the native speaker' (1999: 243). And in EFL, it is important for teachers to be able to do this, for the simple reason that their learners require it of them. These EFL learners thirst for information about English idioms, slang, phrasal verbs, native English accents and suchlike, regardless of the likelihood of their acquiring these items for their own productive use. This is precisely why some EFL learners prefer to study with 'native speakers' of English and are prepared to spend considerable time and money travelling the globe in order to do so. For, regardless of their failings in other areas of language and pedagogy, 'NS' teachers are generally the better equipped as informants in these intuitive respects.

However, learners of this kind are a diminishing breed. Far more common are those learners who require English for international or, in the USA, multicultural communication, and in this context, 'native speaker' intuition is not required of teachers. More important by far is competence as an instructor and this involves not only a solid education in pedagogy but, even more importantly for EIL, an appreciation of 'the foreignness and not the nativeness of the language' (Widdowson 1994b), 'the ability to get into the skin of the foreign learner' rather than that of the 'native speaker' (Seidlhofer ibid.), along with an understanding of what is involved in mutual intelligibility between 'NNSs' rather than in intelligibility for a 'NS'.[19] And these sorts of considerations are especially critical in EIL pronunciation teaching, to which we now turn.

Teaching pronunciation for EIL: 'NNS' teachers and 'NS' teachers

I referred above to the fact that EFL learners wish to be exposed to 'native' accents of English and, notwithstanding the problem of L1 identity which we considered earlier in the chapter, to acquire as close an approximation to one of these accents (often RP or GA) as possible. In EFL classrooms, therefore, 'NS' teachers are more likely than 'NNS' teachers to be able to provide the pronunciation models that learners wish to hear, assuming, of course, that teachers have within their own repertoire the individual learner's preferred target accent. However, this is not to say that 'NS' teachers are necessarily better placed to instruct learners in how to acquire these accents, particularly for productive (as opposed to receptive) use. Unless 'NS' teachers have sufficient familiarity with their learners' L1 pronunciation systems as well as a sound knowledge of articulatory phonetics (and although some do, the majority do not), they will be able to inform but not instruct: to do little more than model their own accent and hope that acquisition will follow by some mysterious magic process.

And once we turn our attention to pronunciation for EIL, the situation changes completely. It is no longer relevant for learners to attempt to approximate 'NS' accents; they need not even concern themselves primarily with their intelligibility for 'NS' listeners, nor with their own ability to understand the latter. Their pronunciation goal is, above all, one of international intelligibility, and here 'NS' teachers' privileged intuitive knowledge becomes largely irrelevant. On the other hand, the privileged knowledge of 'NNS' teachers, gained through their own experience of learning the L2, their background in the L1, and their membership of the EIL community, provides them with a number of distinct advantages. In terms of EIL, then, it is absurd that both 'NS' and 'NNS' teachers continue to regard the former as high status pronunciation authorities and the latter as secondary.

So what, precisely, are the advantages of 'NNS' teachers in dealing with EIL pronunciation? They fall into three main areas: phonological and phonetic knowledge systems; the intelligibility criterion; and classroom pronunciation models. We will take each of these in turn.

222 *The Phonology of English as an International Language*

Phonological and phonetic knowledge systems

Although, as I have already suggested, there are undoubtedly 'NNS' teachers who have a very limited knowledge of their own and the English phonological systems and of articulatory phonetics, they tend to be in the minority. In several European countries, for example, prospective English language teachers study English and pedagogy at university level for several years, during the course of which they look at phonology and phonetics in depth. The average British or American teacher of English,[20] on the other hand, knows little about the phonology of their learners' first language(s) and, in an overt rather than intuitive sense, not much more about that of their own L1. And even those who have learnt a little phonology are unlikely to have studied phonetics, despite the fact that, as Taylor (1991) points out, phonetic knowledge is crucial in EIL, with the need for both teachers and learners to become familiar with a growing range of L2 accents of English.

Taking the British situation, as I pointed out earlier, the majority of teachers do not progress beyond certificate level in their professional development. A typical UCLES certificate course (CELTA) with approximately 50 hours of 'input' is likely to include, at the most, around five one-hour sessions dealing with pronunciation—probably with a session each on the phonemic alphabet, features of connected speech, word stress, rhythm/sentence stress, and intonation. A typical UCLES diploma course (DELTA) devotes around twelve to fifteen hours to phonology. The same five areas are covered in slightly more detail, and there is also likely to be some fairly superficial discussion of interlanguage phonology (though rarely labelled thus) looking, for example, at the causes and effects of different L1 pronunciation problems.

The situation does not improve much on British master's courses. I do not have any precise figures, but as I write, IELTDHE (Institute for English Language Teacher Development in Higher Education) is about to conduct a survey of the amount of language description and analysis included in British master's courses in ELT, TESOL, Applied Linguistics, and the like. A brief show of hands at the IELTDHE 7th Annual Seminar in 1998 suggested that the figures ultimately revealed would be low, ranging from nothing to around thirty hours for the majority. Since these figures are aggregates of time spent on a range of potential language topics (phonology, phonetics, syntax, morphology, semantics, lexis, discourse analysis, and pragmatics), it follows that the amount of time—if any—dedicated to the first two will be minimal in most cases.

But 'NS' teachers tend not only to be less knowledgeable about phonology and phonetics than 'NNS' teachers at the formal level: they also often lack essential knowledge of a less formal kind. As I have already pointed out, 'NS' teachers have intuitive knowledge of L1 English pronunciation. This enables them to act as informants about the L2. For example, they are able to interpret pitch movements as expressions of particular attitudes (though not always at a conscious level), or to state instinctively where weak forms can and cannot be used. 'NNS' teachers rarely have this sort of intuitive knowledge of English, but nor do they need to do so in EIL teaching, where their learners are not aiming to 'get into the skin of the native speaker'. More important by far for EIL are intuitions about the L1 accents of their learners. 'NS' teachers rarely have such intuitions; 'NNS' teachers by definition have them in relation to learners from their own L1 (even if they have not studied their L1 phonology in a formal manner) and often, because they also speak other languages, in relation to learners from other L1s.

Whereas intuitions about the L2 pronunciation system simply make 'NS' teachers better informants, intuitions about learners' L1 pronunciation make 'NNS' teachers better instructors by enabling them to deal more effectively and sensitively with learners' difficulties with English pronunciation. This is because, as speakers (often native) of the same L1, they are aware of the strangeness for their learners of certain English items, perhaps particular sounds or clusters, the use of aspiration, the width of the pitch range, or the difference in length between stressed and unstressed syllables, and so on. They appreciate which items their own L1 group consider to be stereotypical markers of Englishness (i.e. those which they would produce if mimicking an L1 English speaker), and whose production may thus pose a particular threat to learners' L1 identities and risk the ridicule of their peer group and consequent classroom embarrassment. They probably found the same items strange, embarrassing, or threatening to produce at some point in their own learning of English, and are able to recall the feeling and empathize with their learners. This ensures that they will not approach the learning of these features of English in a purely mechanical way—as merely a matter of learners 'getting their tongues round' the items concerned.

Knowledge, both formal and intuitive, of their learners' L1 and the English L2 phonological and phonetic systems thus enables the informed majority of 'NNS' teachers to devise more effective classroom strategies to deal with their learners' problems. In particular, they can make use of articulatory phonetics to demonstrate where and how sounds are produced in the L2 as compared with the L1. And in the context of EIL—where L2 English accents are regional varieties in their own right rather than deficient attempts at reproducing an 'NS' variety—it is important for teachers to be able to focus on both, rather than exclusively on the (unattainable) 'NS' variety. If they are multilingual, 'NNS' teachers can use contrastive work to provide learners with overt exposure to other L2 accents than their own, thus improving learners' receptive EIL pronunciation. In monolingual classrooms, where this type of mutual exposure in a range of L2 accents is not available, teachers can still engage learners extensively in contrastive work by using recorded materials along with their own insights into the L2 English pronunciation of their learners. 'NNS' teachers can also take careful account of the link between L1 accent and identity, so enabling their learners to preserve their L1 identities in L2. And they are far better placed than monolingual—and even bilingual—'NS' teachers to take account of the crucial intelligibility criterion, which we consider next.

The intelligibility criterion

The intelligibility criterion refers to the prioritizing for pronunciation teaching of the features that were designated 'core' in Chapter 6. These features are the ones which emerged from the ILT data as crucial for mutual intelligibility in EIL interaction contexts, that is, between 'NNSs' rather than a 'NS' and 'NNS'. It follows from what I said in the previous section, that those teachers who are intimately familiar with their learners' L1 pronunciation systems are far better placed to identify which core features are already present in the learners' (L1) repertoires (by virtue of being features of their L1 systems) and which core features will have to be added to their EIL repertoires.

In addition, 'NNS' teachers are likely to have experience of using English as a lingua franca with speakers of other L1s. This means that they know at first hand which features of their own English pronunciation are unintelligible to speakers of other L2 varieties of English, and which features of the latters' pronunciation cause them intelligibility problems. This personal experience is then available to these teachers to reinforce the core approach. Even if the Lingua Franca Core is found to need some modifying in the light of future research into interlanguage talk, the principle itself is undamaged: those who speak English in EIL contexts are aware that it is not necessary to reproduce all aspects of L1 English pronunciation to be intelligible to other L2 speakers, and they have a good idea of which features are particularly crucial and which are trivial in this respect.

On the other hand, 'NS' teachers—even if bilingual—cannot put themselves into the shoes of L2 speakers of English and assess which pronunciation features of different L2 Englishes are intelligible and unintelligible to these speakers. They can only gauge intelligibility from their own perspective as 'NSs' of English and guess in respect of 'NNSs'. This regularly results in the 'NS' teacher assumption that whatever features make English pronunciation intelligible to them will also make it intelligible to 'NNS' listeners, and so they present these features in their classrooms as all-purpose, all-context pronunciation essentials. Their personal experience, far from reinforcing the core approach, is likely to militate against it.

A good example of the way in which NSs' personal experience militates against the core approach is a recent electronic mail discussion in which I participated, about the relative importance of segmentals and suprasegmentals, which was hotly debated on both sides of the Atlantic. The discussion grew out of the following quotation from Rosewarne (1999: 46): 'The assertion, commonly made in the early 1990s, that suprasegmental features have the greatest impact upon the intelligibility of EFL [English as a Further Language] speakers, does not appear to have been established empirically, at least not to my satisfaction'. Rosewarne is specifically not talking about intelligibility for 'NS' receivers, as he points out in a footnote explaining his idiosyncratic use of the acronym 'EFL'. Nevertheless, the bulk of the (almost entirely NS) responses ignored the possibility of 'NNS' receivers and, in disagreeing with Rosewarne's position, commented from their own 'NS' perspective. Some comments even focused on *appropriacy* for 'NS' listeners. For example, two participants noted that Chinese speakers of English sound rude and abrupt to 'NSs' because of their staccato rhythm and lack of linking.

Part of the problem for 'NS' teachers is their investment in and emotional attachment to the L1 pronunciation system. It represents their identity, just as it does not represent the identities of L2 speakers. If a particular pronunciation feature of an L2 group sounds rude to 'NSs', unless they have studied sociolinguistics, social psychology, phonology, phonetics, and another L1 (and, as we have already noted, relatively few 'NS' teachers of English have done so), they will regard it as intrinsically rude rather than merely as evidence of an L2 regional variety. In the same way, if they find some aspect of an L2 group's pronunciation unintelligible, they will consider it intrinsically unintelligible and in need of remediation.

The core approach, then, will not appeal to any 'NS' teachers who are not prepared to adopt an EIL perspective and to consider pronunciation from an 'NNS' listener's point of view. These teachers will continue to base their pronunciation decisions on intelligibility and appropriacy for themselves and their peers. Thus, they will continue to teach for production assimilatory features (features of connected speech, such as assimilation, elision, weak forms, linking) and the sounds /θ/ and /ð/ simply because these items are important to them. 'NNS' teachers, on the other hand, do not have an emotional attachment to L1 English pronunciation and are therefore likely to be far more receptive, ultimately, to the core approach.

Classroom pronunciation models

The final and briefest part of this section focuses on the advantages of 'NNS' teachers in providing learners with pronunciation models. In Chapter 1, I discussed Dalton and Seidlhofer's (1994b) distinction between a model and a norm, and argued that in the context of EIL, it is not appropriate to regard RP or GA as a norm against which L2 pronunciation is judged (and inevitably found wanting), but agreed that they can provide useful classroom models or 'points of reference' to prevent learner accents from diverging too far in different directions.

As far as the RP model is concerned, though, we have a problem. If less than three per cent of British speakers of English have RP accents and, assuming that not all of these are engaged in teaching English, RP speakers are in very short supply in the outside world. This means that learners of British English are far more likely to be taught by speakers with other (light) regional British accents. I do not regard this in itself as greatly problematic, since these accents share most of the EIL core features (and a good many of the non-core features) with one another.

However, for completely different reasons, I believe that the optimum pronunciation models for EIL are those of ('NNS') fluent bilingual speakers of English. These are both more realistic and more appropriate than L1 models and yet sacrifice nothing in intelligibility. Fluent bilingual models incorporate all the core features and are thus internationally intelligible. For learners from the same L1 as the teacher, the model also contains a number of L1 features, and is thus more realistic, i.e. attainable in a practical sense.

But more importantly, fluent bilingual models are also more appropriate sociolinguistically and socio-psychologically. In sociolinguistic terms, it is a simple matter of practising what we preach. If we wish to argue that L2 accents (containing the core features) are regional varieties equal in EIL status to 'NS' varieties of English, then we cannot imply that they are somehow less suitable than the latter as classroom models, and thus in some way substandard. For learners who do not share the teacher's L1, there is nevertheless the benefit of exposure to the teacher's accent, which is more useful to EIL learners than exposure to RP. In socio-psychological terms, fluent bilingual teachers are living testimony to the fact that learners can acquire intelligible English accents while retaining their L1 identities.

I have spent a considerable amount of time on the issue of the status of 'NNS' teachers. This is because the balance needs redressing so very badly. 'NS' and 'NNS' teachers alike regard the latter as being far lower in status than the former and no more so than in pronunciation teaching. The 'accent bar' segregating 'NS' and 'NNS' users (Kachru 1992: 67)[21] is still alive and very well. The accents of 'NNS' teachers are constantly evaluated in terms of their proximity to 'NS' standard accents, while no credit is given to the advantages that 'NNS' teachers have in pronunciation teaching, particularly for EIL. In fact, I doubt if many are aware that there are advantages in this direction.

This would go some way to explaining the difficulties encountered by those with L2 English accents in securing teaching positions outside (and even, in some cases, within) their own L1 countries. In this regard, my own experience of working with 'NNS' teachers in Britain has been depressing. For example, L2 speakers on my DELTA (previously DTEFLA) courses have often had difficulties in finding enough temporary teaching work to allow them to fulfil the practical requirements of the course, let alone anything longer-term. Advertisements for teachers in Britain still regularly specify native speakers, and the same is apparently true in the USA. Bonny Norton, referring to her experience of studying job advertisements at the 1996 TESOL Convention in Chicago, says that she was 'struck by the number of advertisements that called specifically for a "native English speaker"' (1997: 422). And very recently there have been adverts in the British press seeking 'native-speaker' teachers for Japan and China.

Nevertheless, as EIL becomes more firmly established and 'NNS' teachers grow in number and confidence, we may one day reach the situation predicted by Eph Tunkle, a co-presenter at a colloquium entitled 'Non-native teachers teaching pronunciation', held at the 1999 TESOL Convention in New York: 'is it not feasible that in a few years, a colloquium will be held on the topic: "Native English speakers teaching pronunciation: where can we put them?"'

Pronunciation learning for 'native speakers' of English

If 'NSs' of English do not want to be left behind in international communication, they will finally have to accept that it is not sufficient that English is their first language, and that they, too, have to expend some effort on learning EIL. Indeed, as Widdowson points out, 'the fact that their own language is so dominant does them a disservice' (see page 217 above). For centuries, 'NSs' have assumed that it is the job of the others, the 'NNSs', to make their English intelligible to NSs. There has never been any question of the opposite scenario. And this situation still obtains in the minds of the vast majority of British and American teachers of English, with the exception of some who teach Business English (though this is not yet overly reflected in Business English teaching materials). But, as Kachru points out, the newer role of English as the language of international communication 'puts a burden on those who use it as their *first* languange, as well as on those who use it as their *second* language'. He adds that 'this responsibility demands what may be termed "attitudinal readjustment"' on the part of 'NSs' (1992: 67; emphasis in original).

The perhaps unpalatable truth for 'NSs' is that if they wish to participate in international communication in the 21st Century, they too will have to learn EIL. For future children, it can be incorporated into the secondary school curriculum as a compulsory component of their existing English studies, and alongside the learning of other languages. The approach currently being developed by Walt Wolfram in the USA (as described in his paper 'Dialect Diversity in TESOL: A Proactive Program', presented at the 33rd TESOL Convention in New York, March 1999) to render children from different states more receptive to each other's dialects (grammar and vocabulary as well as pronunciation) provides useful pointers as to how awareness can be raised. But EIL learning will have to go beyond this to include both L2 varieties and productive accommodation.

For those who have already reached adulthood it will be necessary to attend adult EIL classes in the same way that 'NNS' adults do. These adults, like the school-age learners of the previous paragraph, will need to learn EIL receptively by adding to their 'NS'-oriented receptive repertoires a range of L2 regional accents of English. They will also need to learn EIL productively. This will entail learning the core features, regardless of their own L1 variety. Thus, for example, GA speakers will need to master the production of intervocalic /t/ and RP speakers of rhotic /r/ , so that they are able to produce them in EIL settings. Speakers of both these L1 varieties will have to accept that it may already be better, depending on their EIL interlocutor, to use substitutions of /θ/ and /ð/, and, at the very least, to accept and understand them. In this and other regards (such as the avoidance of assimilatory features where an EIL addressee will have difficulties in interpreting them), 'NSs' also need practice in adjusting their pronunciation according to the demands of their addressee and the speech situation. The development of accommodation skills described in Chapter 7 is thus as appropriate to 'NS' pronunciation education as it is to 'NNS'.

However, before any of this is possible, 'NSs' will require a change of attitude towards their own and L2 accents of English. In 1995 (3 November), the *International Herald Tribune*, an American newspaper produced in Paris, published an article by Mikie Kiyoi, a Japanese speaker of English living in Paris. The title of the article was 'Dear English Speakers, Please Drop the Dialects'. In it she argues that Anglo-Americans need to know 'that the English they speak at home is not always an internationally acceptable English', and asks, 'Dear Anglo-Americans, please show us you are also taking pains to make yourselves understood in an international setting'.[22]

As Tom McArthur points out, 'Such non-native points of view are on the increase, and as the reasonableness of their case becomes apparent, further efforts are likely to be made to regularize whatever we mean by International or World Standard English' (1999: 55). 'NSs' of English are no different in this respect from L2 speakers who wish to use English for international communication. They too will be obliged to learn the regularized forms of EIL which emerge and which, in terms of pronunciation, will most likely take the form of something similar, if not identical to, the Lingua Franca Core. And they will also have to '[take] pains to make [themselves] understood in an international setting', in other words to develop the sort of accommodation skills that they have always expected of 'NNSs', so that they are able to adjust their use of the core to suit individual EIL interlocutors.

There will inevitably be even greater difficulty in convincing American and British 'NSs' that they should make productive and receptive phonological adjustments of this kind in multicultural interaction within their own L1 countries. Nevertheless, in time, the EIL teacher education for 'NSs' of English that I mapped out above ought gradually to affect attitudes towards L2 speakers and their accents at home as well as in international settings.

It will be interesting in years to come to see whether the term 'native' undergoes another change in connotation. In the days of empire, the natives were the indigenous populations and the term itself implied uncivilized, primitive, barbaric, even cannibalistic (see Pennycook 1998). With the spread of English around the globe, 'native'—in relation to English—has acquired newer, positive connotations. 'Native speakers' of English are assumed to be advanced (technologically), civilized, and educated. But as 'NSs' lose their linguistic advantage, with English being spoken as an International Language no less—and often a good deal more—effectively by 'NNSs' (preferably no longer labelled as such); and as bilingualism and multilingualism become the accepted world norm, and monolingualism the exception (see Graddol 1997), perhaps the word 'native' will return to its pejorative usage. Only this time, the opposite group will be on the receiving end.

Notes

1 What Crystal actually states is that the total population of the US is 251,394,000 million and the total number of L1 English speakers 221,227,000 million. But he points out that the assumption that a large proportion of the remainder of the population (i.e. just over 30 million) can be counted as L2 speakers is probably correct.

2 This was the figure given by David Crystal in his plenary talk, 'The Future of English: A Welsh Perspective' at the 33rd Annual TESOL Convention, New York, March 1999.

3 Cambridge Integrated Language Teaching Schemes (CILTS) Bulletin 44, July/August 1996. Since the launching of the CILTS framework, the former pre-service CTEFLA (Certificate in the Teaching of English as a Foreign Language to Adults) and COTE (Certificate for Overseas Teachers of English) have been replaced by CELTA (Certificate in English Language Teaching to Adults), and the former DTEFLA (Diploma in the Teaching of English as a Foreign Language to Adults) and DOTE (Diploma for Overseas Teachers of English) by DELTA.

4 There are a number of more enlightened centres, especially CELTA, who are now prepared to give places to 'NNS' trainees whose accents are 'intelligible'. However, these remain the exception rather than the rule, and intelligibility is presumably interpreted as 'intelligible to 'NSs' of English'.

5 The substance of this presentation is repeated in Jenkins 1998b.

6   As opposed to NS intuitions—which are rarely accurate.
7   We are now firmly in the realm of teacher education. It would be impossible for short teacher training courses to deal in any adequate manner with both sociolinguistics and social psychology. Such courses will inevitably be forced to continue to deal in partial truths.
8   This is not to suggest that the study of these two disciplines is useful only or mainly as preparation for English pronunciation teaching. They are, of course, important in their own right as well as providing important background to a host of other subjects within the general area of applied linguistics. My point is simply that they are essential to appropriate and effective English pronunciation teaching.
9   I am not including here the intranational ESL varieties of English, such as Indian English and Singapore English.
10 The University of Cambridge Local Examinations Syndicate's First Certificate in English (FCE) is generally considered to be of upper intermediate level, and Preliminary English Test (PET) of lower intermediate level. According to UCLES, 'FCE has widespread recognition in commerce and industry, e.g. for contact with the public or secretarial work in banking, airlines, catering etc', while those with PET 'should be able to cope linguistically in a range of everyday situations which require use of English in their own or a foreign country, in contact with native and non-native speakers of the language' (UCLES 2000: 11–13).
11 As Quirk points out, 'Few today would suggest that there was a single standard of English in the world. There are few enough ... that would claim the existence of a single standard within any one of the ENL countries: plenty that would even deny both the possibility and the desirability of such a thing' (1985: 2). And McArthur argues that there is even a 'pecking order' among different Standard Englishes, though the order itself depends on one's personal perspective (1999: 54). See also McArthur (1998: 119–37) for definitions of and comments on Standard English ranging from the 18th to the 20th Centuries.
12 It is, of course, a feature of subtractive bilingualism in minority language situations, but in EIL contexts, L2 speakers are in the majority.
13 Kjellin has subsequently presented a paper on the subject: 'Accent Addition: Effects of prosody on second language learning', at LP (Linguistics and Phonetics) 98, Ohio State University, Columbus, Ohio (Kjellin 1999).
    In the paper, Kjellin cites Amalia Sarabasa as having influenced his own use of the term through personal correspondence and her 1994 paper.
14 Mendelsohn said words to this effect in his presentation at the 1994 TESOL Convention in Baltimore, and again at the 1998 TESOL Convention in Seattle, during his talk, 'Preparing teachers to be teachers of pronunciation' (as part of the Colloquium on the Teaching of

Pronunciation). He compared accent removal with stain removal and commented that neither works.

15 It should be noted that since I wrote this about pronunciation testing in CAE, the descriptors have been rewritten. Although some of the more negative comments about L2 accent have been removed, there is nothing in the new descriptors to suggest that there has been any marked change in the underlying philosophy or, indeed, in the way examiners are assessing pronunciation in practice.

16 Widdowson restricts his argument to the British, but the same is undoubtedly true of the Americans.

17 In the year 1997–98, 7,584 people took UCLES CELTA courses and in the same year, 748 people entered for the UCLES Diploma. The figures for the previous year were very similar (figures provided by UCLES, April 1999).

18 The title EIL has not yet become widely used and there are thus many learners who still refer to their English classes as 'EFL' but who are, nevertheless, learning English for international rather than 'NNS–NS' communication. My discussion at this point concerns EFL in the latter rather than the former sense.

19 I have talked throughout this section as though the definition of 'native speaker' were unproblematic. Obviously this is not the case, as discussed at length, for example, by Davies (1991, 1995), and see also Chapter 1 where I argued that the terms 'NS' and 'NNS' are nonsensical in the context of EIL, and proposed instead NBES and BES).

20 I am not referring here to pronunciation specialists such as writers of pronunciation courses, but to typical British and American teachers who can be found in ELT classrooms in various locations around the world.

21 The term was coined by Abercrombie in 1951 to refer to the phenomenon of judgements being made on people's speech depending on whether or not they spoke RP (see Abercrombie 1951: 13).

22 Reproduced in *English Today* 51, 13/3 page 17 under the heading 'Cosmopolitan English' and in *English Today* 58, 15/2 page 55.

Afterword:
The future of the phonology of EIL

Teach the language we must, for English is the international language and there's an end on't.

Sir John Hanson, Director-General, the British Council, 'English is as English does', review of Pennycook 1994 in the *Times Higher Education Supplement*, 7 July 1995

At the time of writing, the future of EIL is less certain than Sir John Hanson's words suggest. While there is general agreement that the world needs a neutral language of international communication, it is not clear that the language will ultimately be English, or English alone (Graddol 1997). Much will depend on the capacity of the English language to fulfil the dual needs of international intelligibility and local identity. A change of attitude among the world's speakers of English must be a first step in this direction, though categorical statements such as that quoted above do not inspire optimism that change is assured. On the contrary, they provide further evidence of what Kachru (1992) describes as the continuing 'grip on the profession' of the 'traditional paradigm' (see page 196).

The future of EIL is inextricably bound up with its pronunciation, both L1 and L2, and with the attitudes of speakers of L1 and L2 varieties of English to their own and one another's accents. If the 'traditional [pronunciation] paradigm' persists in English pronunciation teaching, then English will not be able to serve the needs of L2 local identity. Furthermore, mutual intelligibility will be restricted pedagogically to minority EFL ('NS–NNS') interaction, with 'NNS's still approximating the accent of the 'NS's as closely as possible. Thus, learners will not develop the ability to make their pronunciation easily intelligible in EIL ('NNS–NNS') interaction. And because L2 speakers of English all speak at least one other language—and often several—they may well switch to another language common to their repertoires to serve as a lingua franca for the purposes of international communication.

The purpose underlying this book has therefore been to try to move pronunciation teaching on from its narrow past and take it into the new century with a perspective relevant to the needs of the world's majority (L2) speakers of English. This means a perspective that embraces both 'NNS–NNS' mutual intelligibility and group identity. And I believe that a core approach does precisely this. The Lingua Franca Core (with possible future refinements) if acquired by EIL speakers (L1 as well as L2) will guarantee mutual phonological intelligibility. The extensive non-core areas will satisfy the demands of L1 identity to all but the 'NS' English minority. And this is a situation which the latter will have to learn to live with: if the core approach succeeds globally, the choice will no longer be theirs.

For the moment, however, we are some way from this situation. Many pronunciation courses are still based on the premise of 'NS–NNS' interaction and neglect the fact that learners are now interacting far more with other L2 speakers. Most pronunciation course books on both sides of the Atlantic still focus on intelligibility for L1 receivers and ignore considerations of identity altogether. Receptively, learners are generally required to make the effort to understand many aspects of 'NS' pronunciation, from sounds through assimilatory features to shades of attitude expressed in pitch movements. No pronunciation book to my knowledge gives learners practice in adjusting their pronunciation to suit the needs of different interlocutors or speech situations, or even discusses the need for them to do so. And nowhere are there publications addressing *L1 speakers of English* and the productive and receptive adjustments they too could be making to facilitate international communication.

The same is even more true of multicultural settings. In the USA especially, the attitude persists that if L2 speakers of English wish to succeed in securing and retaining employment, then it is they who must adjust their accent and conform to something more 'native-like', with little concession being made to their L1 roots. Some American phonologists refer to this process as a type of 'code-switching'—unjustifiably, to my mind, since code-switching tends to involve all participants in switching between two or more codes, rather than some participants in adjusting towards the 'more correct' code of others.

Nevertheless, all is not doom and gloom. In spite of my somewhat negative comments about many pronunciation materials, a small number are beginning to incorporate EIL considerations. Two come particularly to mind. The first, Judy Gilbert's *Clear Speech from the Start* (2000), is a pronunciation course for beginners. Her aim is to avoid the fine details which are regularly included in traditional courses simply because they are features of 'NS' pronunciation, and to prioritize those that are crucial for intelligibility. Although she does not specifically refer to international intelligibility, her priorities are very much in line with this in her promotion of the teaching of consonants, syllable length, and nuclear stress. The second book is a teacher education book, Dalton and Seidlhofer (1994a). The areas covered are those of traditional pronunciation manuals (sounds, connected speech, stress, intonation). Nevertheless, the authors do not take everything for granted in the way that many other courses do. Rather, they evaluate the usefulness of the published activities they discuss and even the validity of certain accepted phonological claims (such as stress-timing). But most important in relation to EIL are their discussions of the link between pronunciation and identity, and of the relationship between attitudes and intelligibility.

Progress is thus being made. But if English phonology is to serve the needs of its international speakers, there is still some way to go, not only in terms of attitudes but also of practicalities. Assuming that there is a place in EIL for the Lingua Franca Core (and this is by no means assured as I write), there are still difficulties. Most importantly, much more research is needed before we can say with confidence where we should draw the line between BES and NBES proficiency in expanding circle varieties of English. In other words, what do we consider to be part of interlanguage phonology and what to be part of an L2 regional accent? If we wish ultimately to be able to codify the phonological varieties of the expanding circle, it is essential to clarify this distinction.

Another problem is the need for empirical evidence from different international groupings to confirm (or not) the detailed claims of the LFC. In this regard, the continued lack of empirical research into phonology in EIL contexts—as compared with 'NS–NNS' contexts—remains disappointing. However, a start has recently been made in Brazil by Ricardo da Silva (1999), who conducted a small-scale study to test my original (Jenkins 1996a) core for its accuracy in predicting the intelligibility of Brazilian speakers' accents for other L2 speakers of English. Much more work of this kind will be necessary before we can be confident that we have identified the definitive core.

If EIL is the future of English, it will be so by virtue of its ability to reconcile the opposing forces of intelligibility and identity. And as far as spoken English is concerned, pronunciation is the common denominator. It is the one feature of the language that will enable speakers to preserve their L1 identity (through acceptable pronunciation transfer) while at the same time promoting their intelligibility (by selecting appropriately from the core in order to accommodate to their interlocutor). Phonology has long been marginalized in the teaching of English to speakers of other languages. But I suspect that it is about to experience a revival as the world's English speakers begin to appreciate the major contribution to international communication made by the phonology of English as an International Language.

Bibliography

Abercrombie, D. 1951. 'RP and Local Accent' in D. Abercrombie (ed.) 1965: *Studies in Linguistics and Phonetics*. Oxford: Oxford University Press.

Abercrombie, D. 1956. *Problems and Principles: Studies in the Teaching of English as a Second Language*. London: Longman.

Ahn, M. 1998. 'The phonological interlanguage of Korean learners of English.' Unpublished PhD thesis, University of Wales, Cardiff.

Ahulu, S. 1997. 'General English.' *English Today* 49, 13/1: 17–23.

Alexander, R. 1996. 'Lingua franca English'. *IATEFL Newsletter* 132: 35, August 1996.

Allwright, R. L. 1979. 'Language learning through communication practice' in C. Brumfit, and K. Johnson (eds.): *The Communicative Approach to Language Teaching*. Oxford: Oxford University Press.

Allwright, R. L. 1984a. 'The importance of interaction in classroom language learning'. *Applied Linguistics* 5/2: 156–71.

Allwright, R. L. 1984b. 'Why don't learners learn what teachers teach? The interaction hypothesis' in D. M. Singleton and D. G. Little (eds.): *Language Learning in Formal and Informal Contexts*. Dublin: IRAL.

Altenberg, E. and **R. Vago.** 1983. 'Theoretical implications of an error analysis of second language phonology production' in G. Ioup and S. H. Weinberger (eds.). 1987.

Anderson, A. and **T. Lynch.** 1988. *Listening*. Oxford: Oxford University Press.

Anderson, J. I. 1983. 'The Markedness Differential Hypothesis and syllable structure difficulty' in G. Ioup and S. H. Weinberger (eds.). 1987.

Anderson-Hsieh, J. 1995. 'Pronunciation factors affecting intelligibility in speakers of English as a foreign language'. *Speak Out!* 16: 17–19.

Andreasson, A-M. 1994. 'Norm as a pedagogical paradigm'. *World Englishes* 13/3: 395–409.

Arthur, B., R. Weiner, M. Culver, J. L. Young, and **D. Thomas.** 1980. 'The register of impersonal discourse to foreigners: verbal adjustments to foreign accent' in D. Larsen-Freeman (ed.) 1980: *Discourse Analysis in Second Language Research*. Rowley, Massachusetts: Newbury House.

Aston, G. 1986. 'Trouble-shooting in interaction with learners: the more the merrier?'. *Applied Linguistics* 7/2: 128–43.

Austin, J. L. 1962. *How to Do Things with Words*. Oxford: Clarendon Press.

Bamgboṣe, A. 1998. 'Torn between the norms: innovations in world Englishes'. *World Englishes* 17/1: 1–14.

Bansal, R. K. 1990. 'The pronunciation of English in India' in S. Ramsaran (ed.) 1990: *Studies in the Pronunciation of English: A Commemorative Volume in Honour of A.C. Gimson*. London: Routledge.

Beebe, L. 1977. 'The influence of the listener on code-switching'. *Language Learning* 27/2: 331–9.

Beebe, L. 1981. 'Social and situational factors affecting the communicative strategy of dialect code-switching'. *International Journal of the Sociology of Language* 31: 139–49.

Beebe, L. and H. Giles. 1984. 'Speech-accommodation theories: a discussion in terms of second-language acquisition' in H. Giles (ed.) 1984.

Beebe, L. and J. Zuengler. 1983. 'Accommodation theory: an explanation for style shifting in second language dialects' in N. Wolfson and E. Judd (eds.) 1983: *Sociolinguistics and Second Language Acquisition*. Rowley, Massachusetts: Newbury House.

Bell, A. 1984. 'Language style as audience design'. *Language in Society* 13: 145–204.

Bell, R. T. 1976. *Sociolinguistics: Goals, Approaches and Problems*. London: Batsford.

Benson, M. 1991. 'Attitudes and motivation towards English. A survey of Japanese freshmen'. *RELC Journal* 22/1: 34–48.

Berkovits, R. 1980. 'Perception of intonation in native and non-native speakers of English'. *Language and Speech* 23/3: 271–280.

Berkovitz, D. 1986. 'The effects of perceived cultural empathy on second language performance'. Unpublished doctoral dissertation, Columbia University.

Berns, M. 1995. 'English in the European Union'. *English Today* 43, 11/3: 3–11.

Bex, T. and R. J. Watts (eds.). 1999. *Standard English. The Widening Debate*. London: Routledge.

Bhatia, V. K. 1997. 'Introduction: genre analysis and world Englishes'. *World Englishes* 16/3: 313–9.

Bisong, J. 1995. 'Language choice and cultural imperialism: a Nigerian perspective'. *ELT Journal* 49/2: 122–32.

Block, D. 1996. 'Not so fast: some thoughts on theory culling, relativism, accepted findings, and the heart and soul of SLA.' *Applied Linguistics* 17/1: 63–83.

Bradford, B. 1982. 'Through the sound barrier. An approach to teaching pronunciation to multi-national groups of adult learners at advanced level'. Unpublished dissertation for RSA Diploma in TEFLA.

Bradford, B. 1988. *Intonation in Context* (Teacher's Book). Cambridge: Cambridge University Press.

Brazil, D. 1994. *Pronunciation for Advanced Learners of English* (Teacher's Book). Cambridge: Cambridge University Press.

Brazil, D. 1996. 'Designing an integrated pronunciation course'. *Speak Out!* 17: 5–9.

Brazil, D. 1997. *The Communicative Value of Intonation in English*. Cambridge: Cambridge University Press. Originally published in 1985 as Monograph 8 by the English Language Research Unit, University of Birmingham.

Brazil, D., M. Coulthard, and C. Johns. 1980. *Intonation and Language Teaching*. London: Longman.

Brodkey, D. 1972. 'Dictation as a measure of mutual intelligibility: a pilot study'. *Language Learning* 22/2: 203–20.

Broselow, E. 1983. 'Non-obvious transfer: on predicting epenthesis errors' in G. Ioup and S. H. Weinberger (eds.) 1987.

Broselow, E. 1984. 'An investigation of transfer in second language phonology' in G. Ioup and S. H. Weinberger (eds.) 1987.

Broselow, E., R. R. Hurtig, and C. Ringen. 1987. 'The perception of second language prosody' in G. Ioup and S. H. Weinberger (eds.) 1987.

Brown, A. 1991. *Pronunciation Models*. Singapore: Singapore University Press.

Brown, A. 1995. 'Minimal pairs: minimal importance?' *ELT Journal.* 49/2: 169–75.

Brown, G. 1974. 'Practical phonetics and phonology' in J. P. B. Allen and S. P. Corder (eds.) 1974: *The Edinburgh Course in Applied Linguistics Vol. 3: Techniques in Applied Linguistics.* Oxford: Oxford University Press.

Brown, G. 1989. 'Making sense: the interaction of linguistic expression and contextual information'. *Applied Linguistics* 10/1: 97–108.

Brown, G. 1990. *Listening to Spoken English.* 2nd edn. London: Longman.

Brown, G. 1995. *Speakers, Listeners and Communication.* Cambridge: Cambridge University Press.

Brown, G. 1996. 'Language learning, competence and performance' in G. Brown, K. Malmkjaer, and J. Williams (eds.): *Performance and Competence in Second Language Acquisition.* Cambridge: Cambridge University Press.

Brown, G., K. L. Currie, and J. Kenworthy. 1980. *Questions of Intonation.* London: Croom Helm.

Brown, G., K. Malmkjaer, A. Pollitt, and J. Williams (eds.) 1994. *Language and Understanding.* Oxford: Oxford University Press.

Brown, P. and S. C. Levinson. 1987. *Politeness. Some Universals in Language Usage.* Cambridge: Cambridge University Press.

Brumfit, C. J. (ed.). 1982. *English for International Communication.* Oxford: Pergamon Press.

Brumfit, C. J. 1984. *Communicative Methodology in Language Teaching.* Cambridge: Cambridge University Press.

Brumfit, C. J. 1995. 'The role of English in a changing Europe: where do we go from here?' *Best of ELTECS.* The British Council.

Bygate, M. 1988. 'Units of oral expression and language learning in small group interaction'. *Applied Linguistics* 9/1: 59–82.

Byram, M. 1989. *Cultural Studies in Foreign Language Education.* Clevedon: Multilingual Matters.

Cauldwell, R. 1996. 'Stress-timing: observations, beliefs, and evidence'. *Eger Journal of English Studies* Vol. 1: 33–48.

Celce-Murcia, M. 1977. 'Phonological factors in vocabulary acquisition: a case study of a two-year-old English-French bilingual'. *Working Papers in Bilingualism* 13: 27–41.

Celce-Murcia, M., D. M. Brinton, and J. M. Goodwin. 1996. *Teaching Pronunciation. A Reference for Teachers of English to Speakers of Other Languages.* Cambridge: Cambridge University Press.

Conteh-Morgan, M. 1997. 'English in Sierra Leone'. *English Today* 51, 13/3: 52–6.

Cook, V. 1993. *Linguistics and Second Language Acquisition.* Basingstoke: Macmillan.

Corder, S. P. 1978. 'Language-learner language' in J. C. Richards (ed.) 1978: *Understanding Second and Foreign Language Learning: Issues and Approaches.* Rowley, Massachusetts: Newbury House.

Coulthard, M. and M. Montgomery (eds.). 1982. *Studies in Discourse Analysis.* London: Routledge.

Coupland, J., N. Coupland, H. Giles, and K. Henwood. 1988. 'Accommodating the elderly: invoking and extending a theory'. *Language in Society* 17: 1–41.

Coupland N. 1984. 'Accommodation at work: some phonological data and their implications' in Giles (ed.) 1984.

Creider, C. A. 1979. 'On the explanation of transformations' in T. Givon (ed.): *Syntax and Semantics 12, Discourse and Syntax.* New York: Academic Press.

Cruttenden, A. 1970. 'On the so-called grammatical function of intonation'. *Phonetica* 21: 182–92.

Cruttenden, A. 1986. *Intonation*. Cambridge: Cambridge University Press.
Cruz-Ferreira, M. 1989. 'A test for non-native comprehension of intonation in English'. *IRAL* 27/1: 23–39.
Crystal, D. 1987. *The Cambridge Encyclopedia of Language*. Cambridge: Cambridge University Press.
Crystal, D. 1988. *The English Language Today*. London: Penguin.
Crystal, D. 1995. *The Cambridge Encyclopedia of the English Language*. Cambridge: Cambridge University Press.
Crystal, D. 1996. 'The past, present and future of English rhythm'. *Speak Out!* 18: 8–13.
Crystal, D. 1997. *English as a Global Language*. Cambridge: Cambridge University Press.
Crystal, D. and D. Davy. 1975. *Advanced Conversational English*. London: Longman.

da Silva, R. 1999. 'A small-scale investigation into the intelligibility of the pronunciation of Brazilian intermediate students'. *Speak Out!* 23: 19–25.
Dalton, C. and B. Seidlhofer. 1994a. *Pronunciation*. Oxford: Oxford University Press.
Dalton, C. and B. Seidlhofer. 1994b. 'Is pronunciation teaching desirable? Is it feasible?' in T. and S. Sebbage (eds.) *Proceedings of the 4th International NELLE Conference*. Hamburg: NELLE.
Dalton-Puffer, C., G. Kaltenboeck, and U. Smit. 1997. 'Learner attitudes and L2 pronunciation in Austria'. *World Englishes* 16/1: 115–28.
Daniels, H. 1995, 'Psycholinguistic, psycho-affective and procedural factors in the acquisition of authentic L2 pronunciation'. *Speak Out!* 15: 3–10. Reprinted in A. McLean (ed.) 1997.
Davies, A. 1991. *The Native Speaker in Applied Linguistics*. Edinburgh: Edinburgh University Press.
Davies, A. 1995. 'Proficiency or the native speaker: what are we trying to achieve in ELT?' in G. Cook and B. Seidlhofer (eds.) 1995: *Principle and Practice in Applied Linguistics. Studies in Honour of H.G. Widdowson*. Oxford: Oxford University Press.
Davies, A., C. Criper, and A. P. R. Howatt (eds.). 1984. *Interlanguage*. Edinburgh: Edinburgh University Press.
Day, R. (ed.) 1986. *Talking to Learn: Conversation in Second Language Acquisition*. Rowley, Massachusetts: Newbury House.
De Bot, K. 1986. 'The transfer of intonation and the missing data base' in E. Kellerman and M. Sharwood Smith (eds.) 1986.
Dickerson, L. J. 1975. 'The learner's interlanguage as a system of variable rules'. *TESOL Quarterly* 9: 401–7.
Dickerson, L. J. and Dickerson W. B. 1977. 'Interlanguage phonology: current research and future directions' in S. P. Corder and E. Roulet (eds.) 1977: *The Notions of Simplification, Interlanguages, and Pidgins, and their Relation to Second Language Pedagogy*. Neuchâtel: Faculté des Lettres.
Dickerson, W. B. 1976. 'The psycholinguistic unity of language learning and language change' in G. Ioup and S. H. Weinberger (eds.) 1987.
Doughty, C. and T. Pica. 1986. '"Information gap" tasks: do they facilitate second language acquisition?'. *TESOL Quarterly* 20: 305–25.
Dressler, W. U. 1984. 'Explaining natural phonology.' *Phonology Yearbook* 1: 29–51.

Eckman, F. 1977. 'Markedness and the contrastive analysis hypothesis' in G. Ioup and S. H. Weinberger (eds.) 1987.

Eckman, F. 1981a. 'On the naturalness of interlanguage phonological rules' in G. Ioup and S. H. Weinberger (eds.) 1987.

Eckman, F. 1981b. 'On predicting phonological difficulty in second language acquisition'. *Studies in Second Language Acquisition* 4: 18–30.

Edwards, J. 1994. *Multilingualism*. London: Routledge.

Edwards, J. R. 1982. 'Language attitudes and their implications among English speakers' in E. B. Ryan and H. Giles (eds.): *Attitudes towards Language Variation*. London: Edward Arnold.

Eisenstein, M. and G. Verdi. 1983. 'The intelligibility of social dialects for working-class adult learners of English'. *Language Learning* 35/2: 287–98.

Ellis, R. 1985. *Understanding Second Language Acquisition*. Oxford: Oxford University Press.

Ellis, R. 1994. *The Study of Second Language Acquisition*. Oxford: Oxford University Press.

Faerch, C. and G. Kasper. 1986. 'Cognitive dimensions of language transfer' in E. Kellerman and M. Sharwood Smith (eds.) 1986.

Ferguson, C. 1971. 'Absence of copula and the notion of simplicity: a study of normal speech, baby talk, foreigner talk and pidgins' in D. Hymes (ed.) 1971: *Pidginization and Creolization in Language*. Cambridge: Cambridge University Press.

Field, J. 1998. 'Skills and strategies: towards a new methodology for listening'. *ELT Journal* 52/2: 110–8.

Flege, J. E. 1987. 'The production of "new" and "similar" phones in a foreign language: evidence of the effect of equivalence of classification'. *Journal of Phonetics* 15: 47–65.

Flege, J. E. and J. Hillenbrand. 1984. 'Limits on phonetic accuracy in foreign language speech production' in G. Ioup and S. H. Weinberger (eds.) 1987.

Flowerdew, J. 1996. *Academic Listening. Research Perspectives*. Cambridge: Cambridge University Press.

Gass, S. and C. Madden (eds.). 1985. *Input in Second Language Acquisition*. Cambridge, Massachusetts: Newbury House.

Gass, S. and E. M. Varonis. 1984. 'The effect of familiarity on the comprehensibility of non-native speech'. *Language Learning* 31/1: 65–89.

Gass, S. and E. M. Varonis. 1985a. 'Variation in native speaker speech modification to non-native speakers'. *Studies in Second Language Acquisition* 7/1: 37–57.

Gass, S. and E. M. Varonis. 1985b. 'Task variation and nonnative/nonnative negotiation of meaning' in S. Gass and C. Madden (eds.) 1985.

Gass, S. and E. M. Varonis. 1991. 'Miscommunication in nonnative speaker discourse' in N. Coupland, H. Giles, and J. Wiemann (eds.) 1991: *'Miscommunication' and Problematic Talk*. Newbury Park: Sage Publications.

Gatbonton, E. 1978. 'Patterned phonetic variability in second language speech: a gradual diffusion model'. *Canadian Modern Language Review* 34/3: 335–47.

Gika, S. 1996. '"Foreign" in English language teaching: meaning, role and appropriateness'. *IATEFL Newsletter* 130: 14–7.

Gilbert, J. 1993. *Clear Speech*. 2nd edn. Cambridge: Cambridge University Press.

Gilbert, J. 2000. *Clear Speech from the Start*. Cambridge: Cambridge University Press.

Giles, H. 1973. 'Accent mobility: a model and some data'. *Anthropological Linguistics* 15: 87–105.

Giles, H. (ed.). 1984. *International Journal of the Sociology of Language. The Dynamics of Speech Accommodation*. Amsterdam: Mouton.

Giles, H. and N. Coupland. 1991. *Language: Contexts and Consequences*. Milton Keynes: Open University Press.

Giles, H., N. Coupland, and J. Coupland. 1991. 'Accommodation theory: communication, context, and consequence' in H. Giles, N. Coupland, and J. Coupland (eds.) 1991.

Giles, H., N. Coupland, and J. Coupland (eds.). 1991. *Contexts of Accommodation. Developments in Applied Sociolinguistics*. Cambridge: Cambridge University Press.

Giles, H., A. Mulac, J. J. Bradac, and P. Johnson. 1987. 'Speech accommodation theory: the first decade and beyond' in M. L. McLaughlin (ed.) 1987: *Communication Yearbook* 10. Beverly Hills, CA: Sage Publications.

Giles, H. and P. Smith. 1979. 'Accommodation theory: optimal levels of convergence' in H. Giles and R. St. Clair (eds.) 1979: *Language and Social Psychology*. Oxford: Blackwell.

Gimson, A. C. 1978. 'Towards an international pronunciation of English' in P. Strevens (ed.): *In Honour of A.S. Hornby*. Oxford: Oxford University Press.

Gimson, A. C. 1994. *An Introduction to the Pronunciation of English*. 5th edn. Revised by A. Cruttenden. London: Edward Arnold.

Graddol, D. 1997. *The Future of English*. The British Council.

Grice, H. P. 1975. 'Logic and conversation' in P. Cole and J. Morgan (eds.) 1975: *Syntax and Semantics 3: Speech Acts*. New York: Academic Press.

Gumperz, J. J. 1982. *Discourse Strategies*. Cambridge: Cambridge University Press.

Hakuta, K. 1974. 'Prefabricated patterns and the emergence of structure in second language acquisition'. *Language Learning* 24: 287–98.

Halliday, M. A. K. 1970. *A Course in Spoken English: Intonation*. Oxford: Oxford University Press.

Hassall, M. 1996a. 'Where do we go from here? TEIL: a methodology'. *World Englishes* 15/3: 419–25.

Hassall, M. 1996b. 'Implementing EIL: the medium really is the message'. *New Zealand Studies in Applied Linguistics* 2: 57–77.

Hecht, B. F. and Mulford, R. 1982. 'The acquisition of a second language phonology: interaction of transfer and developmental factors' in G. Ioup and S. H. Weinberger (eds.). 1987.

Hibbert, L. and S. Makoni. 1997. 'The Plain English Campaign and South Africa', *English Today* 50, 13/2: 3–7.

Hockett, C. F. 1958. *A Course in Modern Linguistics*. New York: Macmillan.

Honey, J. 1989. *Does Accent Matter?* London: Faber and Faber.

Honey, J. 1997. *Language is Power. The Story of Standard English and its Enemies*. London: Faber and Faber.

Honikman, B. 1964. 'Articulatory settings' in D. Abercrombie, D. B. Fry, P. A. D. MacCarthy, N. C. Scott, and J. L. M. Trim (eds.) 1964: *In Honour of Daniel Jones*. London: Longman.

Hymes, D. 1972. 'On communicative competence' in J. B. Pride and J. Holmes (eds.) 1972: *Sociolinguistics*. Harmondsworth: Penguin.

Ioup, G. 1984. 'Is there a structural foreign accent? A comparison of syntactic and phonological errors in second language acquisition'. *Language Learning* 34/2: 1–17.

Ioup, G. and A. Tansomboon. 1987. 'The acquisition of tone: a maturational perspective' in G. Ioup and S. H. Weinberger (eds.) 1987.

Ioup, G. and S. H. Weinberger (eds.). 1987. *Interlanguage Phonology.* Cambridge, Massachusetts: Newbury House.

Jakobson, R. 1968. *Child Language, Aphasia, and Phonological Universals* (trans. A. Keiler). The Hague: Mouton.

James, C. 1998. *Errors in Language Learning and Use.* London: Longman.

Jenkins, J. 1995. 'Variation in phonological error in interlanguage talk'. Unpublished PhD thesis, University of London, Institute of Education.

Jenkins, J. 1996a. 'Changing pronunciation priorities for successful communication in international contexts'. *Speak Out!* 17: 15–22. Reprinted in McLean (ed.) 1997.

Jenkins, J. 1996b. 'Native speaker, non-native speaker and English as a Foreign Language: time for a change'. *IATEFL Newsletter* 131: 10–11.

Jenkins, J. 1997. 'Teaching intonation for English as an International Language: teachability, learnability and intelligibility'. *Speak Out!* 21: 15–26.

Jenkins, J. 1998a. 'Which pronunciation norms and models for English as an International Language?'. *ELT Journal* 52/2: 119–26.

Jenkins, J. 1998b. 'Rethinking phonology in teacher education.' *Vienna English Working Papers* 7/1: 40–6.

Jenkins, J. and J. Kenworthy. 1998. 'Cloning: a means of finding your L2 voice'. *Speak Out!* 22: 34–9.

Jenner, B. 1989. 'Teaching pronunciation: the common core'. *Speak Out!* 4: 2–4.

Jenner, B. 1992. 'The English voice' in A. Brown (ed.) 1992: *Approaches to Pronunciation Teaching.* London: Macmillan.

Jenner, B. 1995. 'On diphthongs'. *Speak Out!* 15: 15–16.

Jenner, B. 1997a. 'International English: an alternative view'. *Speak Out!* 21: 10–4.

Jenner, B. 1997b. 'Articulatory setting: the genealogy of an idea'. *Vienna English Working Papers* 6/1: 19–33.

Jones, R. H. and S. Evans. 1995. 'Teaching pronunciation through voice quality'. *ELT Journal* 49/3: 244–51.

Kachru, B. B. (ed.). 1982. *The Other Tongue. English Across Cultures.* Urbana, IL.: University of Illinois Press.

Kachru, B. B. 1985. 'Standards, codification and sociolinguistic realism: the English language in the outer circle' in R. Quirk and H. G. Widdowson (eds.): *English in the World: Teaching and Learning the Language and Literatures.* Cambridge: Cambridge University Press.

Kachru, B. B. 1991. 'Liberation linguistics and the Quirk concern'. *English Today* 25: 3–13.

Kachru, B. B. 1992. 'Models for non-native Englishes' in B. B. Kachru (ed.) 1992.

Kachru, B. B. (ed.). 1992. *The Other Tongue. English Across Cultures.* 2nd edn. Urbana, IL.: University of Illinois Press.

Kachru, Y. 1993. 'Interlanguage and language acquisition research'. Review of L. Selinker: *Rediscovering Interlanguage. World Englishes* 12/2: 265–8.

Kaltenboeck, G. 1994. '"Chunks" and pronunciation teaching'. *Speak Out!* 13: 17–22.

Kasper, G. 1989. 'Variation in interlanguage speech act realisation' in S. Gass, C. Madden, D. Preston, and L. Selinker (eds.): *Variation in Second Language Acquisition Vol. 1: Discourse and Pragmatics.* Clevedon, N Somerset: Multilingual Matters (pp. 37–58).

Kasper, G. 1997. 'Beyond reference' in G. Kasper and E. Kellerman (eds.): *Communication Strategies. Psycholinguistic and Sociolinguistic Perspectives.* London: Longman.

Kellerman, E. 1979. 'Transfer and non-transfer: where are we now?'. *Studies in Second Language Acquisition* 2: 37–57.

Kellerman, E. and **M. Sharwood Smith** (eds.). 1986. *Cross-linguistic Influence in Second Language Acquisition.* Oxford: Pergamon Press.

Kenworthy, J. 1987. *Teaching English Pronunciation.* London: Longman.

Kershaw, G. 1996. 'The developing roles of native-speaker and non-native-speaker teachers'. *Modern English Teacher* 5/3: 7–11.

Kjellin, O. 1999. 'Accent addition: Prosody and perception facilitate second language learning' in O. Fujimura, B. Joseph, and B. Palek (eds.): *Proceedings of LP'98 at Ohio State University, Columbus, Ohio, Sept. 1998* (Vol. 2, pp. 373–98). Prague: The Karolinum Press.

Kramsch, C. 1993. *Context and Culture in Language Teaching.* Oxford: Oxford University Press.

Kramsch, C. 1998. 'The privilege of the intercultural speaker' in M. Byram and M. Fleming (eds.): *Foreign Language Learning in Intercultural Perspective.* Cambridge: Cambridge University Press.

Krashen, S. 1981. *Second Language Acquisition and Second Language Learning.* Oxford: Pergamon Press.

Krashen, S. 1982. *Principles and Practice in Second Language Acquisition.* Oxford: Pergamon Press.

Kreidler, C. W. 1989. *The Pronunciation of English.* Oxford: Blackwell.

Labov, W. 1966. *The Social Stratification of English in New York City.* Washington DC: Centre for Applied Linguistics.

Ladefoged, P. 1967. *Three Areas of Experimental Phonetics.* Oxford: Oxford University Press.

Ladefoged, P. 1982. *A Course in Phonetics.* 2nd edn. New York: Harcourt Brace Jovanovich.

Ladefoged, P. and **I. Maddieson.** 1996. *The Sounds of the World's Languages.* Oxford: Blackwell.

Lado, R. 1957. *Linguistics Across Cultures.* Ann Arbor: University of Michigan Press.

Lane, H. 1963. 'Foreign accent and speech distortion'. *Journal of the Acoustical Society of America* 35/4: 451–3.

Lanham, L. W. 1990. 'Stress and intonation and the intelligibility of South African Black English' in Ramsaran (ed.) 1990.

Larsen-Freeman, D. 1985. 'State of the art on input in second language acquisition' in S. Gass and C. Madden (eds.) 1985.

Leventhal, C. E. 1980. 'Measuring intelligibility of non-native speakers with white noise'. *TESOL Newsletter* 14/1: 17–8.

Levis, J. 1999a. 'Training teachers to use English as a pronunciation resouce'. *Speak Out!* 24: 16–24.

Levis, J. 1999b. 'The intonation and meaning of normal yes/no questions.' *World Englishes.* 18/3: 373–80.

Lightbown, P. M. and ·**N. Spada.** 1999. *How Languages are Learned.* 2nd edn. Oxford: Oxford University Press.

Lippi-Green, R. 1997. *English with an Accent.* London: Routledge.

Locke, J. 1993. *The Child's Path to Spoken Language.* Cambridge, Massachusetts: Harvard University Press.

Long, M. H. 1985. 'Input and second language acquisition theory' in S. Gass and C. Madden (eds.) 1985.

Long, M. H. 1990. 'Maturational constraints on language development'. *Studies in Second Language Acquisition* 12: 251–85.

Long, M. H. and **P. Porter.** 1985. 'Group work, interlanguage talk, and second language acquisition'. *TESOL Quarterly* 19/2: 207–28.

Lowenberg, P. 1992. 'Testing English as a world language: issues in assessing non-native proficiency' in B. B. Kachru (ed.) 1992.

Lowenberg, P. 1993. 'Issues of validity in tests of English as a world language: whose standards?'. *World Englishes* 12/1: 95–106.

Lynch, T. 1996. *Communication in the Language Classroom*. Oxford: Oxford University Press.

Macaulay, R. 1988. 'RP R.I.P.'. *Applied Linguistics* 9/2: 115–24.

Macken, M. A. and C. A. Ferguson. 1981. 'Phonological universals in language acquisition' in G. Ioup and S. H. Weinberger (eds.) 1987.

Major, R. C. 1987. 'A model for interlanguage phonology' in G. Ioup and S. H. Weinberger (eds.) 1987.

Maley, A. 1985. 'The most chameleon of languages: perceptions of English abroad.' *English Today* 1: 30–3.

Marks, J. 1999. 'Is stress-timing real?'. *ELT Journal* 53/3: 191–9.

McArthur, T. 1998. *The English Languages*. Cambridge: Cambridge University Press.

McArthur, T. 1999. 'The galactic language'. *English Today* 58, 15/2: 52–6.

McCarthy, M. 1991. *Discourse Analysis for Language Teachers*. Cambridge: Cambridge University Press.

McCarthy, M. and R. Carter. 1997. 'Octopus or Hydra?'. *IATEFL Newsletter* 137: 16–17.

McLean, A. (ed.). 1997. *SIG Selections 1997*. IATEFL: Whitstable.

Medgyes, P. 1992. 'Native or non-native: who's worth more?'. *ELT Journal* 46/4: 340–9.

Medgyes, P. 1994. *The Non-Native Teacher*. London: Macmillan.

Milroy, J. and L. Milroy. 1999. *Authority in Language*. 3rd edn. London: Routledge.

Milroy, L. 1994. 'Sociolinguistics and second language learning' in Brown *et al.* (eds.) 1994.

Milroy, L. 1999. 'Standard English and language ideology in Britain and the United States' in T. Bex and R. J. Watts (eds.) 1999.

Modiano, M. 1996. 'The Americanization of Euro-English'. *World Englishes* 15/2: 207–15.

Mortimer, C. 1985. *Elements of Pronunciation. Intensive Practice for Intermediate and More Advanced Students*. Cambridge: Cambridge University Press.

Nash, R. 1969. 'Intonational interference in the speech of Puerto-Rican bilinguals'. *Journal of English as a Second Language* 4/2: 1–42.

Nattinger, J. R. and J. S. DeCarrico. 1992. *Lexical Phrases and Language Teaching*. Oxford: Oxford University Press.

Nayar, P. B. 1998. 'Variants and varieties of English: Dialectology or linguistic politics?' in H. Lindquist, S. Klintborg, M. Levin, and M. Estling (eds.) 1998: *The Major Varieties of English. Papers from MAVEN 97*. Växjö: Acta Wexionensia.

Nelson, C. L. 1982. 'Intelligibility and non-native varieties of English' in B. B. Kachru (ed.) 1982.

Nelson, C. L. 1992. 'My Language, Your Culture: Whose Communicative Competence?' in B. B. Kachru (ed.) 1992.

Nelson, C. L. 1995. 'Intelligibility and world Englishes in the classroom'. *World Englishes* 14/2: 273–9.

Neufeld, G. G. 1978. 'On the acquisition of prosodic and articulatory features in adult language learning' in G. Ioup and S. H. Weinberger (eds.) 1987.

246   *The Phonology of English as an International Language*

Norton, B. 1997. 'Language, identity, and the ownership of English'. *TESOL Quarterly* 31/3: 409–29.

O'Connor, J. D. 1973. *Phonetics*. Harmondsworth: Penguin.
Odlin, T. 1989. *Language Transfer. Cross-linguistic Influence in Language Learning*. Cambridge: Cambridge University Press.
Ogden, C. K. 1930. *Basic English*. London: Kegan Paul, Trench, and Trubner.
Olsson, M. 1978. *Intelligibility: An Evaluation of Some Features of English Produced by Swedish 14-year-olds*. Gothenburg Studies in English Vol. 40. Goteborg: Acta Universitatis Gothoburgensis.
Onions, C. T. (ed.) 1973. *The Shorter Oxford English Dictionary*. Oxford: Clarendon Press.

Parrot, M. 1998. 'A personal response from Martin Parrott'. *The IH Journal* 5: 20–1.
Pawley, A. and F. H. Syder. 1983. 'Two puzzles for linguistic theory: nativelike selection and nativelike fluency' in J. C. Richards and R. W. Schmidt (eds.) 1983: *Language and Communication*. London: Longman.
Pennington, M. 1996. *Phonology in English Language Teaching. An International Approach*. London: Longman.
Pennycook, A. 1994. *The Cultural Politics of English as an International Language*. London: Longman.
Pennycook, A. 1998. *English and the Discourses of Colonialism*. London: Routledge.
Phillipson, R. 1992. *Linguistic Imperialism*. Oxford: Oxford University Press.
Pica, T. and C. Doughty. 1985. 'Input and interaction in the communicative language classroom: a comparison of teacher-fronted and group activities' in S. Gass and C. Madden (eds.) 1985.
Pinker, S. 1994. *The Language Instinct*. London: Penguin.
Pirt, G. 1990. 'Discourse intonation problems for non-native speakers' in M. Hewings (ed.) 1990: 145–55. *Papers in Discourse Intonation*. Monograph 16, English Language Research, University of Birmingham.
Porter, D. and S. Garvin. 1989. 'Attitudes to pronunciation in EFL'. *Speak Out!* 5: 8–15.
Porter, P. A. 1986. 'How learners talk to each other: input and interaction in task-centered discussions' in R. Day (ed.) 1986.
Prodromou, L. 1988. 'English as cultural action'. *ELT Journal* 42/2: 73–83. Reprinted in R. Rossner and R. Bolitho (eds.) 1990: *Currents of Change in English Language Teaching*. Oxford: Oxford University Press.
Prodromou, L. 1996a. 'Correspondence'. *ELT Journal* 50/1: 88–9.
Prodromou, L. 1996b. 'Correspondence'. *ELT Journal* 50/4: 371–3.
Prodromou, L. 1997. 'From corpus to octopus.' *IATEFL Newsletter* 137: 18–21.

Quirk, R. 1982. 'International communication and the concept of Nuclear English' in C. J. Brumfit (ed.) 1982.
Quirk, R. 1985. 'The English language in a global context' in R. Quirk and H. G. Widdowson (eds.) 1985.
Quirk, R. 1990. 'Language varieties and standard language'. *English Today* 21: 3–10.
Quirk, R. and H. G. Widdowson (eds.) 1985. *English in the World: Teaching and Learning the Language and Literatures*. Cambridge: Cambridge University Press.

Rampton, B. 1990. 'Displacing the "native speaker": expertise, affiliation and inheritance'. *ELT Journal* 44/2: 97–101.

Ramsaran, S. (ed.) 1990. *Studies in the Pronunciation of English: A Commemorative Volume in Honour of A.C. Gimson.* London: Routledge.

Riley, P. 1989. 'Who do you think you're talking to? Perception, categorisation and negotiation processes in exolinguistic interaction' in V. Bickley (ed.): *Languages in Education in a Bi-lingual or Multi-lingual Setting.* Hong Kong: Education Department, Institute of Language in Education.

Rimmer, W. 1997. 'Dictation for teaching and testing pronunciation'. *Speak Out!* 21: 36–8.

Riney, T. 1997. Review of Mehmet Yavas (ed.): *First and Second Language Phonology. Applied Linguistics* 18/2: 237–9.

Ringbom, H. 1987. *The Role of the First Language in Foreign Language Learning.* Clevedon, N. Somerset: Multilingual Matters.

Roach, P. 1982. 'On the distinction between "stress-timed" and "syllable-timed" languages' in D. Crystal (ed.) 1982: *Linguistic Controversies.* London: Edward Arnold.

Roach, P. 1991. *English Phonetics and Phonology.* 2nd edn. Cambridge: Cambridge University Press.

Rosewarne, D. 1996. 'Changes in English pronunciation and some implications for teachers and non-native learners'. *Speak Out!* 18: 15–21.

Rosewarne, D. 1999. 'Review of "Teaching Pronunciation: A Reference for Teachers of English to Speakers of Other Languages" by M. Celce-Murcia, D. M. Brinton, and J. M. Goodwin'. *Speak Out!* 23: 45–56.

Rost, M. 1990. *Listening in Language Learning.* London: Longman.

Rost, M. 1996. *Listening.* London: Penguin.

Rulon, K. A. and **J. McCreary.** 1986. 'Negotiation of content: teacher-fronted and small-group interaction' in R. Day (ed.) 1986.

Sajavaara, K. 1986. 'Transfer and second language speech processing' in E. Kellerman and M. Sharwood Smith (eds.) 1986.

Sarabasa, A. 1994. 'Perception and production saturation of spoken English as a first phase in reducing a foreign accent'. Paper presented at ISLP 1994, Yokohama, Japan: Accoustical Society of Japan Vol. 4: 2015–8.

Sato, C. J. 1985. 'Task variation in interlanguage phonology' in S. M. Gass and C. Madden (eds.) 1985.

Saville-Troike, M. 1996. 'The ethnography of communication' in S. L. McKay and N. H. Hornberger (eds.) 1996: *Sociolinguistics and Language Teaching.* Cambridge: Cambridge University Press.

Saxton, S. 1997. 'Gut reactions'. *Modern English Teacher* 6/2: 46–9.

Schachter, J. 1974. 'An error in error analysis'. *Language Learning* 24: 205–14.

Schachter, J. 1983. 'A new account of language transfer' in S. M. Gass and L. Selinker (eds.) 1983: *Language Transfer in Language Learning.* Rowley, Massachusetts: Newbury House.

Schmidt, R.W. 1977. 'Sociolinguistic variation and language transfer in phonology' in G. Ioup and S. H. Weinberger (eds.) 1987.

Schwartz, J. 1980. 'The negotiation for meaning: repair in conversations between second language learners of English' in D. Larsen-Freeman (ed.) 1980: *Discourse Analysis in Second Language Research.* Rowley, Massachusetts: Newbury House.

Scovel, T. 1998. *Psycholinguistics.* Oxford: Oxford University Press.

Seidlhofer, B. 1999. 'Double standards: teacher education in the Expanding Circle'. *World Englishes* 18/2: 233–45.

Seidlhofer, B. and C. Dalton. 1993. 'The pragmatics of pronunciation.' *IATEFL Conference Report* 1993: 23.

Seidlhofer, B. and C. Dalton. 1995. 'Appropriate units in pronunciation teaching: some programmatic pointers'. *International Journal of Applied Linguistics* 5/1: 135–46.

Selinker, L. 1972. 'Interlanguage'. *IRAL* 10: 209–31.

Selinker, L. 1992. *Rediscovering Interlanguage*. London: Longman.

Sharwood Smith, M. 1994. *Second Language Learning: Theoretical Foundations*. London: Longman.

Shockey, L. 1984. 'All in a flap: long-term accommodation in phonology' in H. Giles (ed.) 1984.

Simo-Bobda, A. 1999. 'Pertinent, but not a contradiction of Kachru'. *English Today* 58, 15/2: 29–30.

Smith, L. E. 1983. 'English as an International Auxiliary Language' in L. E. Smith (ed.): *Readings in English as an International Language*. Oxford: Pergamon Press.

Smith, L. E. 1992. 'Spread of English and issues of intelligibility' in B. B. Kachru (ed.) 1992.

Smith, L. E. and J. A. Bisazza. 1982. 'The comprehensibility of three varieties of English for college students in seven countries'. *Language Learning* 32: 259–70.

Smith, L. E. and C. Nelson. 1985. 'International intelligibility of English: directions and resources'. *World Englishes* 4/3: 333–42.

Smith, L. E. and K. Rafiqzad. 1979. 'English for cross-cultural communication: the question of intelligibility'. *TESOL Quarterly* 13/3: 371–80.

Smith, N. V. 1973. *The Acquisition of Phonology*. Cambridge: Cambridge University Press.

Sridhar, K. K. 1996. 'Societal multilingualism' in S. L. Mackay and N. H. Hornberger (eds.): *Sociolinguistics and Language Teaching*. Cambridge: Cambridge University Press.

Stampe, D. 1969. 'The acquisition of phonetic representation' in Chicago Linguistics Society, 5: *Papers from the Fifth Regional Meeting*.

Starks, D. and B. Paltridge. 1994. 'Varieties of English and the EFL Classroom: a New Zealand Case Study'. *The TESOLANZ Journal* 2: 69–77.

Strevens, P. 1980. *Teaching English as an International Language*. Oxford: Pergamon Press.

Suenobo, M., K. Kanzaki, and S. Yamane. 1992. 'An experimental study of intelligibility of Japanese English'. *IRAL* 30/2: 146–56.

Sure, K. 1992. 'Falling standards in Kenya?'. *English Today* 32: 23–8.

Sutter, J. 1999. 'Prisons, panopticism and dividing practices: hegemony in ELT and the role of teacher training'. Unpublished MA Dissertation, King's College London.

Swan, M. and B. Smith. 1987. *Learner English*. Cambridge: Cambridge University Press.

Takahashi, T. 1989. 'The influence of the listener on L2 speech' in S. Gass, C. Madden, D. Preston, and L. Selinker (eds.) 1989: *Variation in Second Language Acquisition Vol. I: Discourse and Pragmatics*. Clevedon, N. Somerset: Multilingual Matters.

Tarone, E. 1978. 'The phonology of interlanguage' in G. Ioup and S. H. Weinberger (eds.) 1987.

Tarone, E. 1979. 'Interlanguage as chameleon'. *Language Learning* 29/1: 181–91.

Tarone, E. 1980. 'Some influences on the syllable structure of interlanguage phonology' in G. Ioup and S. H. Weinberger (eds.) 1987.

Tarone, E. 1982. 'Systematicity and attention in interlanguage'. *Language Learning* 32: 69–82.
Tarone, E. 1983. 'On the variability of interlanguage systems'. *Applied Linguistics* 4/2: 143–63.
Tarone, E. 1988. *Variation in Interlanguage*. London: Edward Arnold.
Taylor, D. 1991. 'Who speaks English to whom? The question of teaching English pronunciation for global communication'. *System* 19/4: 425–35.
Taylor, D. 1993. 'Intonation and accent in English: what teachers need to know'. *International Review of Applied Linguistics* 31/1: 1–21.
Tench, P. 1997. 'Towards a design of a pronunciation test'. *Speak Out!* 20: 29–43.
Thakerar, J. N., H. Giles and J. Cheshire. 1982. 'Psychological and linguistic parameters of speech accommodation theory' in C. Fraser and K. R. Scherer (eds.) 1982: *Advances in the Social Psychology of Language*. Cambridge: Cambridge University Press.
Thornbury, S. 1993. 'Having a good jaw: voice-setting phonology'. *ELT Journal* 47/2: 126–31.
Tiffen, B. 1992. 'A study of the intelligibility of Nigerian English' in A. van Essen and E. I. Burkart (eds.) *Homage to W. R. Lee. Essays in English as a Foreign and Second Language*. Dordrecht: Foris.
Todd, L. 1997. 'Ebonics: an evaluation'. *English Today* 13/3: 13–7.
Trudgill, P. 1998. 'World Englishes: Convergence or divergence?' in H. Lindquist, S. Klintberg, M. Levin, and M. Estling (eds.) 1998: *The Major Varieties of English. Papers from MAVEN 97*. Växjö: Acta Wexionesia.
Trudgill, P. 1999. 'Standard English: What it isn't' in T. Bex and R. J. Watts (eds.) 1999.

UCLES. 2000. *Cambridge Examinations, Certificates and Diplomas: Regulations 2000*. Cambridge: UCLES.
Ufomata, T. 1990. 'Acceptable models for TEFL (with special reference to Nigeria)' in S. Ramsaran (ed.) 1990.

Van Els, T. and K. De Bot. 1987. 'The role of intonation in foreign accent'. *The Modern Language Journal* 71/2: 147–55.
Varonis, E. M. and S. Gass. 1982. 'The comprehensibility of non-native speech'. *Studies in Second Language Acquisition* 4/2: 114–36.
Varonis, E. M. and S. Gass. 1985a. 'Non-native/non-native conversations: a model for negotiation of meaning'. *Applied Linguistics* 6/1: 71–90.
Varonis, E. M. and S. Gass. 1985b. 'Miscommunication in native/non-native conversation'. *Language in Society* 14: 327–43.
Vaughan-Rees, M. 1997. 'Full marks for not teaching rules of pronunciation?'. *IATEFL Newsletter* 139: 9–10.
Vaughan-Rees, M. 1999. 'Word-stress rules'. *Speak Out!* 23: 38–9.

Weinberger, S. H. 1987. 'The influence of linguistic context on syllable simplification' in G. Ioup and S. H. Weinberger (eds.) 1987.
Wenk, B. 1986. 'Crosslinguistic influence in second language phonology: speech rhythms' in Kellerman and Sharwood Smith (eds.) 1986.
Wennerstrom, A. 1994. 'Intonational meaning in English discourse: a study of non-native speakers'. *Applied Linguistics* 15/4: 399–420.
West, M. 1953. *General Service List of English Words*. Harlow: Longman.
Widdowson, H. G. 1982, 'What do we mean by "International Language"?' in C. J. Brumfit (ed.) 1982.

Widdowson, H. G. 1984. 'Theoretical implications of interlanguage studies for language teaching' in A. Davies, C. Criper and A. P. R. Howatt (eds.) 1984.

Widdowson, H. G. 1990. *Aspects of Language Teaching*. Oxford: Oxford University Press.

Widdowson, H. G. 1991. 'The description and prescription of language' in J. E. Alatis (ed.) 1991: *Georgetown University Round Table on Language and Linguistics, Language, Communication and Social Meaning*. Washington DC: Georgetown University Press.

Widdowson, H. G. 1993. 'Proper words in proper places'. *ELT Journal* 47/4: 317–29.

Widdowson, H. G. 1994a. 'The ownership of English'. *TESOL Quarterly* 28/2: 377–89.

Widdowson, H. G. 1994b. 'Pragmatics and the pedagogic competence of language teachers' in T. Sebbage and S. Sebbage (eds.): *Proceedings of the 4th International NELLE Conference*. Hamburg: NELLE.

Widdowson, H. G. 1997. 'EIL, ESL, EFL: global issues and local interests'. *World Englishes* 16/1: 135–46.

Wilkinson, G. 1995. *Introducing Standard English*. Harmondsworth: Penguin.

Willis, D. 1996. 'Accuracy, fluency and conformity' in J. Willis and D. Willis (eds.) 1996: *Challenge and Change in Language Teaching*. London: Macmillan Heinemann.

Wode, H. 1986. 'Language transfer: a cognitive functional and developmental view' in E. Kellerman and M. Sharwood Smith (eds.) 1986.

Wolff, H. 1959. 'Intelligibility and inter-ethnic attitudes'. *Anthropological Linguistics* 1/3: 34–41.

Wolfram, W. 1991. 'Interlanguage variation: a review article.' *Applied Linguistics* 12/1: 102–6.

Zuengler, J. 1982. 'Applying accommodation theory to variable performance data in L2'. *Studies in Second Language Acquisition* 4: 181–92.

Zuengler, J. 1987. 'Effects of "expertise" in interactions between native and non-native speakers'. *Language and Communication* 7: 123–37.

Zuengler, J. 1989. 'Assessing an interaction-based paradigm. How accommodative should we be?' in M. R. Eisenstein (ed.) 1989: *The Dynamic Interlanguage: Empirical Studies in Second Language Variation*. New York: Plenum.

Zuengler, J. 1991. 'Accommodation in native-nonnative interactions: Going beyond the "what" to the "why" in second language research' in H. Giles, N. Coupland, and J. Coupland (eds.) 1991.

Index

Published in this series: